CAN'T TAKE

MY EYES

OFF OF YOU

1 MAN

7 DAYS

12 TELEVISIONS

CAN'T TAKE

MY EYES

OFF OF YOU

JACK LECHNER

 CROWN PUBLISHERS   NEW YORK

Grateful acknowledgment is given to the Newberry
Library, Chicago, to reprint an excerpt from "Prayer to
His Bosses" by Ben Hecht.

Published by Crown Publishers, New York, New York.
Member of the Crown Publishing Group.

Random House, Inc. New York, Toronto, London,
Sydney, Auckland
www.randomhouse.com

CROWN is a trademark and the Crown colophon is a
registered trademark of Random House, Inc.

Printed in the United States of America

Design by Barbara Sturman

Library of Congress Cataloging-in-Publication Data
Lechner, Jack.
    Can't take my eyes off of you : one man, seven days,
twelve televisions / by Jack Lechner.—1st ed.
    1. Television programs—United States.   I. Title.
PN1992.3.U5 L35   2000
791.45'75'0973—dc21   00-35855

ISBN 0-609-60681-6

10 9 8 7 6 5 4 3 2 1

First Edition

For Sam,

who never should have given me that

personalized *TV Guide* cover

CONTENTS

CAN'T TAKE

MY EYES

OFF OF YOU

In April 1967, a man named Charles Sopkin performed a dangerous experiment upon himself. He brought six television sets into his New York apartment, and proceeded to spend an entire week watching them, from *Sunrise Sermonette* to *The Late, Late Show.* The result of Sopkin's experiment was a book called *Seven Glorious Days, Seven Fun-Filled Nights.* It provides not only a snapshot of the state of popular culture during one week in the late Sixties, but also a moment-by-moment account of an otherwise sane man doing something completely crazy.

In September 1999, thirty-two years after Charles Sopkin watched

Seven Glorious Days...

Channel 2 sign off at 6:12 A.M. with the traditional shot of the flag and the National Anthem—stations went off the air in those days—I decided to repeat Sopkin's experiment.

The obvious question is: Why?

Like television itself, the answer is complex and multifaceted. One reason is that *Seven Glorious Days* was a cherished book of my youth, which probably gives you a good idea of my youth. I was already obsessed with the media at ten years old, and I was happy to learn that someone else was equally obsessed. Besides, the book was sitting around our house in the first place because my mother *knew* Charles Sopkin. After graduating from Wellesley, she lived in Manhattan with a girl named Judy Simon. Judy had a brief romance with Sopkin, an editor at various magazines and publishing houses. It ended badly, but that's another story. (As a kid, the part I wanted to hear about was how Mom and Judy lived next door to a trained chimpanzee named Kokomo, who kept them awake riding his unicycle at all hours.)

Another reason for my foolhardiness is that both the world and television have changed a lot since 1967—could anyone then have imagined the sheer number of channels available today?—and a week of TV immersion in 1999 might prove as revealing about the state of American popular culture now as Sopkin's week did then.

This is a time of transition for television. The original networks are being watched by fewer people than ever before—although they charge higher ad rates than ever before too. Young people turn increasingly to computers for relaxation, and while they certainly watch television, it doesn't have the same claim on their lives that it did on my generation. But when they do watch, they have more options, because the number of channels has grown exponentially. Our local cable system on the Upper West Side of Manhattan features seventy-five different channels, and downtown you can get ninety-two. Only ten years ago, when Bill McKibben analyzed a single day of television in his book *The Age of Missing Information,* he continually referred to "the cable channels" as if they were a vast, undifferentiated sea of low-budget mediocrity. Now the cable sea is differentiated and higher-budget, and some of it isn't even mediocre.

By contrast, Charles Sopkin's six-channel universe of 1967 looks relatively orderly. Of course, he didn't think so at the time. Every generation since the time of ancient Rome has complained that things are deteriorating—check out Horace and Juvenal if you doubt me—and Sopkin was no exception to the rule. At the end of *Seven Glorious Days, Seven Fun-Filled Nights*, he despaired at the state of a medium that surely couldn't get much worse. "I naively expected that the ratio would run three to one in favor of trash," he wrote. "It turned out to be closer to a hundred to one." The question is, does Sopkin's ratio still apply? And even if it does, what kind of trash is it, anyway? As archaeologists know well, trash can be as revealing as treasure.

There's yet another reason I felt compelled to follow Sopkin's trail. While watching fifteen hours of TV a day may be standard operating procedure for any number of people, it takes genuine effort for me. I'm a natural multiprocessor; my wife complains that I can't tie my shoes without reading a book, listening to the radio, or both at once. What's always bugged me about television is that it doesn't tend to reward intense concentration, but it's too distracting to relegate to the background.

It's especially distracting for me, because of what I bring to it. I've worked in both film and television for fourteen years, most recently as head of development at Miramax Films. When it comes to watching TV, I'm like a guy who's worked at the hot dog factory, and rarely eats a hot dog because he knows a little too much about the ingredients. It's not snobbery—it's that I can't turn off the analytical side of my brain. All I see is the stuff that doesn't work, and I start thinking immediately of ways to fix it. When I left Miramax in June of 1999, it occurred to me that the Sopkin experiment might act as a kind of shock treatment to get me back in front of the screen, after spending years behind it. Perhaps I could turn my inside knowledge into an advantage instead of a hindrance. Unlike most TV critics or TV-studying academics, I would be looking at a week of television from a practical, real-life perspective, without retreating into theory, scorn, or spin. And maybe, by bombarding my senses into submission, I might learn how to enjoy watching TV again, the way I did when I was a kid.

Unlike Charles Sopkin, who was already fifteen years old when network TV began to take off, I grew up on television. I once read a book about the history of *I Love Lucy*, which contained a complete episode guide. It was humbling to realize that I had watched every single episode of the show—all 179 of them—before I was out of elementary school. Show me an episode guide for *The Dick Van Dyke Show* or *Batman* or even *The Brady Bunch*, and I'll probably recognize every one of those episodes too.

When I say I grew up on television, I mean that quite literally. My mother has spent her entire adult life working on a high-school quiz show called *It's Academic*, and some of my earliest memories are of the WRC-TV control room in Washington, D.C. The shows were all shot live-to-videotape, with the harried director barking orders simultaneously at the cameramen, the stage manager, and anyone else within earshot. "Camera Two, move in on Mac. Take Two. Three, pan right. Take Three. Take One. Can somebody get me a goddamn cup of coffee?" It was the next best thing to Mission Control during an Apollo launch.

Meanwhile, my father's involvement in the civil rights movement led to a political career in Virginia. He spent two terms in the House of Delegates, then ran for lieutenant governor and for Congress—no easy task for a Jewish liberal in the cradle of the Confederacy. Dad's campaigns were covered often on local TV news, where the reporters invariably screwed up all the relevant facts and misspelled his name.

Especially after Dad's first race, when I was eleven years old and my sister Eve was six, we never watched any TV show without knowing that someone had put it together—and not always very well. In sixth grade, my friends and I were addicted to a syndicated afternoon show called *Johnny Sokko and His Flying Robot*. I was the one who decoded the show's bizarre aesthetic (heroic Asian kids versus swarthy, mustachioed villains) by figuring out that the Japanese producers had filmed it on the cheap in Mexico. I still have a copy of the letter I wrote a few years after that to Charles Schulz, complaining about the declining quality of the "Peanuts" specials and movies. Schulz wrote back on Snoopy stationery to say he agreed, but couldn't do anything about it. This proved to be a useful lesson in applied show business.

I studied film in college, then worked at a number of production companies and studios in Los Angeles, New York, and London. As I climbed the movie ladder, I watched less and less television. There were always scripts to read and critique, screenings to attend, and family and friends to see in whatever time was left. Besides, I got married in 1987, and it was hard enough to balance the demands of a marriage and a job without making additional time for TV. For years, my closest connection with television was to watch disgruntled feature-film people trooping off to make ten times my salary working on sitcoms.

But during the 1988 writers' strike, when I was unemployed—along with nearly everyone else I knew—it was television that bailed me out. I won four games on *Jeopardy!* before losing the fifth to a transit cop from Brooklyn, who was faster on the buzzer. (Playing *Jeopardy!* may be about recalling knowledge, but winning *Jeopardy!* is all about eye-hand coordination.) In my third game I set a still-unbroken record for losing the most money in Final Jeopardy, by betting $15,000 on the category of British Royalty. Did you know Mary I was the granddaughter of Ferdinand and Isabella of Spain? Well, I didn't.

The strike ended, and we all went back to work. Eventually, I ended up in TV myself—first at Channel Four in London, then at HBO in New York. I began to understand the medium from the inside, and in London I even started to watch TV again, for the novelty of experiencing another culture through the lens of television. (I still miss a program called *One Man and His Dog*, which applied the focused attention of network sports coverage to competitive sheep-herding trials.) But in 1996, I returned to feature films as head of development at Miramax, where I supervised as many as seventy-five projects at once; I scarcely had time to read the newspaper, let alone watch TV. After three exhilarating but exhausting years, I decided to leave before I burned out entirely. When people asked me what I was going to do with my new-found free time, the answer came naturally: "I'm going to watch a lot of television." Which brings us up to date, as I stand poised on the brink of doing just that.

While the television universe has grown vastly more complicated in the thirty-two years since Sopkin's book, the human eye and brain can still only take in the same finite amount. I couldn't possibly follow Sopkin's example in having a TV set for every channel, so I decided to compromise by doubling his stakes, from six sets to twelve. My plan was to pick an average week of television to watch and study, specifically avoiding the "sweeps" months when the networks load their schedules with specials and stunts to boost ratings (and thus the ad rates for their local affiliates). Instead, I wanted to see the range of daily-grind, garden-variety TV—the shows that even professional TV critics rarely watch. I chose the week of September 26, 1999, near the beginning of a new television season. In the Sixties the networks would roll out their new shows all at once; but these days the debuts are staggered over the course of a full six weeks, sometimes longer. (For instance, the new season of the long-running drama series *NYPD Blue* wouldn't start until January 2000.) During my week, some shows would be premiering, others still in reruns, and still others on their second or third episode of the new season.

My plan was to keep seven of the twelve sets tuned to the terrestrial networks (NBC, ABC, CBS, Fox, WB, UPN, and PBS), while the other five covered various cable channels. Outside prime

CAN'T TAKE MY EYES OFF OF YOU

time, I was prepared to abandon even that structure, and look at everything: soap operas, game shows, talk shows, music videos, old stand-up routines, old movies, old detective shows, sports, news, sports news, cartoons, wrestling, infomercials—the gamut. My only restriction was to ignore the stream of recent movies on cable channels like HBO and Showtime, as well as the slightly less recent movies on other channels, on the grounds that movies are movies and deserve to be studied in their own habitat.

Knowing how addled my brain might become under this onslaught, I pored over *TV Guide* the week before I started, and constructed elaborate grids to designate which program would run on which set for every half-hour available. I staggered the grids to cover most of the schedule; I would start by waking up early and going to bed early, and with each day I would get up later and retire later. Like Sopkin, I planned to focus on one or two shows at a time, while dutifully noting the competition. With more ground to cover, however, I expected to do more channel-surfing, especially since I would have something Sopkin didn't: a remote-control. (Since 1967 the explosion of channels has drastically changed what people watch, and the invention of the remote has made an equally drastic difference to *how* they watch.) Inevitably I would miss some things, but I planned to take in as much as any one person could.

My wife, Sam Maser, programs a film series at the Tribeca Film Center downtown, where she has an office. She also works on her own writing several days a week, in our two-bedroom apartment near Columbia University. She was supportive of my plans to replicate the Sopkin experiment until I explained that I wanted to bring the TV sets into our apartment. "Then I'm moving to a hotel for the week," she said. "And don't expect me to prepare any food, either. I'm not your handmaiden. If you think I'm going to run to the kitchen to bring you root beer, you've got another think coming." Sam is a smart and sarcastic Jewish girl from Philadelphia who has no patience for foolishness—although she sees nothing foolish in wearing a gorilla costume to surprise me at my office birthday party. After much wrangling, we negotiated an agreement: Sam would remain in the apartment, and join me in front of the sets to interpret her favorite shows (*ER* and *The Price Is Right*) for the episodic-series-impaired (me). However, she would leave me alone for much of the week, in the company of our snuffling, snorting, banana-obsessed pug dog, Cosmo. (Cosmo has chosen to ignore television since the time *The Adventures of Milo and Otis* ran on Fox Family Channel, when he kept hurling himself at the set to sniff the mysteriously unscented pug onscreen.)

Before I could get started, there were numerous practical considerations to deal with. The twelve televisions were first on the list. Sam suggested that I ask TV manufacturers to lend me the sets for the week, which made sense. When I contacted John Taylor, VP of Public Affairs at Zenith Electronics in Chicago, he delighted me by grasping the idea immediately, and even more by agreeing to the loan.

I encountered similar good fortune when I called Time Warner Cable. After navigating through one of the more byzantine voice-mail systems of modern times, sheer luck landed me with one Ricardo Palacios. I explained my plan to him, and there was silence on the line for a moment. Finally, Ricardo spoke up: "I have to put it to you, sir—I won't say it's crazy, but it is a world record. Will you have medical assistance ready?" Ricardo personally supervised all the complications of my order, with a touching concern for my health and well-being. "You're going to need some sort of heat extraction or ventilation," he said the next time I called. "Twelve TVs and cable boxes are going to generate a lot of heat, don't you think? You're going to have a lot of psychic load on you, but you don't want to add a physical load to that." Taking his advice seriously, I prepared to include several electric fans in my increasingly elaborate rearrangement of the living room.

Looking at our existing outlets, Sam and I realized that even if we added surge protectors and power strips, we were likely to overload our electrical circuits and black out the entire apartment, if not the building, if not the block. I did some research and settled on a company called The Electric Connection, who could install as many grounded outlets as we needed. It wouldn't be cheap—at all—but at this point Zenith had already shipped the TV sets, and I knew I was past the point of no return. Sam's sister Sally, visiting from Philadelphia, was highly amused by the whole thing. Sally plays Ultimate Frisbee every weekend, and she would no sooner spend a week watching TV than I would spend a week playing Ultimate Frisbee. "I want to measure you before and after you do this," said Sally as the three of us walked down Broadway. "To see if it stunts my growth?" I said. "No," she chortled, "to see how much your ass spreads from sitting on it for a whole week!"

On Monday, September 20—which happens to be our wedding anniversary—Sam and I were awakened at 8:15 by a buzz from the lobby. "I got twelve TV sets for you from Zenith," said a man over the intercom. This was not the romantic awakening I had anticipated. I threw on clothes, hijacked the service elevator, and proceeded to haul twelve huge, heavy boxes upstairs. Sam snapped into commanding-officer mode, determining where to put them. "I figured these were going to a hospital," said the puzzled moving guy as he entered our apartment. "It's not a hospital *yet*," responded Sam.

Shortly after Sam left for work that day, electrician Harold Howard showed up to install the new outlets while I made lunch. As he opened the circuit breaker box, Harold accidentally dislodged a large hanging sign on our kitchen wall. The sign knocked over a bottle of red wine vinegar, spraying glass and vinegar throughout the kitchen. Startled by the noise, I spilled a bowl of pea soup all over the dining-room table, all over the floor, and—most unfortunately—all over the pug. Luckily, Sam didn't call until I had managed to clean up the results of this Rube Goldbergian chain reaction. "And I'm going to be leaving you home alone for a week?"

she moaned, mulling the alternatives. "How much more damage can I do?" I replied. "Oy," she said eloquently.

The next afternoon, Donovan Dawkins from Time Warner arrived to install the cable boxes. Originally from Jamaica, Donovan proved to be unflappable when faced with a job that would leave a lot of people flapped. For my part, I had to open the boxes and start unpacking the television sets. Before I knew it, twelve shiny black Zeniths were squatting in my living room like the vanguard of an alien invasion. As Donovan, Sam, and I connected the cable boxes to the sets, I began to glimpse what I was in for. Even three TVs tuned to different channels produced a dizzying load of information. There was a cut every few seconds, and images piled on top of each other in ways unimaginable outside the work of video artist Nam June Paik. It was a bowl of electronic fish, a wall of fireworks, popcorn for the eyes. Every additional set added to the intensity, until all twelve were alight with the visage of Keanu Reeves in *Speed.* "This is a good movie for twelve televisions at once," I told Sam. "The only good movie for twelve televisions at once," replied my wife, "is Derek Jarman's *Blue,*" which is ninety minutes of an unchanging blue screen. "I just can't believe the uproar," she continued. "I feel like I'm living at Circuit City!"

At last the stage was set. Seven Zeniths and cable boxes sat on tray tables I had bought in a frantic last-minute trawl of New Jersey discount stores, while the other five sat on the floor beneath the tables. Only one task remained—to learn about any unforeseen pitfalls ahead, by consulting people who had firsthand knowledge of the original experiment. I was saddened to learn that Charles Sopkin had died a few years earlier, but I tracked down his son Nicholas, an investment banker in New York. Nicholas proved to be extremely gracious and helpful. "I didn't read the book until I was older," he said. "I think I was eighteen or nineteen. I still don't think I appreciate it as much as some other people, who read the book every five years or so."

His father's TV immersion took place before Nicholas was born, so he kindly put me in touch with Alexandra Mayes Birnbaum, Charles Sopkin's sister-in-law, who is a recurring character in *Seven Glorious Days*. At first, Ms. Birnbaum professed to remember very little about Sopkin's TV week—but soon the memories came back in a flood. "My most vivid memory is what Charles looked like around Day 3," she said. "It seemed to me he wore the same thing for a twenty-four-hour period, or however long seven times twenty-four is—which was, if memory serves, a sort of once-French-blue terrycloth bathrobe that seemed to get grittier as the days went by. I don't remember what he drank, but it was either scotch or bourbon or something. And I remember breezing in at one point when he was watching Konrad Adenauer's funeral. There was an attempt at, 'Should we stand up, should we not stand up?' But he started to babble after about Day 4. He was becoming fairly incomprehensible; he had a running stream of conversation with the television sets." I think I gulped at this point, picturing my own imminent descent into the same hell, but Ms. Birnbaum continued in full flow. "I wasn't with him twenty-four hours a day, and he was in great spirits, but, boy, did he need to be taken out and hosed down when it was over. That I can tell you. I mean, there was no question, the man had to be dry-cleaned after that."

I spoke to Alexandra Birnbaum on September 16, 1999, and the image of Charles Sopkin babbling in his bathrobe has haunted me ever since. Now it's September 25, the day before my voyage begins. I sit on the living-room couch and contemplate the reality—and possible insanity—of what I'm about to do. A producer friend named Jonathan Weisgal has sent over thirteen TV dinners, which are now sitting in my freezer. There are twelve television sets in front of me, and tomorrow I'm going to start watching them for an average of fifteen hours a day, for a full week. Will I survive with my faculties intact? My first job out of college was reviewing video games for *Games* magazine, and I remember all too well the way my eyes seemed to bungee in and out of their sockets at the end of each day. I can only hope that years of seeing six movies at a stretch at Sundance and Cannes have strengthened my eye muscles in the interim. As for my brain . . .

Enough. I take a deep breath, and let it out. I'm as ready as I'll ever be—to boldly go where one man has gone before. ⏹

I wake up every few hours, but drift back to sleep each time. As usual, Cosmo spends most of the night on the pillow above my head, like a furry cap with paws for ear flaps. Then Sam and I both wake spontaneously at 8:10 A.M., five minutes before the alarm would have gone off. She gets *The New York Times* and brings it back to bed. "Wow," she exclaims. "The headline on the Metro section says, 'Man on Upper West Side Attempts Foolhardy Stunt.'"

My plan is to start watching at 9:00 A.M., in time for the Sunday-morning talk shows, then to skip around the schedule all day and get the lay of the land. Nevertheless, I block it all out

"Man on Upper West Side Attempts Foolhardy Stunt"

of my mind and read the newspaper until 8:40, which is roughly when pleasure stops and procrastination begins. "You'd better get in the shower," says Sam. "It'll take you five minutes just to turn the damn things on." I write this down, and Sam raises an eyebrow. "If this turns you into someone who decides to chronicle every action of their life, I may divorce you. I just want you to know that." I write that down too.

The first unpleasant surprise of the day comes in the shower—no hot water, at least at first. I take the quickest shower in memory, and don't even sing, which is most unusual for a karaoke enthusiast like me, who not-so-secretly wishes he were Frank Sinatra. Chilled but clean, I dress, enter the living room gingerly, take a deep breath, and turn on the Zeniths. The noise is like a gathering roar, or—more charitably—like an orchestra tuning up. Unready to conduct just yet, I dash to the kitchen and grab some cereal from a huge box I bought months ago over Sam's objections. "Just to make you happy, I'm eating Apple Jacks," I tell her. She shrugs. "I think you need as much sugar as you can get," she says.

The orchestra is tuned and ready to play. I mute everything except *CBS Sunday Morning*, and begin. Here are the headlines: Five days after the Taiwan earthquake, two brothers have been pulled from the wreckage. They survived by eating apples and drinking their own urine. (I'm eating Apple Jacks and drinking orange juice, but I can sympathize with their plight.) Judith Exner is dead. She was the mistress of JFK and Sam Giancana—and the ex-wife of William Campbell, who played Koloth the Klingon on a memorable episode of the original *Star Trek*.

I have more urgent things to worry about. "Sweetie—this is so stupid—I forgot a spoon for my cereal." "Oh, Christ," says Sam as she gets it for me. "Day 1: I am Spoon-Bearer. I should keep my own diary of this week."

Senator Paul Wellstone is on *Meet the Press*, touting the virtues of Democratic presidential contender Bill Bradley. "Do you believe in this theory of Clinton fatigue?" asks ruddy-cheeked, russet-haired Tim Russert. Wellstone responds, "I think people really became very tired of all they were hearing about, and they want to end that." In other words, yes. In the opposite chair is Secretary of Energy Bill Richardson, who supports Vice President Gore. Richardson is Hispanic, and Russert asks him cheekily if Gore will take on a Hispanic running mate—for example, Bill Richardson. "I'm not gonna get into that," says Richardson, who knows what's good for him. Wellstone joins in the teasing until Russert finally changes the subject, smirking like an attorney who's just withdrawn an inflammatory statement.

Now that I have my bearings, I venture a tentative glance at the other sets. The Sunday-morning talk shows are all doing the political thing. Philadelphia mayor Ed Rendell is on ABC's *This Week*, while Pat Buchanan is on *Fox News Sunday*. A slug on the screen below him reads, "Buchanan worked for Nixon from 1968–1974." Is this like the warning on a pack of cigarettes? I approve of this idea; every politician should come with warning labels.

Immediately, I run into remote trouble. With twelve TVs, every time you mute one, you unmute three others. Trying to fix the problem only makes it worse, and soon I feel like the Sorcerer's Apprentice. After several exasperating minutes, I get up and apply the remote directly to each set, muting the politicians and unmuting *Men In Toolbelts* on The Learning Channel. The eponymous men are preparing to hook lighting fixtures into ceiling beams. "It's very important to use these," says a burly man, pointing to a bunch of little black circles. "They're not Wallaces, they're grommets. One grommet, two grommet. I may have to vomit. I made a poem up!" He has the appearance and demeanor of a professional wrestler. His partner, by contrast, is a bushy-haired guy who looks like an Ed Koren *New Yorker* cartoon come to life. Is he there to stand in for thoroughly unhandy urbanites like me? No, he actually seems to know something. "We recommend shellac when the natural beauty of the wood doesn't need to be altered by colors," says the bushy-haired guy. I stare in incomprehension.

Men In Toolbelts is a perfect example of the multichannel TV universe in action. In Charles Sopkin's day, the only measure of a program's success was the ratings—how many people watched the show. But over the next few decades, networks and advertisers discovered the power of demographics. What mattered wasn't the sheer number of viewers, but whether they were the viewers the advertisers wanted to reach. These days the gospel is that each program—and sometimes entire channels, such as Lifetime (for women) and Nickelodeon (for kids)—should be tailored to a specific demographic, and it's this idea of "narrowcasting" that has driven the cable explosion. The cable channels settle for much smaller audiences than do the traditional networks, but in exchange they deliver an exquisitely preselected bunch of ready consumers to their advertisers. So The Learning Channel doesn't mind that I'm not gripped by *Men In Toolbelts*, as long as real-life men in toolbelts are—and as long as they stick around for the Home Depot commercials.

Meet the Press has segued to a panel discussion on Edmund Morris's new biography of Ronald Reagan. I unmute it. Russert is asking Reagan's old spokesman Marlin Fitzwater if Reagan was "an airhead, a cultural yahoo." "He didn't spend a lot of time putting himself on the couch," admits Fitzwater. "The least interesting subject for Ronald Reagan was Ronald Reagan," says former Reagan aide Michael Deaver, who's on too. Who's next, Ed Meese?

On Channel 9, I spy another Ronald. It's an ad for McDonald's, in which Ronald McDonald meets what seems to be the whole Grimace family, including the dragified Mrs. Grimace and Mama Grimace. Oddly, they're not in the kandy-kolored studio world of McDonaldland, but outdoors in a meadow. I attribute this to the influence of *Teletubbies*, a meadow-set British kids' show that I'll check out tomorrow.

My first half hour is already over, in the blink of an eye. Clearly, time is going to move differently now.

I check out *Bobby Jones* on BET. It's a panel show, and the guests are talking about "breaking into the business." What business? The music business? Ah, it's the *gospel* music business. I suddenly remember that Sunday morning doesn't only mean political punditry. Here's a gospel DJ—he's articulate and slick, and could be mistaken for a Top 40 guy until he starts quoting Scripture.

There's a gauzily romantic commercial for Viagra on CBS. I guess they figure the average viewer for the Sunday-morning talk shows is either Bob Dole's age, or Bob Dole himself. If that's true, Bob Dole is probably watching *Meet the Press*, which has pundit William Safire talking about—what else?—the presidential race. I guess Sunday television is like a perpetual reunion for ex–Nixon staffers. "All of us are jumping on the excitement of a fight," says Safire. The guy next to him—Michael Kinsley of Slate.com— observes, "We're not just jumping on it, we're creating it." Safire agrees, I agree, and yet they keep talking as if nobody has pointed out that it's September 1999. Even the Iowa caucuses are still four months away. Russert asks Safire, "If you had to bet today, will it be Gore or Bradley as the Democratic nominee?" Safire won't take the bet. "Smart man, Safire," says Russert, smirking again. Are these shows all about goading people into making statements they'll rue in the future?

There's a very well-put-together woman on ABC. I turn up the sound, and her voice lets me know she's Cokie Roberts. I only know her from National Public Radio. Roberts is talking about the other topic of the morning, the Reagan biography. Apparently, Edmund Morris creates a fictional persona who observes Reagan's life along with the reader. It's a deviation from the traditional practices of biography, but it doesn't seem like such a big deal on TV, where movies-of-the-week take outrageous liberties with true stories all the time. The other panelists are columnist George Will, former Clinton adviser George Stephanopoulos—and Sam Donaldson, the sight of whom causes me to tune out what everyone else is saying. I can't be the first person to become totally distracted by Donaldson's hair. It's like a plastic helmet—silver, stiff, complete with sideburns. If it isn't a rug, he should change his barber. I only snap out of it when Donaldson signs off, hair immobile: "Until next week, that's *This Week.*" It's already 10:00 A.M.—time flies when you're watching twelve TVs at once, regardless of what you're watching.

On Channel 47, here's Rod Parsley, the pastor of the World Harvest Church in Columbus, Ohio. "Today I conclude my soul-searching message—are you Rapture-ready?" asks Reverend Parsley. He's full of fire and brimstone, preaching before a packed-looking—and huge-looking—church. He warns us that just as the flood surprised everyone but Noah, the Rapture will surprise us. Not everyone is going up to heaven on the first load. "Repentance is the key!" says a card on screen. Next, we see a picture of a suburban kitchen, complete with Mom and kid. Then the people disappear, leaving the dishes in the sink. A newspaper headline reads, "Millions Missing!" It's a promo for Rod's audiotapes about the Rapture, which can be had "For Your Love Gift of $20 or More." An announcer tells us, "There's not another event that has to take place before Jesus returns. Don't be left behind!"

Back in the pulpit, Rod gets into the begats. "What a book—what a book, the Bible. Like a diamond laying on a velvet couch, the revelation of Enoch." To my mild embarrassment, I start to lose interest. As a lapsed Jew, I know too well that if the Rapture happens, I'm not likely to disappear from the kitchen. I decide to find some godless programming for agnostics.

Here's the ticket—on USA Network, it's the World Wrestling Federation. Since wrestling is more popular than ever, and monopolizes hours of TV every week, I unmute the sound to experience the phenomenon. Two big guys in comic-book outfits tussle in the ring. A hold. A flip. Then one wrestler wallops the other one onto the mat with a metal folding chair, and I gasp audibly. Can this be legal, even in a fixed sport? Sam calls out from the bedroom—"That's the first thing I've heard you react to out loud." The chair-bashing seems to end the match, with the bashee lying flat on the canvas. Suddenly, I feel sickened. I was expecting harmless cartoon fun, but this is just brutality, even if it's fake brutality. Then, on the coming attractions for next week, one wrestler forces another to eat Alpo. When I asked for godless programming, I didn't mean it literally! I repent! Cut to a commercial—for WWF action figures, of course. No tiny little metal folding chairs are in evidence.

The wrestling I remember from my own youth is ancient history for the screaming crowd in today's arena. I distinctly recall sitting with my sister in the late Seventies and watching the adventures of such comparatively benign figures as Hulk Hogan and the late, lamented Andre the Giant. Sure, they were walking cartoons even then, and we had no illusions that wrestling was anything other than broad entertainment. But I can hardly believe the intense mean-spiritedness of the WWF action on the set before me. They've pulled off the astonishing feat of identifying the lowest common denominator and going even lower.

I try to stick it out, but it's no use. Eventually I abandon all journalistic diligence and retreat to PBS. The intriguingly named *Zooboomafoo* turns out to be an animal-themed kids' show, today featuring lessons on how to wash dogs. Host Martin has a sidekick, a skunk puppet who grabs the hose and sprays it everywhere. Hilarity ensues. Martin is drenched. "Thanks, Zabu," he says. (Or is it Sabu, like the star of *The Thief of Bagdad*? Seems unlikely.) In fact, there are two human hosts—the other one, Chris, says to grab some towels before the dogs shake. Of course, he's too late, and everyone gets drenched all over again.

Sam comes in before taking the dog for a morning walk. She's smitten by *Zooboomafoo*, where Chris and Martin are now playing with some pigs: "Look how cute they are!" She's referring to the pigs, not the hosts; Sam has been completely animal-crazy since childhood. Chris and Martin swing out on ropes like Tarzan, then drop into the mud and crawl around with the pigs. They're remarkably chipper, considering the indignities of their job. The skunk falls in the mud too. How many puppets do they have? Next, Zabu narrates a stop-motion animation segment about his home in Zabu-land. Between the replacement puppets and the animation, my mental calculation of the show's budget keeps going up and up like a taxi meter. Sam still hasn't walked the dog—she could happily watch *Zooboomafoo* all day. In fact, it's pretty good, and I feel revived after my nasty brush with wrestling. Wait, Zabu is hopping. He's not a skunk, he's a monkey of some kind. A marmoset? A lemur?

Things become a little clearer when the show finally ends. It's Zoboomafoo—and that's his name. It's supported by HealthTex, "Viewers Like You," and McDonald's. We see an animated Ronald opening a book, out of which comes a flying Happy Meal. This is what PBS calls "enhanced underwriting," and I call a commercial. It's enhanced enough to make me long for the days when *Mobil Masterpiece Theatre* was just called *Masterpiece Theatre*.

Now that I'm in the PBS kids' bag, however, it's time for *Zoom*, and I'm not going to miss it. The original show is a cherished memory of my childhood, and they've revived it only recently. It looks like the old set, although the costumes are hipper—T-shirts with *Zoom* logos, and blue jeans. The multiethnic kids who host the show are out in the streets of Boston asking other kids, "What will fashion and music be like a century from now?" Polka dots, says one. Music will sound terrible, says another. "If you want to watch TV, there'll be a little screen in your pants or your jacket." Just what we need. Next, the Zoom kids do a skit in Ubbi Dubbi, a variant of pig Latin popularized by the original show. "Hubbi, frubbiends!" It's nice to know one dead language survives on television.

I glance over to wrestling long enough to see two busty female wrestlers; the one with the most pronounced cleavage is named Chyna. A male wrestler lies on the mat, groaning. Then another wrestler—his partner?—hits Chyna with a frying pan.

Fortunately there's golf on NBC, in which the only things hit by metal objects are golf balls. I should tell you right now that I'm a virtual sports illiterate. I'm not snobbish about it, just detached. I've never been able to make the leap of association that would allow me to feel that a particular team or player represents me—and without that leap, it's all just noise and motion. But you don't have to care who wins to enjoy watching golf on television. It's a soothing, green oasis in the cathode desert, and it should last most of the day, hooray.

Bob Doll from Merrill Lynch talks about money on *Money Talks* on ABC. Can you imagine the trouble he has with people thinking his name is a typo? ABC should have him debate a stockbroker named Bill Clanton.

After two hours of taking notes, my left hand starts cramping badly. Being a bit of a hypochondriac, I immediately picture myself with a crippling case of repetitive strain injury, unable to finish my experiment or do much of anything else. So far, I've chosen to sit in our comfiest overstuffed chair, with my Macintosh PowerBook on my lap for note-taking. If I lean back, I can't take notes; if I lean forward, I get no support from the chair. Eventually, I'll probably have to bring my computer desk and an upright chair into the room to prevent permanent nerve damage.

"E-mail for Z-mail!" goes the closing rap on *Zoom*. It includes the Web address, along with the singsong *"0-2-1-3-4"* coda from my youth. (It's the show's zip code.) I'm delighted by the new *Zoom*. This is how to update a classic, with respect for the original but openness to the present. Funding comes from the National Science Foundation, "America's Investment in the Future"; the Corporation for Public Broadcasting; and the inevitable Viewers Like You. Then, just as I think we might avoid it, that goddam McDonald's ad again. It seems to be a blanket support of kids' programming on Channel 13, so it runs after every show. It's possible that this is especially disturbing to me because I was tormented as a child by a recurring series of nightmares that Ronald McDonald was trying to eat me. (When I was twelve, my dream self got the jump on him and beat him to a bloody pulp. This remains one of the most satisfying moments of my life, so maybe I'm protesting too much about the wrestlers.)

Sam comes in, concerned for my well-being. "Do you need an open window? The weather's nice. How about a little fresh air in here?" I grunt, and she opens the window as I check out the alternatives at 11:00 A.M. On A&E, it's their flagship show, *Biography*, which can reduce even the most eventful life to sixty minutes including commercials. As someone who's worked on numerous movies inspired by true stories, I'm envious of the freedom inherent in A&E's format. They don't have to fit the life into a narrative structure, or argue about how much artistic license to take; they just have to lay it all out, depending on what they can illustrate with still photographs, archive footage, and interviews.

In this case the show starts with a photo of a very old woman. I guess Rose Kennedy, but it's Coco Chanel. We hear the sonorous voice of host Peter Graves: "Chanel's carefully cultivated public image made her fortune. But behind that image lay a very different private life, which she went to great lengths to conceal." Okay, I'm hooked. I know almost nothing about Coco Chanel, except that she designed dresses, created Sam's favorite perfume, and was bisexual. Are they going to go there?

During the first ad, I check out *Robocop* on the Sci-Fi Channel, a series based on the film. I love the original movie, but not as much as my mother-in-law does. She judges every movie by its body count—the higher, the better—and once dragged my sister-in-law to the Philadelphia Auto Show to have her picture taken with a guy in a Robocop suit. My late father-in-law shared her predilections; they must have watched *Blue Thunder* ten times.

Biography is back. After a childhood of poverty and an adolescence of performing in nightclubs, Coco Chanel attracts a seemingly endless string of wealthy lovers. One sets her up in a boutique, and another introduces her to the chemist who invents Chanel No. 5. We see video footage of her salon, which is stunning—trust the French to preserve it as it was. "I don't think this is fair," says Sam. "You've actually found something engrossing."

Having settled into the life of Chanel, I realize that my setup is impractical and impossible. The Mac is starting to heat up, and my thighs are feeling it. I lug my computer desk into the living room and couple it with a dining-room chair. But there's a problem: the PowerBook screen blocks out four or five TVs, including the one I'm watching. I turn the desk sideways, which works fine, except that we have to move more furniture to let people walk easily from the living room to the dining room. When I finally sit down at my new command post, Cosmo wants to play fetch with his giant stuffed bone, and I acquiesce. He's a happy dog. He seems to ignore the TVs entirely; not for the first time, I envy his savoir-faire.

It's 11:30 already. How is this possible? Meanwhile, if Chanel was bisexual, *Biography* isn't dealing with it. The Duke of Westminster, the richest man in England, is her next conquest. We see still photos of the aristocracy of prewar Europe, when aristocracy really meant something. After that comes a real coup for the A&E researchers: an early newsreel of a fashion show at Westminster's palace.

Still playing fetch, I accidentally toss the bone onto a shelf. I apologize to Cosmo, retrieve it myself, and throw it really far down the hall, to his scampering delight. When I come back to the sets, *Biography* is up to World War II. Chanel proclaims, "This is no time for fashion," and closes her boutique. Good for her. But she sleeps with Nazis. Bad for her. The liberation of Paris, seen previously in *The Sorrow and the Pity*, is here recapitulated in thirty seconds. Chanel is spared humiliation—shaved heads don't go with tailored suits—and she moves to Switzerland for nine years. "But in 1953, rumors reached Paris that Chanel was planning the impossible—a comeback." The suspense!

Once the comeback is safely under way, I turn to BET, where Johnnie Cochran now has a talk show. The subject of today's colloquy is violence on television. At once, I think of the classic Saul Steinberg drawing of the artist drawing himself drawing himself drawing himself, and so on. Could it be that the ultimate subject of television is television itself?

Cochran's guest is Steve Allen, onetime TV provocateur and now honorary chairman of the Parents Television Council, which recently took a full-page ad in *The New York Times* headlined, "TV Is Leading Children Down a Moral Sewer." Allen is sort-of-debating Mike Wilson, a long-haired guy in his late twenties who develops computer video games. Wilson argues that video games are an easy target. Then, with no explanation, we see a clip of actor-director Stanley Tucci on some panel somewhere, saying there's too much sex and violence in the media. "Children don't have enough choices," says Tucci. BET segues from this directly to an ad for *Body and Soul*, a compilation of sensual soul classics like "Let's Get It On." Under the scroll of titles is a foxy lady sliding around beneath satin sheets, who wriggles as a muscular man embraces her from behind. Someone at BET must be having a good laugh about this.

The Chanel bio is on its last legs, and so is Chanel; old age isn't kind to her. "A woman who isn't loved is lost," she says. "She might as well be dead." Cut to black-and-white footage of a carousel, with calliope music playing—what does this have to do with Chanel? Continuing in this vein, Chanel's death is narrated over a long overhead pan of Paris at night, also black and white. In their scramble for appropriate footage, the *Biography* team has gotten downright impressionistic.

"Virus of Violence" finishes up on BET. Needless to say, Steve Allen gets the last word. The irony is thick here, not least because Johnnie Cochran became famous for defending that sterling role model for children, O.J. Simpson. Cochran closes the show with a sort of benediction: "Good night, keep the faith, and let's stop the violence and the hate." And if it doesn't fit, you must acquit.

Noon. Determined to watch something I would never see if I weren't engaged in my foolhardy stunt, I go to domestic goddess Martha Stewart's show on the Food Network, *From Martha's Kitchen*. To my delight, today's topic is pizza. I love pizza. In fact, I met Sam by placing a personals ad in *The Village Voice* that described me as being "into pizza, movies, and Motown," and fifteen years later it's still accurate. Martha starts out making pizza dough from scratch in her kitchen. She sprinkles yeast into a measuring cup of water. "Watch the magic occur. You can see how alive and fluffy it is." I know too much about Martha, having read a dishy biography called *Just Desserts*, which was actually depressing rather than delicious; if the book is to be believed, everyone who gets close to Martha ends up hating her, suing her, or both. As the pizza takes shape and the pug snores at my feet, I realize I'm getting hungry. I've been watching for three hours plus, so it's no wonder.

Okay, I give up—it's lunchtime. True to form, Cosmo springs awake as soon as I head to the kitchen, and waits patiently for scraps that do not appear. Meanwhile, I'm listening to Martha in the next room as she takes phone questions about pizza. This show sure isn't live, so it must be the old dodge where anyone who calls in gets assigned a date to call later. But how do they get people to ask about pizza specifically? Could these callers be peons in Martha's empire, pretending to be viewers? "I have a beehive oven in my old 1810 farmhouse," says Martha, "and I make my pizzas right in the oven." Sure you do. Like Martha Stewart has time to cook for herself. Is she using the royal "I"?

Sunlight streams through the windows. It looks like a gorgeous day, or is that just because I'm stuck here indoors? I eat lunch and settle in to watch *Hercules*, the syndicated hit on Channel 11. Kevin Sorbo, who plays the mythical hero, is a big man who looks the part—he could be an ex–football player—but he has a pleasantly offhand, underplayed delivery. Sorbo's manner says to relax and not take the show too seriously, the way James Garner's wry affect used to color *The Rockford Files*. Violent or not, I'd let my kid watch this, whatever Steve Allen thinks.

The story is that Hercules is having unearthly visitations from a dead friend (whose name I don't catch), warning him that the end of the world is at hand. Confusingly, the friend refers to the upcoming event as "Armageddon"—whose mythology is this, anyway? Then another, rowdier, friend refers to Herc and the dead guy as "the Dynamic Duo." Clearly they don't worry about anachronisms on this show. As if to confirm this, here come the Four Horsemen of the Apocalypse, and I *know* they're not in Edith Hamilton's *Mythology.* "War," says Herc. "What's it good for?" asks his pal. "Absolutely nothing," replies Herc.

I finish lunch at 1:00 P.M. Sam takes Cosmo to a birthday party in Central Park for Tibby, another pug. Should I do the dishes and miss the rest of *Hercules,* or leave them in the sink like a slob? I vote for slob. According to my laboriously prepared grid, I'm supposed to change a bunch of channels now, but I'm sluggish with post-lunch brain chemicals, and I decide to leave them be, just like the dishes.

Battle Dome, on Channel 9, looks like the latest variation on *American Gladiators.* Like that show, which was a phenomenon several years ago, *Battle Dome* is halfway between wrestling and a triathlon on Mars. Cartoonish as it is, it's still enough like sports that I can feel my attention preparing to wander. The champion is a spangly guy in a toga, flanked by three equally spangly cheerleaders who knead his muscles. He and the challenger don masks, and they both grab on to a metal grid that lifts off the ground. The object is to knock your opponent off the grid, which the champion does in no time flat, to enthusiastic caresses from the gals. You couldn't get away with this blatant T&A stuff only ten years ago—but now they just call it postmodern.

Speaking of postmodernism—and how often do you get to use *that* segue?—there are Chuck Close paintings on Channel 75, with their photorealistic faces broken down into tiny abstract squiggles. Sam and I went to his retrospective at MoMA, and this looks like the same show. The camera pulls in and out, giving the full effect of both the portraits and the squiggles. This is good television, as in both good for you and good to watch. I turn up the sound, just in time for the end of the segment.

There's a different take on the art world in a commercial for air freshener, which features a cigar smoker who makes his print of

Edvard Munch's *The Scream* scream. After the smoker installs a Glade Plug-In, the screaming figure starts dancing and singing, "Plug it in, plug it in." Hey, maybe Merrill Lynch could do something similar with Pablo Picasso's *Guernica*—after all, there's a bull in the painting. Timex, meet Salvador Dali. Lysol, meet Andres Serrano.

I return to *Hercules* as the story wraps up. I'm not clear on the details, but I think that by forgoing his chance at full godhood—in a surprising bit of fidelity to the Greek myth, Herc is half-mortal, half-divine—Herc saved the world and brought his pal back from the dead. I still don't know the pal's name, but the rowdy guy seems to be named Ares. Is he actually Ares, god of war? Maybe he's Aries, like the constellation? Maybe he's from Buenos Aires?

Let's check out *The Gossip Show* on E! The format is to cut from one gossip columnist to another, as each gives a bit of dish. "Cybill is the new face of menopause," says a woman with an Australian accent. Another columnist tells us that the venerable band Aerosmith was offered two mil to play one night for a Saudi prince, but they've turned it down to play for their fans at an already-booked concert date. The source? Steven Tyler, the lead singer. Some gossip.

HBO's animated multicultural fairytale series, *Happily Ever After*, features "The Sissy Duckling," written by Harvey Fierstein of *Torch Song Trilogy* fame. While more-macho ducklings play baseball, duckling Elmer stages puppet shows for the smaller ducklings. His mother complains that Dad won't stop the kids from calling their son a sissy, but Dad says it's true—"Thanks to him, I'm the laughingstock of this whole flock!" Fierstein also provides Elmer's voice, and his gravelly rumble doesn't sound very sissy. Maybe that's the point, but I think it's just bad voice casting. Carl Reiner once created a sitcom called *Head of the Family*, and starred in the pilot. Producer Sheldon Leonard took one look at the pilot and told Reiner, "You're not right for what you wrote for yourself." Thus *The Dick Van Dyke Show* was born.

Elmer redeems himself by saving his father's life, and Papa Duck finally tells off a macho blowhard duck who's been making fun of Elmer. The credits reveal that, wittily, the straight duck parts have all been cast with openly gay actors: Mama Duck is voiced by lesbian singer Melissa Etheridge, while the macho duck is Dan Butler from *Frasier*. I miss the credit for Papa Duck—is it Ian McKellen? Rupert Everett? Trying to think of possibilities only points up how few openly gay male actors there are, even now, years after Rock Hudson's outing. It's easy to make fun of political correctness, but I find myself hoping some gay kids will take courage from "The Sissy Duckling"—and maybe some famous gay adults as well.

A headline on A&E reads, "Big Diamonds Really Are Unlucky." It's a documentary on the Hope Diamond. Where's Sam when you need her? She loves jewelry. However, this exclusively didactic approach to documentaries is bugging me. It's informative, sure, but after living for three years in London, I can imagine what someone from Channel Four or the BBC thinks when they see this stuff. On British television, the range of documentary programming is nearly as vast as the range of drama and comedy. It embraces cinema-verité, point-of-view pieces like Ross McElwee's very personal film essays, and even the occasional multipart prime-time documentary series. But in America, it's as if the people who make children's educational shows in Britain were responsible for the entire schedule. The traditional PBS documentary is just-the-facts-ma'am, with an omniscient narrator and only the slightest suggestion of an individual point of view. (There are a few exceptions, like the valiant series *P.O.V.*, which hives off a tiny corner of the PBS schedule for first-person work.) With so many cable channels showing documentaries, there should be room for more approaches to the form—but no, A&E and Discovery and their spin-off channels are mostly happy to follow PBS's lead. What's even more frustrating is that, because of the lure of American co-production dollars, didactic documentaries are multiplying on British TV as well.

Xena: Warrior Princess starts on 11. After *Hercules*, I should give equal time to its even more successful sister show. Within minutes, Xena and her friends are fighting off a Roman legion, in a furious action sequence that makes *Hercules* look poky by comparison. Xena vows to kill Julius Caesar, who sent the baddies. Kevin Sorbo may be a good sport, but the wonderfully named Lucy Lawless is a force of nature. No wonder she beats him in the ratings.

Both *Xena* and *Hercules* seem to use the same algorithm with which my old Hollywood boss Art Linson produced movies like *The Untouchables* and *Heat*. Instead of starting with something smart and dumbing it down, like most Hollywood product, they start with something dumb and smarten it up. It's a lot more fun that way. (Art always insisted that if you start with something smart *and* make it in a smart way, you won't make money. Much of my subsequent career in the movie business has been dedicated to challenging this assertion—and, to my chagrin, Linson's Law has won out almost every time.) What's remarkable is that Xena and her blond sidekick, Gabrielle, are clearly a couple, although I doubt we'll ever see them between the sheets. This certainly explains why most of my lesbian friends are *Xena* devotees. Xena and Gabrielle have a third friend, Amarice, a troublemaker. It's the same formula we just saw on *Hercules*, although the homoerotic charge on that show is considerably lower.

Now Xena is face to face with Caesar's mistress, a vixen who has captured Gabrielle. I miss the rest of the scene because I'm distracted by Cosmo, who's stopped playing fetch and wants to sit on my lap. But it's more than Cosmo that's distracting me. I've been at this for four and a half hours now, and I'm getting woozy. How can it be so exhausting just to sit and watch television? Then I remember the immortal words of the perpetually unemployed alcoholic father of one of my college girlfriends: "The problem with doing nothing is, you can't take a vacation."

Xena goes to see Brutus, and delivers a different set of immortal words: "Beware the ides of March." "Why the ides of March?"

asks Brutus. "Because on that day," says Xena, "Caesar will declare himself emperor." Brutus is skeptical, but Xena won't let up. "Come on, Brutus. Gabrielle saved your life once. Give me a chance to save hers." Yond Xena hath a lean and hungry look.

Then Caesar tells Brutus that Gabrielle will be executed on the ides of March, and the penny drops for Brutus. Caesar seems more like a Malibu beach bum than an emperor, but that's probably part of the fun here. There's a big fight as Xena tries to free Gabrielle and Amarice from prison. The vixen throws a discus and cuts Xena down in mid-battle, as Gabrielle watches in horror. Gabrielle goes nuts and stabs a centurion to death, but then she stops, traumatized by the blood. Cut to an Almond Joy commercial.

A *Max Headroom* rerun on Bravo. This was hip for, what, two minutes in 1987? But during that time it was the biggest thing in the world—merchandising, diet Coke ads, parodies in "Doonesbury," you name it. Twelve years later it's barely a footnote. All TV crazes are subject to the same dictum King Solomon had on his ring: "This too shall pass." Gather ye rosebuds, Pokémon.

Close-up on Xena, barely alive. Gabrielle cradles her head and kisses her brow. "Don't cry," says Xena. "I won't," says Gabrielle. The centurions march Xena and Gabrielle through the snow, while the vixen gloats that Caesar will become emperor, and her puppet. Oh my God, they're tying Xena and Gabrielle to crosses! At least they're not using nails. "You're the best thing in my life," Xena tells Gabrielle. "I love you, Xena," says Gabrielle. Wait, they *are* using nails! Meanwhile, Caesar makes his speech, while Brutus readies for the kill. The centurion raises his hammer just as Brutus raises his knife. William Shakespeare could never have envisioned this—it's a nail-driving, Forum-stabbing, cross-cutting extravaganza! "And you, Brutus?" says Caesar. (No Latin here—Ubbi Dubbi is the only dead language on American TV.) We dissolve from Caesar's lifeless body to Xena's point of view on the cross as the soldiers march away. This is pretty heavy; they never crucified anyone on TV when I was a kid, except on Easter specials. It looks like the end for Xena, but just then her body is surrounded by the kind of animated sparkles that usually accompany the words "Our Feature Presentation." Xena's spirit form reaches out to Gabrielle's spirit form. They ascend to heaven, sparkling away like Leonardo DiCaprio at the end of *Titanic*, leaving their earthly bodies hanging. I gape at the screen dumbfounded as we cut to a promo for next week's season premiere of *Xena: Warrior Princess:* "The battle for their bodies is lost, but the battle for their souls is about to begin!" I can only imagine what Reverend Rod Parsley would make of this show. It transcends kitsch; it has the charge of pure pop absurdity, like *Batman* in its Sixties heyday, and I can see why it's a hit.

It's 2:30. On Fox Family Channel, the adventures of Shirley Holmes, a descendant of Sherlock. On MTV, *The Tom Green Show.* Tom is an elfin, bearded Canadian who has remained a naughty little boy long after most naughty little boys have packed it in. The face of Tom's sidekick, Glenn, appears on a TV screen, positioned above the body of a dummy that just sits there. Today, Tom is investigating lifetime guarantees. He does this by going to stores and smashing the merchandise with a sledgehammer. It's a variation on the old schtick invented by Steve Allen—in the days before TV was leading children down a moral sewer—and perfected by David Letterman.

But Tom Green seems tame compared to the horror of *The New Addams Family* on Fox Family Channel. It's a brand-new color update of the classic series, with no-name actors trying to look like the actors from the movie, who were trying to look like the actors from the TV show, who were trying to look like the cartoons from *The New Yorker.* Even the non-Addamses are mugging it up. Watching this travesty, it's hard to remember that the original show was pretty sophisticated.

Suddenly, I can take no more. "How did this happen?" I yell, surrounded by the evidence of my folly. I flee to the kitchen for some rice pudding, the comfort food to end all comfort foods. Charles Sopkin would have had a cocktail at this point, but I'm not Charles

Sopkin. Yet. When I return to the living room, I take drastic measures by muting everything except Kurt Masur conducting Tchaikovsky's Fifth Symphony on PBS. Instantly, I feel better; this isn't just high culture, it's sanity personified. I get up and stretch, trying to ignore the Jesse Ventura action figures on Channel 9. I really want to take a nap—and I don't tend to take naps. It would be so easy to lie down on the couch and listen to soothing Tchaikovsky . . .

Just as I'm about to succumb, I am rescued by the appearance of the notorious Emeril Lagasse on the Food Network. Emeril seems like unlikely casting for a chef; he looks more like a counterman at a diner, or a bartender. This contrast seems to be part of his appeal, at least for the appreciative women who make up a big chunk of his live audience. He talks about adding chopped garlic, and for some reason the audience applauds. "Pow!" he says. Emeril has a number of catch phrases—including "Let's kick it up a few notches!" and "Bam!"—and they have the traditional Pavlovian effect on audiences, like *Laugh-In*'s "You bet your sweet bippy!" and *Saturday Night Live*'s "We are two wild and crazy guys!" Strangely, "Add a few cloves of garlic" seems to be another one, although it's not as catchy. Emeril's a showman, and I admire anyone who can enthrall a live audience with an hour of cooking. However, I remember Sam saying that the *New York Times* food section couldn't get any of his recipes to come out right.

Emeril is now making chili. "Rice and beans, rice and beans. You know what I mean?" Emeril has a sound-effects man, Doc, who plays a percussion instrument when Emeril uses the pepper grinder. And boy, does he use it. "Now we're going to add some chili powder," says Emeril. "Bam!" yells a wisenheimer in the audience. "You said it," Emeril shoots back. Then he smothers the chili with tortilla strips to "kick it up a few notches," which seems to be his code for "let's drown it in something." I really am getting punchy— I imagine Emeril leading the congregation in a rhapsody about the Rapture, and Rod Parsley making something with parsley in the

SUNDAY

CAN'T TAKE MY EYES OFF OF YOU

kitchen. Preaching, cooking, it's all performance when it's on TV. The patron saint of television should really be the late director-choreographer Bob Fosse, for his steadfast conviction that everything is show business.

On Channel 2, James Brolin stars in a syndicated series about Navy pilots—*Baywatch* meets *Top Gun*, as they say in Hollywood—called *Pensacola Wings of Gold*. What a title! It's like that infamous product of the New York newspaper mergers of the Sixties, the *World Journal Tribune*. It's easy to imagine that the producer wanted to call it *Pensacola*, the network wanted to call it *Wings of Gold*, and the diplomatic Brolin suggested a compromise. (He must be diplomatic, because he's married to Barbra Streisand.) That may not be how it happened, but I bet it's not far off. And what about the show, anyway? We see a hunky flyboy bantering with a bony blonde in a negligee. She coyly offers him a Pringles chip from a carefully displayed can.

Charles Colson, of all people, has been dredged up on C-SPAN's *Book TV*. I was right—Sunday is the day for ex–Nixon staffers on television. *Book TV* is a no-frills show that plunks down a video camera in a bookstore or anywhere an author is doing a reading, and broadcasts the whole thing. Colson has co-authored a book called *Now How Shall We Live?*, and he's speaking at the Christian Booksellers Association conference. "Our job is to give them eyes with which to see, and ears with which to hear," Colson tells the booksellers. That was probably his rationale for the Watergate bugging too—giving Nixon ears with which to hear Larry O'Brien at the Democratic National Committee. "There is no way for the law to have authority unless the law is based on the Law beyond the law," continues Colson. A title onscreen points out helpfully that "Charles Colson served seven months in prison for his involvement in Watergate." I guess the idea is that nobody knows more about ethics than a reformed sinner.

A first-season *Partridge Family* episode succeeds the Addamses on Fox Family Channel. I can tell it's first-season because the youngest boy, Chris—the drummer in the family band—is played by dark-haired Jeremy Gelbwaks instead of blond Brian Forster. This should give you an idea of how I spent the early Seventies, along with several million other kids. The show wasn't even on my Sunday grid, but, wearied by Emeril, I set my course for the Partridge Family.

The guest star is William Schallert, who played Patty Duke's father on her "cousins identical cousins" show, and who appeared on the same episode of *Star Trek* as Judith Exner's ex-husband William Campbell. In long-hair wig and mustache, Schallert plays a country singer named Red, whom the Partridges meet in a small town and bring home like a stray puppy. "It appears I don't got much choice," drawls Red. "Tracy here has growed right upon my knee." Back at the Partridge homestead, they have an old-fashioned sing-along. Shirley Jones's voice isn't lost in the mix, the way it is on the Partridge Family records; for a moment we hear the bell-clear soprano she displayed in *Oklahoma!* and *Carousel*. Where is this episode going? They can't be setting up beady-eyed William Schallert as a potential love interest for Shirley.

Next morning, Keith—the one and only David Cassidy—persuades the band's manager, Reuben Kinkaid, to make Red the opening act at their next gig. Cassidy's erotic appeal is still evident thirty years later; he's got a self-enclosed narcissism that makes you love him the way he loves himself. But Susan Dey as Laurie Partridge is the real catch here, as always. Is she really the prettiest girl in the history of TV sitcoms, or is it just my nostalgia talking? Comes the gig, and the family band is onstage doing "I Can Feel Your Heartbeat" from the first album. It's their heaviest number, which isn't saying much. Red watches from backstage, then grabs his guitar and walks out. Commercial.

Emeril is still kicking it up a few notches, but I'm lost in a Partridge Family reverie, remembering the lunchboxes, the issues of *Tiger Beat*, and the way I accidentally left the first album sitting under a desk lamp and came home to find an abstract sculpture in black vinyl.

Red explains himself to Shirley and the kids. "I've always been a bum with a guitar and a hat," says Red. "People paid me if they liked me. People paying me before they knew they liked me—that just isn't my style." But Keith thinks Red has plain old stage fright, and he and Laurie persuade Reuben—was he supposed to be Jewish?—to book him another gig. Sure enough, Red does great this time, bantering with the audience before singing "The Wabash Cannonball." It sounds as if Schallert does his own singing. Backstage, Reuben tells Red the club wants to book him for three weeks, but Red turns it down: "That ain't singing anymore, that's business." For the tag, the Partridges perform with Red at a church. Unlike Schallert, David Cassidy's vocals are massively produced—echo chambers, harmonizers, you name it. It's not that he can't sing, he's just *processed*, the way teen idols always have been, still are, and probably always will be. They're selling perfection, and nobody's perfect.

This *Partridge Family* episode strikes me as a textbook example of old-school series construction, circa 1970. Then as now, a show would make most of its money in syndication to local stations after its initial network run. But in those days the local stations would show the episodes in no particular order, and so most network series eschewed any sort of episode-to-episode continuity. The main characters were static; they needed guest stars to go through dramatic arcs, so they wouldn't have to do it themselves. This all changed after *Hill Street Blues* and *Cheers* imported soap-opera continuity to prime-time dramas and sitcoms respectively. (I'm not counting unabashed prime-time soaps like *Peyton Place*, *Dallas*, and even the parodic *Soap*.) Now, most network series have some sort of developing story line. That may be why the best of television is better than ever; developing characters and stories in multiple installments is something TV can do far more easily than any of the other performing arts. But because the main characters are allowed to change, guest stars don't carry the same weight they used to. It's not uncommon to see an entire episode of a modern network series in which no guest star has more than one scene.

Now James Taylor is on CNN, a real-life version of Red with even less hair than Schallert under that wig. But his voice is still like a warm blanket, and he looks a hell of a lot healthier than he used to. I guess he's clean and sober now, like everybody in showbiz over the age of thirty except the unrepentant Jack Nicholson. "I don't think this business is any more ruthless than any other business, really," says Taylor. He stays focused on playing live music for real people. That ain't business anymore, that's singing!

Again, I plan to switch from Fox Family Channel to something else, but again I'm sucker-punched by a surprise. The theme music and the look of the credit sequence are familiar, but the lyrics are different: "It's a new life for two girls named Brady . . ." And they can't afford to live apart, so they move in together with their new husbands—it's a rerun of *The Brady Brides*, a short-lived attempt to extend *The Brady Bunch* into adulthood. This is like a *Saturday Night Live* skit, except it's real. Florence Henderson guest-stars, and Ann B. Davis as dowdy housekeeper Alice is still cleaning up after the Brady girls. But times have changed since *The Brady Bunch*, which was a one-camera show with a laugh track, like *The Partridge Family*. *The Brady Brides* is a three-camera show "filmed before a live studio audience," early Eighties style, which just feels weird.

At this point, Sam and Cosmo come home from the pug birthday party, where Sam's new pug earrings got many comments. As a result, I miss the setup for the episode, but for some reason the Brady Brides have a gigantic stuffed gorilla in their living room. Alice sees it, and screams like Fay Wray. What a trouper. What a lousy show. At least on the original *Brady Bunch*, Robert Reed was complaining about the scripts. Here, there's nothing to stop the creative reign of terror committed by father-and-son producers

Sherwood and Lloyd Schwartz. According to *The Complete Directory to Prime Time Network and Cable TV Shows,* by Tim Brooks and Earle Marsh, *The Brady Brides* ran for two months in 1981. Two months seems generous—this is crap, unredeemed even by nostalgia. I'm changing the sound.

On goes the *Mrs. America* pageant on Pax TV, Channel 31, direct from Hawaii. That's Mrs., not Miss. "They're prettier than a lot of the young ones," says Sam of the contestants, and she's right. Their costumes, however, are outrageous: Mrs. Ohio is a butterfly, Mrs. North Dakota is "amber waves of grain," and Mrs. Rhode Island is an uncomfortable-looking captain's wheel to symbolize the Ocean State. "I'm surprised Mrs. Nevada didn't represent the state of legalized prostitution," says Sam. The pageant's hosts are former MTV VJ Downtown Julie Brown, and former *Wheel of Fortune* host Chuck Woolery. What a pair!

There's a talking toilet on Channel 9. "Oh yeah, that's the ad for blue Vanish or whatever," says Sam. Actually, it's Clorox. Now the toilet is burping flowers. What did Madison Avenue do before computer-generated imagery? Increasingly, commercials seem to take place in some cybernetic netherworld that has little or nothing to do with life as we know it. I wonder if there are any studies on the efficacy of this kind of advertising. Speaking as one idle commercial-watcher, I can barely keep any of the supercharged, computer-assisted ads and products straight in my head. If I'm in the supermarket, I may remember the burping toilet—unless I'm lucky enough to forget it—but I bet I'll have forgotten again which brand it represents.

It's 4:30. After standing over the sets for a moment, switching channels as my grids demand, I decide to give in to my inner sloth and lie down on the couch, which gives my back some relief. I'm exhausted from sitting and typing for seven and a half hours straight, and I switch to a yellow legal pad. Cosmo is happy to cuddle with me, until he hears some noise outside our front door and jumps off the couch to check it out.

I'm struck by a rerun of the series *Party of Five* on Fox. The star, Neve Campbell, could be David Cassidy's daughter. Their eyes have the same fetching squint, but they also share the same center-parted hair, and the same gloss of teenage perfection. You should hate them, but you just can't. Meanwhile, a guy imitates Joe Cocker on *Your Big Break* on 9. Come on, nobody's going to get their big break as a Joe Cocker imitator. Give it up, kid. But imitation seems to be the way of *Your Big Break*; next, two guys do the Blues Brothers. In 1999? Why not just retitle the show *Your Ticket to Obscurity*?

Back to *Mrs. America*. Big surprise—while there are a few full-time mothers, most of the contestants are professional models. This is a question that doesn't come up in the *Miss* America pageant, because those women are younger and presumably haven't launched their careers yet. The gals frolic at the Hilton Hawaiian Village, "the island's premier resort," which is mentioned by name frequently. They take hula lessons, water-slide in the Luau Lagoon, and generally indulge in the same sorts of activities that the Brady Bunch enjoyed in their two-part Hawaiian episode before Vincent Price stole their tiki doll. There's a lengthy plug for the resort's Rain Soft water system, which puts an end to bad-hair days. And cosmetics are supplied by Mrs. Ernest Borgnine: "Tova has the right products for the contestants, and she has the right products for you too!" How many plugs can they squeeze into this pageant? Did Pax TV have to put up any money at all, or was the show in profit even before they started selling ads?

"And now, please welcome Chief Soolaiye Moolavi and the fire dance!" The traditional Hawaiian fire dance is impressive, as always. And yet that's one of my biggest frustrations with television: however impressive anything is, there's always something else coming up, and soon the wondrous becomes commonplace. This is probably why I prefer to work in feature films, where the world is magnified thirty feet high and it's the commonplace that becomes wondrous. So what's *really* impressive on television? A guy hitting another guy with a metal folding chair? I may enjoy the fire dance, but I certainly don't react out loud to it.

The five finalists for Mrs. America are all stunning, and they present a pleasant alternative to the prevailing standard of TV beauty, the Skinny Teenager. I'd much rather watch the married women, being married to a married woman myself. Chuck Woolery tells us that tonight's winner will compete in the Mrs. World pageant this December, to be held in Israel—"the official destination of the millennium." This show has more plugs than Elton John's scalp. The winner will receive two tickets on El Al (I can't help wondering whether the first runner-up will get *four* tickets on El Al), a lifetime of tooth whitening from Bright Smile, and, finally, a complimentary lifetime subscription to an Internet service provider called Mayberry, USA, "offering access to the World Wide Web without access to any harmful material. Mayberry is a great place to raise a family!" Well, yeah, it was a great place for Andy and Aunt Bee to raise Opie, but that was three decades ago. And who decides what's harmful—Steve Allen?

Drum roll—the fourth runner-up is Mrs. Illinois! "She's got a big butt," says Sam approvingly. The third runner-up, Mrs. Texas! "She's not very pretty." The second, Mrs. Massachusetts! "She's very classy-looking. Beautiful. She's got a pair of knockers on her too. She didn't win? Who's gonna win?" Sam predicts it'll be Mrs. Alabama, but she's wrong. As Downtown Julie Brown puts it, "It's Mrs. Utah, from the state of—of course—Utah!" The Hawaiian crooning is soothing, but it's no "There She Is." The new Mrs. America is joined by her husband. "Oh, he's cute," says Sam, "he should be *Mr.* America." Chuck Woolery signs off, "We thank you for joining us in celebrating our greatest national treasure, the American married woman."

It's 6:00 P.M., and the Hawaiian theme continues. It's not just *Baywatch* anymore—it's *Baywatch Hawaii*! Do they use the studios that *Magnum, P.I.* inherited from *Hawaii Five-O*? Sam watches the tanned, trim lifeguards and sighs. "Wow. You don't look like that. I don't look like that. This show's useless. This is like how to feel bad about yourself." I completely agree, and I feel bad enough already after nine hours of TV. I'm switching.

Flipping around, I get to CNBC, which has an interview with *Saturday Night Live* producer Lorne Michaels, plugging tonight's prime-time special for the show's twenty-fifth anniversary. This is NBC-CNBC synergy in action. Tim Russert shows up again as the host, but they spend more time running clips than talking, which suits me fine. Here's Dan Aykroyd as Nixon, railing at a portrait of JFK: "Someday they'll find out about you—having sex with women, within these very walls! That never happened while Dick Nixon was in the White House!" What an inexhaustible source of ridicule and satire Nixon was. I feel for anyone writing for *SNL* or *The Tonight Show* nowadays. We had giants of opprobrium then.

On the set below *Baywatch*, a Hasidic Jew named Jack Lefkowitz is on Channel 25's *Lawline*. The moderator looks Jewish too. Says Sam, "They're probably talking about how great it is that they're going to have the Mrs. World competition in Israel." In fact, they're talking about real estate. What does this have to do with law? They should call it *Loanline*.

At 6:30, I notice that the esteemed biographer Robert Caro is on *Open Mind* on Channel 25. This is something I might actually want to watch, in that ever-more-distant sphere I now think of as real life—i.e., when I'm not watching twelve televisions. But just as I prepare to unmute Caro, I see something on another channel. Knowing my wife, I yell, "Pug! Pug! Pug!" Sam logs off AOL and runs in to watch with me. Mimi, Drew Carey's grotesque nemesis, is carrying a pug around on a rerun on Channel 5, and this trumps even Robert Caro. If you have a pug, you'll understand. "See all the trolls on Mimi's desk?" Sam points out. "This might be the episode where she dresses a pug up as a troll." It is indeed. Cut to Drew and his buddies singing onstage at the lounge of an airport Ramada Inn. "This is our show," says Sam, knowing my predilections as well as hers. "Pugs and karaoke." In fact, I like Drew Carey a lot, not least because he seems to genuinely enjoy his good fortune as the star of not one but two prime-time shows—and because both shows are reliably funny.

ABC News at 7 shows a picture of artist Damian Hirst's dead shark in a tank of formaldehyde, and I know they must be covering the "Sensation" exhibit that's about to open at the Brooklyn Museum. Sam and I saw the show in London, and while some of it was indeed sensationalist, there were pieces that have really stayed with me, like Rachel Whiteread's translucent casts of the spaces under chairs. Mayor Giuliani has condemned the exhibit, singling out Chris Ofili's painting *The Holy Virgin Mary*, in which an African-ized Mary has a breast fashioned out of elephant dung. In a blatant maneuver to inflame the Catholic voters he'll need in his upcoming Senate race, Giuliani keeps describing this as a painting of the Virgin Mary smeared with excrement, which just isn't true. Giuliani is a putz, but I wouldn't want to hang out with Damian Hirst either.

Sam has retired to the kitchen to make chili, determined to beat Emeril at his own game. The irresistible aroma draws me away from the couch and the Zeniths to check it out. When I get to the kitchen, I'm so happy to be out of the living room that I finally do the dishes. "This is a perfect job for you," says Sam as she stirs the pot. "What, the dishes?" I ask. "No," she says, "the TV experiment. It's constant stim, it's total information overload. You're not bored. Whatever you are, you're not bored." I realize that she's right, and suddenly I am full of resolve to keep going.

When I return to the sets, *60 Minutes* is covering the Reagan biography. Edmund Morris turns out to look remarkably like Steven Spielberg. And who knew he was British? (Actually, he's South African. By the end of the week, I will know every superficial fact about Edmund Morris.) He reads aloud from Reagan's final address, about his Alzheimer's, and breaks into tears. "You said, 'I kept my objectivity,' but this is really distressing to you," says interviewer Lesley Stahl. "This would be distressing to any human being,"

Morris replies. He tells a truly horrifying story about Reagan in his dotage, clutching a toy White House. Nancy pried it from his fingers and asked him about it. "I don't know what it is," he said, "but I think it's something to do with me."

Chili time. I need something I can watch without feeling as if I have to take notes. I decide on *King of the Hill*, a smart animated show I've enjoyed the few times I've watched it. Of course, without notes, I can't remember a damn thing about it, except the indelible sight of young Bobby Hill rocking a baby, singing, "When you get lost between the moon and New York City..." in a thick Texas drawl.

The premiere of *Felicity* pops into view on the WB, and I can't ignore it. I've developed a mild crush on actress Keri Russell through her still photos in various magazines, while never having watched her show or even heard her voice. Plus, I know two of the producers, and as a result I've felt guilty about missing the entire first season.

In the cliff-hanger at the end of last season, our collegiate heroine had to make a choice between spending the summer with Ben or Noel. Now Felicity is telling an older Hispanic guy named Javier what she decided. It turns out Keri Russell has a great voice too. Low. She sounds like the young Lauren Bacall. Just as she gets to the good part, Felicity halts her story to go to a meeting for resident advisers. Javier is frustrated, on behalf of the audience: "Tell me what happened, or I will kill you." "I promise to come back and tell you everything," she says. This is the coming-up-next mechanism that rules television, here revealed in all its glory. Felicity is a video Scheherazade, withholding the end of the story until we've watched enough commercials.

And so this mini-cliff-hanger is followed by an ad for the Gap, aimed squarely at the *Felicity* demographic. In this spot, a phalanx of blank-faced teens sing Depeche Mode's "Just Can't Get Enough" before a white background. "Everybody in leather" is the message. Am I the only one who detects a hint of totalitarianism here? The other Gap campaign running now is "Everybody in vests," which links up with efforts by Gap subsidiary Old Navy to push multipocketed "tech vests." All I can think is that some hapless temp at Gap headquarters was supposed to order a thousand vests, but added a couple of zeros by accident. The CEO goes ballistic. "What are we going to do with fifty warehouses full of vests? *Nobody* wears vests!" There's only one thing to do . . .

Back to *Felicity*—that hair, those eyes, that voice. She's sitting in her empty new dorm room, recording a letter on tape to "Sally." She's worried about how she's "going to deal with the consequences of what I did this summer." They're going to tease us until halfway through the show, aren't they? But then she kisses a guy who seems to be Ben—I guess he won the Felicity lottery. Although he's supposed to be her classmate, Ben looks easily mid-twenties. According to a recent *New York Times Magazine* article, there aren't enough attractive teenage actors to satisfy the booming market in teen programming. This accounts for the "teenage" son on the new show *Once and Again*, Shane West, a subject of said story, who plays sixteen, is twenty-one, and looks twenty-five.

Finally, Felicity tells Javier—and us—the whole story about this summer. She was heading to JFK to accompany Noel to somewhere overseas, but she changed her mind at the last minute and went back to the city to be with Ben. "You got an incredible buffet of men," says the obviously envious Javier. I really didn't think we'd learn the answer this soon. Then Felicity rejoins Ben. "So are you sorry that you went with me?" he asks. "I'm sorry you spent the rest of the summer in Mexico," she replies. He did *what*? Clearly this man is not worthy of our Felicity. Now that the mystery is resolved, the rest of *Felicity* becomes a blur before my increasingly bleary eyes. Noel is pissed off at Felicity, but she's too deep into Ben to care much. There are further indications that Ben is cute but shallow, and I have a feeling it'll take the rest of the season for Felicity to figure this out.

On Fox, they're doing an elaborate parody of *Titanic* on *Futu-*

rama, the new animated series by *Simpsons* creator Matt Groening. The show looks genuinely cool, and I may actually choose to watch it in the future, which is appropriate because it's set in the future. Besides, although my crush on Keri Russell is only stronger now that I've heard her voice (and seen that she can actually act), I'm unlikely to watch *Felicity* again. It's not bad—in fact, it's well made—but it just doesn't stir the mind or the emotions in more than a superficial way. Except for a brief discussion of *The Blair Witch Project*, there's no suggestion that these supposed college students are doing anything other than hooking up, breaking up, and brooding. What are they studying? What are they reading? Is anyone politically active? Not to mention that this show is set at a college in New York City—is anyone getting blitzed at a rock club and throwing up in an alley?

Up next on ABC is the premiere of *Snoops*, the new show by prolific writer-producer David E. Kelley. It seems churlish not to watch this, since I've seen Kelley's show *Ally McBeal* only once or twice, and his other show, *The Practice*, a grand total of never. But I really have to check out *The Saturday Night Live 25th Anniversary Special*.

This is a historic occasion, after all. *Saturday Night Live* was the first TV show to cross the firm generational lines separating Them from Us, culture from counterculture, the children of the Depression from the baby boomers. I'm a generation younger than Lorne Michaels and the original cast, but I still remember the electric jolt of seeing something on television that shared my own cultural references. Now, of course, TV is no longer a monolith with a single crack; it's splintered into hundreds of shards, each reflecting a specific audience as closely as the producers can manage. In this fractured universe, it's possible that no TV show will ever again pack the revolutionary punch of the early *SNL*.

The special starts with Bill Murray's smarmy lounge singer at an Indian casino—a new sketch! He's performing the old Raiders hit "Indian Reservation": "So proud to live—so proud to double

CAN'T TAKE MY EYES OFF OF YOU

down and let it ride!" Murray walks into the glittery audience and serenades various celebrities before he finds original SNL cast member Garrett Morris—what, they couldn't bring Morris on stage? Twenty-five years later, and he's still the Indian on this reservation. But he gets a standing ovation, which must be a belated payback for the humiliation he suffered over all those years as the Black Guy. Finally, Murray gives the traditional invocation, "Live from New York, it's *Saturday Night!*" with Morris in a bubble yelling it again for the hearing-impaired.

Announcer Don Pardo announces the endless string of performers for the evening: Dan Aykroyd, Alec Baldwin, the Beastie Boys, Candice Bergen, David Bowie—and I'm still in the B's. Suffice it to say this special features anyone who's ever performed in any entertainment medium over the last twenty-five years, including everyone who's ever been an *SNL* cast member except Charles Rocket, who said "fuck" on live television. No wonder they left Garrett Morris in the audience. If each person had five minutes on stage, the show would run straight through the night into Monday morning. Eventually Pardo gets to Archimedes Zzzyandottie and Zelmo Zzzzzip, and without further ado he introduces Chris Rock, who is the logical guy to kick things off at this particular point in time. Rock strides onstage and brings down the house by telling the absolute truth: "Twenty-five years on the air, and four funny. I mean, look around this room. I'm looking at some of the most overrated people in the history of comedy. Some of the worst movies ever made were made by people in this room."

The fake commercial is for "Schlitz Gay," with the late Chris Farley and the lately very wealthy Adam Sandler. Then the band takes us into the real commercial—but it seems the segue is another fake-out. Instead of a real ad, we get a brilliantly executed parody ad for exactly the kind of movie Chris Rock was talking about: *Deuce Bigalow, Male Gigolo,* starring *SNL* alumnus Rob Schneider. Schneider is gutsy to use his real name in this context, considering that his own career hasn't exactly thrived since *SNL. Deuce Bigalow* is every moronic formula comedy of the last ten years thrown into a blender; they must have spent a fortune filming all the individual bits to make up this completely accurate pastiche. Then the final card reveals that this is in fact a real commercial for a real movie opening soon. They actually did spend a fortune. I'm reeling.*

This sudden shift of perspective refocuses me on the practicalities of my mission. I ascertain that my back is okay (it is), my eyes are still focused (they are, barely), and my posterior is free of the familiar ache that Sam calls "buttosis." I look around at the other sets. The CBS schedule was delayed when the football game ran over, so only now does the network start a TV movie called *Song of My Heart*, starring gospel singer Amy Grant as a blind cellist. They're hitting all the demographics at the same time with this concoction. Curiously, it was a CBS executive who once told me he sat in the front row at an Amy Grant concert just so he could look up her dress.

Paramount is seizing the opportunity of the *SNL* special to run multiple ads for the latest *SNL* spin-off movie: *Superstar*, starring Molly Shannon as horny Catholic schoolgirl Mary Kathleen Gallagher. Or did Lorne Michaels construct this whole special just to attract attention to the movie? Anything is possible in the world of corporate synergy.

Half an hour has already gone by, and on Fox it's the controversial new sitcom *Action*, which I really do want to see. I've missed the setup. *SNL* alumnus Jay Mohr, playing a slimy studio executive named Peter Dragon, introduces himself to Salma Hayek, playing herself. "I've been waiting for this moment for a long time," she says. "Of course you have," he replies, beaming smugly. She slaps his face. "I guess you would have no recollection of drawing a little face on your little penis and asking me to put on a puppet show." *Action* is an odd hybrid; there's no laugh track, but it's got conventional sitcom lighting instead of the deadpan film look that allowed HBO's *Larry*

---

*I reeled even more at the end of the year, when it went on to become a considerable hit.

CAN'T TAKE MY EYES OFF OF YOU

Sanders Show to get away with this kind of vicious inside-Hollywood material. Also, unlike *Sanders*, it's not very funny. After ten minutes, Sam is bored. "This is going to fail miserably," she declares.

At the next commercial, I switch back to *SNL*. Don Pardo introduces the Three Amigos: Martin Short, Chevy Chase, and Steve Martin. Only Chevy wears the elaborate Amigo costume. "Didn't we have a conference call about this?" he asks forlornly. They introduce a selection of clips from the early days, which are as funny as the recent stuff is not. This isn't nostalgia, it's an empirical statement of fact. It's like The Spot pizzeria in New Haven—every time I go back to visit, I confirm that my college hangout actually does have the best pizza in America. Sam sits bolt upright as Andy Kaufman sings along with the "Mighty Mouse" theme, remembering, "I thought this was the most hilarious thing I'd ever seen." Word association. Bass-O-Matic. Candice Bergen in a sketch. "Look how young she is," says Sam. Land shark. Coneheads. Lorne's offer to the Beatles to reunite for three thousand dollars. "Look how young he is," says Sam. Cheeseburger. Mr. Bill. Dan Aykroyd as Julia Child, spurting blood all over the chicken. This recitation is like the story about the comedians' convention, where everybody knows all the jokes, so they just refer to them by number—but each number makes me smile nonetheless. What has happened to Aykroyd's career? He's really the star of this clipfest—his range and timing are impeccable. Here are Aykroyd and Laraine Newman on stage, tributing John Belushi. She's gained weight, which is flattering; she's also had work done, which has made her more conventionally pretty but robbed her face of its character. "She's barely recognizable," says Sam.

Reluctantly, I turn off the sound on *SNL* and turn up the season premiere of *The Practice*. I've never seen it, and it won the Emmy for Best Drama Series in 1999, beating the most acclaimed show of the year, *The Sopranos*. Defense attorney Dylan McDermott—what is his character's name?—faces off against a diminutive DA. "*Res ipsa* pipsqueak," quips McDermott. While it's a pleasure to hear even mangled Latin—I guess Ubbi Dubbi isn't the only dead language on TV after all—this seems awfully catty for our protagonist. Assistant DA Lara Flynn Boyle calms the pipsqueak down. In another courtroom, Camryn Manheim is defending a doctor who kept a severed head in his medical bag. Why is this guy not in jail? I guess you had to watch last season.

Commercial break. On the *SNL* special, some recent female cast members whom I can't identify—Molly Shannon? Cheri Oteri? I'm just guessing here—present a tribute to Gilda Radner. I turn it up. Todd (Bill Murray) is liquoring up Lisa Loopner (Gilda) so he can put the moves on her. Lisa is tempted, but resolute: "I can't marry you until I finish college and become a concert pianist and the first female open-heart surgeon." "I'll wait for you," says Todd. "I'll wait for these too," he says about her flat chest. Frankly, this sketch seems truer to late adolescence than anything I saw tonight on *Felicity*.

The Practice is back. Henry Winkler is a dentist accused of murdering a woman. The murder victim's mouth was filled with grape jelly, and it seems Winkler had jelly on his gloves and clothes. Henry, whose character's name is also Henry, sits at the dinner table with his family and one of the lawyers, a rotund guy who tells him to stick to yes or no when he gets on the stand. "I didn't have an affair with her," Henry insists, but his wife doesn't believe him. Then the lawyer opens a cupboard and sees three jars of grape jelly. Hmmm. Next day, the DA ambushes Henry on the witness stand, and he admits that he has a bizarre sexual fetish. The deceased stepped on bugs when she came to his office, and then Henry "gratified" himself. But he didn't kill her. I'm amazed that this show beat *The Sopranos*. Maybe I've already missed the glory days of *The Practice*, but it seems like a conventional courtroom drama—albeit a conventional courtroom drama that turns on a bug-squashing fetish.

Just as Paramount is pushing *Superstar* on *SNL*, Warner Brothers is pushing Dylan McDermott's new flick *Three to Tango* on *The Practice*. It looks lame. Next, Sarah Ferguson, Duchess of York, advertises Weight Watchers. I think of the ladylike British producer who called me at Miramax to pitch a movie, saying that Fergie was attached to play the lead. "Forgive me," I said, "but why would the Duchess of York want to star in a movie?" The producer was unfazed. "Why, for money," she replied, "I think she would do just about anything."

Back on *The Practice*, an expert witness explains the "crush fetish": "As a toddler, Dr. Olson saw his mother step on a bug." Yeah, and? Apparently, Henry met the victim through the Internet, and they traded bug crushing for dentistry. Do I buy this? Maybe I've led a sheltered life. Maybe there are legions of crush fetishists out there. But maybe David E. Kelley is just a tad overworked.*

Dylan McDermott, a.k.a. Bobby, proposes a plea bargain to poor Henry, whose wife is now convinced he's guilty: "You're sick, you're just a sick person, and our children are going to have to read about this . . ." But will they develop a crush fetish from seeing their mother step on their father? Meanwhile, Camryn Manheim kisses George, the doctor with the severed head in his medical bag. It's not fair that the talented Manheim—who is the standard bearer for non-anorexic women on prime-time TV—only gets to have relationships with psychos, here and in Todd Solondz's film *Happiness*.

Henry confides to the rotund lawyer, Jimmy, that the real killer is Steven, his teenage son. "He doesn't even know I know," says Henry. But does Bobby know Jimmy knows? We don't know. In the courtroom, Bobby closes with a verbal tap-dance: "We know he's a little twisted. He gets aroused by women squashing bugs, what is that? It looks really bad. But he didn't do it." Across town, Camryn Manheim tells George she feels weird about the kiss. His feelings are hurt—watch out for flying scalpels!

The jury finds Henry guilty. "I didn't do it!" moans Henry as they drag him away. "*Res ipsa* prison," snaps the pipsqueak to Bobby,

*It turns out I *have* led a sheltered life; on December 9, 1999, President Clinton signed a bill outlawing the sale of crush-fetish videos. Honestly.

delighted to have the last word, and in Latin too. "Next on *The Prac-tice*," says the announcer. Oh, Jimmy didn't tell Bobby about the son, and when he does, Bobby hits the roof.

A promo for the local news trails a truly horrifying story: a bride is gunned down before her own wedding. But even with head-lines like that, I've got to get some sleep. I turn off the sets, savoring the feeling of release as one by one they click to black. I remember this feeling from when I broke my arm in third grade. This is how I felt at night when I could finally take off my sling. ♉

Cosmo's rules are simple: When the pack sleeps, he sleeps, and when the pack wakes, he wakes. However, the rules don't seem to apply when we get up at 6:30 in the morning, which is much earlier than usual. To our amazement, Cosmo remains a snoring lump on the pillow while Sam and I bustle around the apartment. It's only when she leaves for the gym that he finally rouses himself.

After showering, dressing, and feeding the pug, I don't get in front of the sets until almost 7:20. Morning is not my thing.

At this time of day, the sets are equally divided between talk/news shows and kids' shows. I start by glancing

"He's the Uncle of His Girlfriend's Daughter's Lover"

around the former, with mild trepidation; I worry that some cata-strophic event will preempt a day's programming and force me to start the week over. Fortunately, it's business as usual today. Dan Quayle has dropped out of the race for the Republican presidential nomination, finally. On NBC's *Today*, Katie Couric—the Mary Sunshine of morning television—interviews William Donohue of the Catholic League and Norman Siegel from the ACLU. The subject, of course, is Mayor Giuliani and the "Sensation" exhibit. Next up: Brooke Shields, plugging the new season of her sitcom *Suddenly Susan*.

Meanwhile, Senator John McCain appears on *Good Morning America* on ABC, then on *This Morning* on CBS. He's formally announcing his presidential candidacy today, and where better to get started? McCain is running the most press-friendly presidential campaign since John F. Kennedy. I can't speculate on whether his chumminess with reporters is genuine or calculated, but either way, it's working. The other candidates seem to view the press as a mob, while McCain singles them out as individuals. The result of this unprecedented personal attention is that they're giving him unpre-cedentedly positive coverage. I'm skeptical only because a candi-date's deftness with the media doesn't tell us much about his ability to govern—although the media seem to have a hard time making that distinction.

Headlines out of the way, I check out the fun stuff. On *Sesame Street*, Elmo is trying to roll down a recalcitrant window shade. "Elmo's having a bad shade day," he sighs. Elmo joined the cast of *Sesame Street* long after I stopped watching, and he's become hugely popular and central to the show. As a result, *Sesame Street* doesn't feel quite like the show I watched as a kid, just the way *Happy Days* lost its zing for me once Chachi became prominent. However, watching Elmo, it's easy to grasp his appeal; he's an adorable four-year-old kid who happens to be a monster with bright red fur.

The WB has a funny animated show called *Histeria*, from the folks who brought you *Animaniacs*. A screechy girl named Pepper

Mills and a more sensible little girl start out discussing the famous Kennedy-Lincoln similarities—but Pepper insists there are even more remarkable similarities between Lincoln and Charles Darwin, who shared the same birthday. Pepper: "It doesn't stop there!" Other girl, wearily: "Yes, it does." But Pepper pushes on: "They both had beards! They both wore shoes! Lincoln started a revolution, while Darwin wrote about evolution! Lincoln wore a stovepipe hat, while Darwin liked to smoke his pipe in front of the stove!" Pepper Mills is hard to take for more than a few minutes, but fortunately, that's how long the segment lasts.

I return to the world of talk, news, talky news, and newsy talk. On *Good Day New York* on Channel 5, the two hosts discuss acupuncture, the subject of their next segment: "Have you ever had acupuncture?" "Yes." "Did it work for you?" "Um . . . sort of." "That's how I felt too. Maybe we didn't do it long enough." "But it is working for a lot of people, as you'll see when we come back." With a testimonial like that, I can hardly wait.

Today and *Good Morning America* both have front windows opening onto the sidewalks of New York. Al Roker on *Today* is taking full advantage of his, interviewing a set of identical sisters. By contrast, the *GMA* window, one story above street level, seems more like a giant billboard for the show than *Today*'s flow-through valve. It's as if they want to get closer to the audience—but not *too* close.

Meanwhile, Diane Sawyer and Charles Gibson of *GMA* are on their folksy, country-inn-ish set, which looks less like a Sheraton hotel lounge than it used to in the days of David Hartman and Joan Lunden. In a bit of synergistic pluggery, they're interviewing one of their own: Sam Donaldson, "Internet Pioneer." It seems the man with the hypnotic hair is going to start doing regular live broadcasts directly on the ABC website. "I'm going to be the Captain Kirk of the Internet!" says Donaldson with forced gaiety. I love that he cited a character played by famous toupee-wearer William Shatner. Donaldson is framed in a little box on a full-screen Web page. Perhaps because she's full-screen and Donaldson is in a box, Sawyer makes a rather sarcastic crack about Donaldson scaling "the highest levels of journalism . . . right up there with Edward R. Murrow." Donaldson says ruefully that he "jumped out of a cake the other day. Would Edward R. Murrow have done that?" This is what TV news has come to at the end of the millennium: three genuinely talented journalists sitting around on a morning show talking about what TV news has come to at the end of the millennium. You can see Donaldson's yearning to be a real working reporter again instead of a talking head; and his hope, however vain, that this newfangled electronic medium might free him the way TV freed Murrow and Cronkite from the strictures of radio. But to do it, he has to turn himself into a literal talking head—in his little box, he reminds me of Jambi the Genie on *Pee-Wee's Playhouse*.

On *Good Day New York*, anchorman Jim Ryan seems to be equally unhappy with his lot—but unlike the folks on *GMA*, he doesn't even have the status of a network job. Witness this exchange with Robyn Carter, the show's gossip columnist. Robyn: "So do you have plans after New Year's Eve?" Ryan (for whom New Year's seems a long way away): "Uh, yes." Robyn: "Then that puts you in good company with Mick and Jerry." Silence from Ryan. Robyn (gamely): "They have plans too." More silence. Nobody seems to be having a good day on *Good Day New York* except me. It's like Kathie Lee Pinter.

A bit rattled by her anchorman's lack of enthusiasm, Robyn goes into her segment, "Robyn's Buzz." The first bit is about how, despite their separation, Mick Jagger and Jerry Hall will spend New Year's Eve together for the sake of the kids. Next, Robyn tells us that Michael Douglas gave a dinner for Catherine Zeta-Jones, and it might have been an engagement party. She shows a *New York Post* photo of the two, which shows a ring on Catherine's hand—but Jim Ryan demurs. It's her left hand, and you'd wear an engagement ring on your right. Silence from Robyn, until she sees a way out: "Then maybe it's a friendship ring." "Well, that's the end of that story," says Ryan, snickering. Barely keeping it together, Robyn goes on to an item about Regis Philbin, but Ryan smells blood: "Well, I just don't know how you read what you write, because nobody else could read it." Robyn (now on the ropes): "When I type, I'm dyslexic, I must be." Ryan (closing in for the kill): "So, as I understand it, Michael Douglas is or isn't getting married." Robyn (on her last legs): "Well, there's a little problem with divorce, but he's working on it." I have never seen such open rancor on a news show in my life. (What's more, according to Sam, you would indeed wear an engagement ring on your left hand, so there.)

John McCain appears on *Today*, completing his lap of the three morning shows. Meanwhile, *Good Morning America* runs a short report at 8:07 on the violence in East Timor—is this the first foreign news we've seen this morning? Of course, they have to make up for it by segueing to a feature on the Pokémon craze. I'm curious to watch, if only because I don't really know what Pokémon is. A major cultural phenomenon is all around me, and I'm out of the loop. The *GMA* piece is about a parent who is suing Nintendo over their Pokémon cards, which he characterizes as a form of gambling. But I don't see how different they are from baseball cards or Wacky Packages in my own childhood. *GMA*'s parenting contributor, Anne Pleshette Murray, says she's "the mother of a recovering Pokémon addict." She sympathizes with the aggrieved parents, but thinks there are positive aspects to collecting, "although I wish he knew 159 animal species instead of these 159 imaginary species."

On *This Morning*, Mark McEwen interviews Scott Turow about his latest novel, *Personal Injury*. If you want to read an excerpt, you can go to the website, of course. *This Morning* is the Rodney Dangerfield of network morning shows—it gets no respect. Nobody watches it, nobody talks about it, and the personable McEwen and his cohorts seem resigned to this state of affairs. Considering that CBS is already hatching a brand-new morning show with Bryant Gumbel, which will put most of these people out of work, their professionalism is commendable.

Good Day New York has a reporter at the Second Avenue Deli, for some reason. Would that I were there. He's eating matzoh ball soup—at 8:50 in the morning?—and signing off: "And we know now that Catherine Zeta-Jones either is or is not getting married." Guess he's in league with the anchorman.

Carl Reiner is on *Good Morning America* with Charles Gibson, pushing a new book. I venerate Carl Reiner, not only for his routines with Mel Brooks and his movies with Steve Martin, but primarily for creating and producing *The Dick Van Dyke Show*, which is still one of the high-water marks of situation comedy. Gibson asks Reiner what he thinks of television writing today. "Some of it is brilliant, some of it is hilarious, and some of it is no good, like everything," says Reiner. "The level of excellence is still at the same one percent, except that we have hundreds and hundreds of shows now." Well, that's it in a nutshell, and I wonder if I'll be able to put things any better by the time I finish my week of immersion. However, he names David E. Kelley as an example of the good stuff, clearly not having seen last night's episode of *The Practice*.

At the end of *Today*, Katie is feeding a baby tiger from a bottle with magicians-slash–animal trainers Siegfried and Roy, who are promoting their new IMAX movie. They're outside, surrounded by the window crowd. Katie looks like a natural tiger mommy.

Nine A.M. Left to my own devices, I would go back to bed right now. I'm starting to feel like Bill Murray in *Groundhog Day*, condemned to repeat this same day's activities five more times after today. But I take a deep breath and carry on, because it's time for *Regis & Kathie Lee*. This is a very successful morning talk show starring TV journeyman Regis Philbin, who has finally come into his own as the host of the prime-time game show *Who Wants to Be a Millionaire*; and living legend Kathie Lee Gifford, who is famous for saying absolutely anything at any time. Today, Kathie Lee has a bizarre big-hair-do that looks as if it wandered off the head of Rod Stewart. Regis is teasing Kathie Lee about having her own record company, which is called On the Lamb, but she's very, very serious about it: "I'm doing a soundtrack album to my life, and at some point I realized that by doing a soundtrack to my life, I'm doing a soundtrack for everybody's life." She goes on until Regis finally asks himself, "And how was *your* weekend, Reege?" I suspect this exchange encapsulates the entire show.

I glimpse the wintry face of Martha Stewart on Channel 9, and I have a moment of déjà vu before I realize that Martha has a daily syndicated show as well as her weekend show on the Food Network. The line between network and cable channels continues to blur—whatever you're watching, you're watching Martha. Martha is dealing with a whole menagerie today—a turtle, a rabbit, various exotic birds, and a hungry-looking cat—and has a cockatoo on her shoulder. She looks none too pleased. Then her animal guy brings in an enormous tortoise. Sam returns from the gym just in time to hear the animal noises, and she rushes in, asking, "Is this how to make your own petting zoo from scratch?" The animal guy explains that the tortoise is loaded with parasites. Now Martha looks *really* happy. "Why is Martha feeding tortoises?" asks Sam. I think Martha will be asking the same question as soon as she's off the air.

Florence Henderson survived the indignity of *The Brady Brides*, and now seems to be co-hosting *Later Today* with two younger women. She looks great. Later today on *Later Today*, Andre Agassi will give us "Hollywood dish about his life on and off the court," only an hour or so after his ex-wife Brooke Shields appeared on *Today* proper. *Later Today* looks like the kind of show that's run in this time slot since my childhood, following in the house-slippered footsteps of *Girl Talk* with Virginia Graham and *Dinah's Place* with Dinah Shore. What's shocking is that—unlike *The View*, or even *Regis & Kathie Lee*—they've done nothing to bring it up to date. It's the same old kitchen with the same old topics.

Sam upbraids me for not watching *Jerry Springer*. "I thought that's what the whole point of this was." Well, it wasn't, but I grit my teeth and unmute it anyway. In case anyone on the planet doesn't know, Jerry is a former mayor of Cleveland who hosts the scrappiest, sleaziest talk show on television—which is saying something.

Today's topic is "I'm Having a Sizzling Affair." Three black women sit on stage with a guy who fancies himself a player. "I ain't your woman, and I ain't no girl!" says one of the women. Now her other boyfriend, Derrick, comes onstage, having just found out his woman is cheating with the player, who is his best friend. Jerry looks weary, but determined to get to the bottom of this serious social problem. "First of all, if he's your best friend, you know he's a player," Jerry tells Derrick. "But he should know better, though!" says Derrick. Of course, if he knew better, there wouldn't be a show.

Meanwhile, rapper/actress Queen Latifah has her own talk show on Fox. "She looks so pretty," says Sam. She also seems too inherently sensible to be hosting this kind of show for much longer. A couple sits onstage, and are joined by a woman who looks like the pop singer Jewel ten years from now. It seems she's the first wife, who claims that the guy never visits their kids. "Are you sure these kids are yours?" asks Latifah—presumably of the guy. The talk shows could just declare each day's topic to be "People Who Should Know Better," and be done with it.

The world's largest rubber-band ball rolls out on *Regis & Kathie Lee*. It's about four feet tall; those are some big rubber bands. This is followed by an even larger tinfoil ball, which is nearly as tall as Regis. In 1999 you don't see wonders like this just for the hell of it—it's a promotion for a new CD-ROM for "Ripley's Believe It or Not."

A rerun of *Wonder Woman* turns out to be the episode introducing Debra Winger as Drusilla, a.k.a. Wonder Girl. It's bizarre and oddly wistful to see Winger as a wide-eyed ingenue in her early twenties, especially considering her inexplicable career slump in recent years. "This even *sounds* Seventies," says Sam, referring to the wah-wah guitars on the soundtrack. What's even funnier is that the series is set in the Forties, during World War II—but Seventies it still is, just as *Happy Days* is more Seventies than Fifties. It can't be helped.

Regis and Kathie Lee are hosting a dazed and mummified-looking Burt Reynolds. Time and alimony haven't been kind to him. "You look good, Burt," says Regis, but he's lying. "You're like Cary Grant, you know what I mean?" It turns out Burt knew Cary Grant; he tells a long anecdote about going to the racetrack with Grant and Dom DeLuise, which isn't nearly as funny as he thinks it is. Then Regis pulls out a tall, slim object under a black cloth, which he holds on his lap before giving it to Burt. "That's from *Boogie Nights*, isn't it?" cracks Kathie Lee. That's the secret of Kathie Lee's appeal right there: she's the gospel-singing good girl with a wicked edge. It turns out to be a tennis trophy Regis won, playing doubles with Andy Williams against Burt and Dinah years ago.

The week is crawling, but the half hours are flying. I feel as if every time I blink, it's half an hour later.

Channel 13 has been showing a test pattern for five minutes now—what gives? Where are the Teletubbies? Just as I consider calling WNET to complain, the show begins at last. As connoisseurs of children's television all know by now, *Teletubbies* isn't just weird, it's positively hallucinatory. This accounts for its surprising popularity with drugged-out clubgoers who watch it after returning from all-night raves, and *then* go to bed. The show is mostly set in an idyllic meadow, where real rabbits gambol under a glowing sun with a baby's face. We cut to Teletubby headquarters, which looks like the inside of the mother ship at the end of the special edition of *Close Encounters*. Meet the Teletubbies, four costumed whatsits with antennae on their heads and screens on their bellies. Each has a different color and a differently shaped antenna—and, as Jerry Falwell has made famous, purple Tinky Winky also carries a purse. Why the reverend is offended by this is beyond me, since the Teletubbies seem as free of gender as they are of logic.

The Tubbies listen to a periscope-type thing, which "Trot trot trot" until they're all trotting in place. It's like a kids' show in *Brave New World*. Then a shot of a spinning pinwheel aboveground. "Uh-oh!" they exclaim, and run outside to play. They lie on their backs wriggling, and the TV sets on their bellies sparkle like Xena and Gabrielle on their crosses. It seems they're about to receive a transmission. Dipsy, the green one, displays a short film on his/her Teletummy, about a four-year-old named Emily and her pony Chester. Confusingly, the film is narrated by some *other* little girl, who remains unseen. When the film ends, the Teletubbies yell, "Again! Again!" To my astonishment, they start the film all over again, from the top, with no additional editing.

Burt finally exits *Regis & Kathie Lee* with a wave to the audience. For a guy who made his rep by being charming on talk shows, I think he's slipping. The next guests are Siegfried and Roy, on their second show of the day. Sam is astonished to see them: "Oh my God, look at how much face work this guy has! He needs his eyebrows drawn on!" Roy, the extrovert of the pair, explains that they've done plenty to keep white tigers from becoming extinct. They bring out Magic, the same baby tiger Katie Couric fed this morning, and Kathie Lee takes over as bottle-feeder. Magic's paws are each the size of my head, and when he grows up, he's going to be six hundred pounds, according to Roy. And he can tell all his tiger friends that he once got fed by Katie Couric and Kathie Lee Gifford in the same morning.

The talk shows are recruiting guests for future episodes. "Is jealousy ruining your relationship?" Call Queen Latifah. "Are you afraid to tell someone you have a crush on them because you feel you are a plain Jane?" Call Montel Williams.

It's 10:00 A.M. On Channel 7 it's *The Rosie O'Donnell Show*, which is a deliberate throwback to happier talk-show days of yore. I love the retro animated opening, which conjures up memories of *Bewitched* and *I Dream of Jeannie*; I'm sure that's deliberate too, since Rosie is obsessed with old television. Rosie is excited this morning, because she has her very own Rosie O'Donnell Barbie doll going on sale this week. This must be the ultimate celebrity perk—until you get to the level where the ultimate celebrity perk is *refusing* to be made into a Barbie doll.

On 4, Maury Povich tackles "My Teen Daughter Is Addicted

to Sex." Fifteen-year-old Heather says she has slept with more than fifty men. I learn all this without putting on the sound; on Maury's show, everything is written onscreen. Next up is Julie, fifteen, who's slept with about twenty guys and is proud of it: "I'm not ashamed of anything I've done." "But you've sought help," says Maury. "Why would you seek help for something you're not ashamed of? Do you feel you have an uncontrollable desire?" "I can control it, I just don't want to," says Julie. Her hapless mother is appalled by everything Julie says and does, but why is she airing it all on TV? Does anyone actually think an appearance on *Maury* will prove therapeutic? This makes Lucy's five-cent psychiatry stand in the comic strip "Peanuts" look like Freudian analysis.

On Channel 5 it's *Divorce Court*, one of six courtoom shows that will air today. *Divorce Court* was the original courtroom show; years ago it was done with actors, but now the stars are real people who have agreed to transfer their hearings from the American justice system to the home entertainment system. Regardless, today's couple seems genuinely aggrieved. He says she was learning to be a phlebotomist, and kept sticking needles into him for practice, but then she got pregnant and gave it up. Tears run down her face. "Did you support me then?" she cries. "You did not support me!" The bailiff hands her a tissue as she pours out her tale of woe. Her husband tries to interrupt, and the judge snaps his head off. Maybe I'm simply not the audience for this—my parents are divorced, and I don't slow down to rubberneck at accidents on the highway—but personally I'd prefer the version with actors. Knowing that these are real couples in pain, I find it unbearable to watch.

Judge Mathis is on 11. A woman says a female "customer" complimented her breast implants, so she kissed the customer on the cheek. A customer where? In moments I learn that although the woman is dressed like a librarian, she's a stripper. The next day her boss accused her of kissing the customer on the lips, and they got into a fight in the dressing room. The boss claims he couldn't have broken her nose, because she looks fine now and it couldn't have healed that fast. I throw up my hands. Military strategist Carl von Clausewitz defined war as the continuation of politics by other means; courtroom shows seem to be the continuation of trashy talk shows by other means.

Rosie's first guest is Brooke Shields, who is clearly making the talk-show rounds along with Siegfried and Roy. But I've left one talk-show stone unturned, and I unmute Roseanne, the former sitcom star who now has her own syndicated talk show. For some reason she's wearing a red velvet crown on her head. Roseanne is thinner these days, and barely recognizable as the spherical housewife comedian I remember from fifteen years ago. However, she's let her voice return to its old nasal squawk, after conscientiously lowering it for the last seasons of her sitcom. Maybe that's because she's ad-libbing now, instead of delivering lines that she could rehearse. Roseanne has two couples changing into each others' clothes behind screens—it's like a racier update of something you'd see on the old Art Linkletter *House Party* show. Couple number one wins, although he can't button his wife's shirt. "As television goes," says Sam, "that's mildly amusing." This would make a great title for a prime-time show: *That's Mildly Amusing!*

Rosie O'Donnell has a remote from this year's "Hands on a Hardbody" contest in Texas, in which whoever keeps their hands on a pickup truck the longest wins the truck. This piece speaks more to my own situation than anything else I've seen so far. The record of ninety-four hours was shattered by Brian Root, who now joins Rosie in the studio. He's a scrawny guy with a beard. Rosie gives him a hug—"One hundred seven hours! Did you have a strategy?" "I ate fruit the whole contest," says Brian. "Nothing but fruit." I ask Sam to pick up some nectarines when she goes to the market later. Brian continues, "When it gets down to the end, it's pretty intense . . . the delirium sets in near the end." Unlike Brian, I'm taking breaks to sleep, so I pray that I'll avoid delirium before I finish my week of "Hands on a Hot PowerBook." Then Brian lets slip that he's won twenty previous cars in contests like this. "You're a professional?"

shrieks Rosie. They must not have covered this in the pre-interview backstage. Brian admits it—he has no job, and trades in most of the cars for cash. "I cannot believe that people actually do this," concludes Rosie. "And the fact that you do this for a living—frankly, it frightens me." Me too.

An anti-smoking commercial features the memorable slogan, "Tobacco. Tumor-causing, teeth-staining, smelly, puking habit." This is the best anti-smoking spot I've seen since "kick the habit" thirty years ago. Many of the new ads are oddly unconvincing, perhaps because they're paid for by the tobacco companies themselves, as part of their massive lawsuit settlements. One of my upstairs neighbors is a psychologist who specializes in nicotine addiction, and he notes that the Philip Morris anti-smoking ads have a particularly devious approach. In the guise of discouraging teen smoking, they posit smoking as an adult thing, like driving a car or having sex. What teen doesn't want to do the adult thing? Needless to say, there doesn't seem to be any tobacco money behind "tumor-causing, teeth-staining, smelly, puking habit."

Megaplatinum recording star Britney Spears is Rosie O'Donnell's next guest, and she performs a number. Clearly, she's as much a dancer as a singer—I guess that's what it takes these days in the post-Madonna age. The song does nothing for me, and neither does Britney. Then Britney sits down with Rosie and shows off her doll collection. I expect either antiques or something of sentimental value, but it turns out she bought them on the home shopping channel QVC. This is a collection? But Rosie is all ears. She tells about calling QVC and giving her credit card, but they wouldn't take the order because nobody believed it was really her. It's bizarre to hear two celebrities on television talking about television as consumers rather than as the consumed.

Maury ends with an update: promiscuous Heather's mom says that Heather was embarrassed by the things that came out on the show, and that it had a huge impact on her. See, it is therapeutic! This is followed by a promo for *Sally Jessy Raphael*, which is also covering teen prostitutes today. Then a dual promo for *Judge Judy* and *The People's Court*, the latter of which is now hosted by Judge Judy Sheindlin's husband, Judge Jerry Sheindlin. You can just imagine them at home, overruling each other.

Eleven A.M. brings more talk shows: the sassy coffee-klatsch of *The View* on ABC, *Sally Jessy*, *Ricki Lake*, and an entirely different episode of *Jerry Springer*. Tired of all this chatter, I check out the new *National Enquirer* magazine show on 5, hosted by toothy gossip columnist Mike Walker. Today's topic: "Phobias of the Rich and Famous." Kim Basinger suffers from acrophobia, but conquered it before winning the Oscar. Howie Mandel is germophobic; he wouldn't even shake his guests' hands when he had his own talk show.

The other significant alternative to talk shows is *The Price Is Right*, still going strong after decades on CBS. Like the Mrs. America pageant, the show is a steady stream of plugs. All the games involve guessing the correct price on a product, so announcer Rod Roddy has to tell you about each and every product—and if you guess right, you win more products! What makes it all work is the venerable Bob Barker, a TV showman par excellence. As someone who grew up on the set of a quiz show, I know what I'm talking about when I say that this kind of hosting is the toughest job in show business that doesn't involve heavy lifting. You're running from setup to setup, you're working with nonprofessionals, and you're finding ways to involve the audience in the challenges faced by said nonprofessionals, all without tripping over either your tongue or the sets. If you flag, the show flags. Bob Barker *never* flags, and he's seventy-five years old this year.

Sam comes running when she hears the *Price Is Right* theme music. She also loves the show, but for different reasons. Sam says it's quintessentially American. You don't have to answer any questions or display any skills—you just have to know how much things cost. It's also the only place on TV to see ordinary working people who aren't experiencing some trauma or other. They're trying to win things most of them couldn't usually afford, and seeing that makes Sam cry.

The show goes to a commercial, and we look around. Ricki Lake has brothers who belong to rival gangs. "I love you, man," says one gang-banger to another. "I love you to death, but I'm not your brother." There are a lot of bleeps, so it's hard to make out much of what they're saying.

At the opposite end of the spectrum, Mr. Rogers is on Channel 13, silver-haired but otherwise just as I remember him from my childhood. It all comes rushing back to me in a wave of pure, pre-intellectual nostalgia; Fred Rogers is a Proustian madeleine for the eyes. Charles Sopkin grew up on radio, so for him children's TV was merely a subject for research; but *Mister Rogers' Neighborhood* has real emotional meaning for me. The show is positively poky compared to the whiz-bang of *Sesame Street*—the antithesis to Mr. Rogers's thesis—but its slowness is deliberate and meaningful. Watching Mr. Rogers, I feel myself adjusting to his rhythm, and I relax into the show just as he intends. Let's take off our suit jacket and put on a cardigan. Let's take off our work shoes and put on sneakers. Let's feed the fish. The effect is even more pleasant than it was thirty years ago, when my life was less cluttered and I didn't want or need to relax. Maybe Mr. Rogers should start making shows for stressed-out adults.

The little red trolley exits Mr. Rogers's house and emerges in the Neighborhood of Make-Believe, whose very name gives you an idea of Mr. Rogers's deliberate style. Once *Sesame Street* began to interweave human characters with Big Bird and Oscar the Grouch, *Mister Rogers'* seemed old-fashioned for ghettoizing the fantastic into its own neighborhood. But now that the borders between reality and fantasy have all but collapsed on kids' TV, that caution seems prescient. And the Neighborhood of Make-Believe itself is still charming. I recognize all the puppet characters at once: King Friday the Thirteenth, X the Owl, Henrietta Pussycat. I now realize that the voices are all done by Fred Rogers, in a way that wasn't obvious to me when I was a kid; he's not a vocal chameleon like the Muppet guys. Now that the death of Shari Lewis has led to the retirement of Lamb Chop, these are the only pre-Muppet puppets still on the air, and their design is entirely different from any we've seen since Jim Henson established a new template for TV puppetry. This isn't to take away from Henson's brilliance. My friend Mark Saltzman, a former *Sesame Street* writer, puts it this way: "Jim Henson had the ability to put two halves of a Ping-Pong ball and some felt together in just the right way to make a four-year-old fall in love with it." The second part of that brilliance was the technological advance of using hands, rods, *and* strings to operate the Muppets. By contrast, Mr. Rogers's puppets are traditional hand puppets any kid could operate, and as such, they're antiques. But *Mister Rogers' Neighborhood* isn't about technology—it's about the love and respect for his audience that flows through this one man more convincingly than it does through just about anyone else on TV.

Sam and I depart the Neighborhood to watch the Showcase Showdown that concludes *The Price Is Right*. Bob Barker delivers his traditional sign-off about getting your pets spayed or neutered, and suddenly it's noon. Sam goes out to pick up lunch. In accordance with my grid, I change channels on half the sets. Once the sound is off, the silence is louder than anything I've heard so far today. I stare at the sets without focusing and just marvel at them, like a kid watching an ant farm. So much motion, so much activity, and what does it all add up to in the end?

I'm simply overwhelmed. Out of sheer self-preservation, I leave the sound off and lie down on the couch with the pug, gathering my strength. Cosmo licks my face for a moment, then promptly goes to sleep on my lap. Satisfied that I'm not missing anything vital—if there's anything vital to miss—I finally surrender to the lure of *The New York Times* and pretend there aren't twelve TV sets in the room. On page A4, there's a story about an Iranian man who lost his passport in 1988 and has been living in Charles de Gaulle Airport ever since. I think I know how he feels.

At 12:37, I finish the newspaper and suffer an attack of guilt. I've let the side down for thirty-seven minutes. "I can do this!" I yell. "I can do this!" I return to my chair, dislodging the startled Cosmo, and boldly turn up the sound on *Sunset Beach,* a soap opera on NBC. A greasy-looking man with an indeterminate accent stands behind a bosomy gal who looks like the blank-faced ingenue Denise Richards. "Sometimes I don't know how I get through the day," he says. You and me both, pal. "Then I think of the smell of your hair." He moves in for a clinch, but she backs away. "Don't move any closer. Don't you dare," she warns him. He looks very surprised by this turn of events.

There's a girl recovering from something on the *Leeza* show. (I'm so old, I remember when Leeza still had a last name—Gibbons—just as Groucho Marx knew Doris Day before she was a virgin.) The girl realized at some point "this is just like an abusive marriage, and I knew I had to get out." Get out from what? Sure enough, she's yet another teen prostitute. Maury, Sally Jessy, and Leeza may be motivated by genuine concern for the plights of these fallen angels, but covering teen prostitution for three consecutive hours suggests that something other than healing is going on. Who's doing shows about teenagers who are exploited in nonsexual ways—by the fast-food industry, or by sweatshops in Asia? I think of Ed Murrow's classic CBS documentary about migrant workers, *Harvest of Shame,* and wonder if those workers would have to turn tricks to get an hour of TV coverage in 1999.

Suddenly, an apparition on Comedy Central. I quickly turn up the sound on the postmodern game show *Vs.,* because one of the contestants has the largest bosom I have ever seen in my life. It's not even sexual, it's just bizarre. The show's premise is that wildly divergent teams compete for cash—for instance, Dykes on Bikes versus Hooters Waitresses. Today's show turns out to be Ventriloquists versus Phone Sex Operators. I'm disappointed that the woman with the gigantic knockers isn't one of the ventriloquists. Can you imagine her act?

Just then, my college classmate Penny arrives, and her eyes widen at the sight of the twelve TVs. Since Penny stopped practicing law to raise her two small children, she's become a regular watcher of the ABC soap-opera lineup, and I've invited her over to interpret for the soap-impaired. Sam walks in minutes after Penny, bearing a chicken burrito, which I try to eat while Penny fills me in on the background of our first subject today: *All My Children.*

Penny says Tad and Dixie are "the traditional soap couple," i.e., gorgeous and not likely to subscribe to *The New York Review of Books.* Tad hosts a talk show called *The Cutting Edge,* which looks a lot more wholesome than the talk shows I've been watching. Dixie works at the same TV station; "she gave a kidney to her brother, and has two kids by two different people," says Penny. This is already so much information that I can barely take anything in, but Penny is just getting started.

Now a woman with a British accent accuses a guy of pushing someone to his death. I ask Penny who they are, and she takes a deep breath. "This is very complicated," she begins. The British woman is named Alex, and the man is named Edmund. The guy they're talking about is Dmitri—"Dmitri is his brother and her husband. Everything Alex says could be a lie. She's a very mysterious character." She was a doctor who was helping Dmitri through a strange neurological ailment. "She tried an experimental treatment with a baby's umbilical cord—which opens up doors for other characters, because the baby's parentage is in question." But that was two months ago, and Dmitri died. Why is Alex blaming Edmund for his death? Says Penny, "She wanted him to stay in the hospital, but Edmund insisted on bringing him home to be with his family, and it was too much for him." Got it, I think.

During the commercial, I take furious notes on the above while Sam tells Penny, "This is perfect for Jack. He loves overstim." "Yeah, but this is *over*-overstim," I moan.

Next we meet the obligatory rich couple in their obligatory mansion. He's a silver-haired elder statesman, and she's a bodacious blond babe. I'll let Penny narrate: "Adam Chandler is the big tycoon in town. He's been married to every woman on the show. This is his current wife, Liza. Before they got married, she was a single woman who decided she wanted to have a baby, so she went to the sperm bank. She asked Tad's brother, Jake, to be the donor. But Adam, the tycoon, wanted to be the father of her child, so he switched the sperm samples." Now Adam is scared that Liza is going to find out the baby is his. This is the kind of crisis you can only encounter on a soap opera. "So when Dmitri needed an experimental treatment with an umbilical cord, Jake and Liza—the ostensible biological parents—said sure, you can use the baby's umbilical cells, and Adam said no no no because he was afraid the truth would come out." Penny listens for a moment, and gleans something from the latest snatch of dialogue that would have flown right by me: "Oh, Dmitri's not dead." He's not? No, says Penny, he's just missing. "That's how they always do it on soaps. The guy who plays Dmitri used to be on *Dynasty*, so this is sort of a comedown for him. He's asking for more money, and now his character is missing until they know whether they can make a deal."

Just as I try to absorb this latest barrage, we go to an ad. "Genital herpes doesn't have to rule your life," says a woman who, for some reason, is boxing. I can't help laughing, because it's like the old joke about the kid who wants a box of Tampax "because with Tampax, you can go horseback riding, and skiing . . ." I laugh harder when the next ad is for Tampax itself, with cheerleaders enjoying the same freedom to which the kid in the joke aspires.

There's a new couple on *All My Children*, picnicking on the beach. It's the same actor who plays Adam, playing a double role as his guileless twin brother, Stuart. Penny explains that the woman is Stuart's wife, Marian Colby, who happens to be Liza's mother. I try gamely to keep up: "You mean Marian is Adam's sister-in-law *and* his mother-in-law?" "That's right," says Penny, happy that I'm beginning to get the hang of soap dynamics. "Marian used to be a huge slut, and slept with, among others, Tad." Even more confusing, Marian looks as if she's the same age as her daughter Liza. Penny says Marian should be a spokeswoman for BOTOX injections; she has no wrinkles, because her facial muscles have been paralyzed at great expense.

Next we meet a Hungarian princess named Gillian, a cousin of the missing Dmitri. In come Alex, the mysterious Brit, and Edmund, the rugged hunk. While Gillian sits fretting about whether Dmitri will show up, Alex and Edmund resume their argument about who's responsible for Dmitri's death, if indeed he is dead. Unable to win the argument—perhaps because of the lack of evidence—Alex goes off riding. "You're upset," Edmund warns her. "You're going to spook the horse!" Gillian urges Edmund to go after her, "for Dmitri." The unseen Dmitri dominates these proceedings like Godot.

Commercial. Two computer-generated fish swim in competing plastic sandwich bags. The fish in Glad is fine, but the one in Brand X is running out of water fast. I feel for that fish. I switch one TV over to *The New Zoo Revue*, a kids' show my friends and I loathed in elementary school, just to see if nostalgia will improve it. But no, it still sucks. However, human hosts Doug and Emmy Jo look exactly as I remember them; they haven't aged a day in twenty-five years. Then I realize these are the same episodes I watched back then. Nobody gets old in reruns.

Back to the beach on *All My Children*, where Stuart is painting Marian in the nude. Then Marian sees Alex riding in the distance—we never see the horse, just as we never see Marian below the neck—and she begins to narrate the offscreen action: "Oh, Stuart, he's throwing the rider!" Sam, passing through the living room, is incredulous. "This isn't television, this is radio!" she exclaims. But the budget savings are awesome, and I wonder if cost-conscious Hollywood studios might adopt this same technique. Bruce Willis can just tell his sidekick, "There's a tremendous fireball! The building is collapsing!" That'll save five million dollars right there.

When we finally see Alex, she's sitting prettily on the sand, her hair still immaculate despite her accident. "I'm a doctor," she insists to Edmund and the police, "I don't *need* a doctor." Stuart and the now-clothed Marian arrive to help. It seems Alex really is okay—but Edmund announces portentously that the horse's leg is broken. Naturally, the horse is still offscreen.

That's it for today's *All My Children*. I shake out my arms like a swimmer, stunned by the amount of detail I've had to take in—and by the far greater amount of detail Penny carries around in her head.

Before I even have time to catch my breath, we're on to *One Life to Live*. Says my guru Penny, "*One Life to Live* isn't as well done as *All My Children*. It has the best actors, but the least good scriptwriting, because it doesn't connect on enough levels." By this she means the levels of society and the different families on the show—nobody expects levels of meaning here. In another bit of soap-opera intertextuality, Adam Chandler's grown daughter Skye is on this show, which allows for a certain amount of back-and-forth. Indeed, we see Skye at a resort hotel somewhere, yelling on the phone to Adam: "Why don't you go meddle in Hailey's marriage? She's the daughter you really care about!" "I assume she is a spoiled brat?" I ask Penny. "Yeah," she confirms.

Next we meet Vicki and Ben, who are in some other exotic location. Says the inexhaustible Penny, "Vicki used to be a multiple personality. She combined all her personalities, but now we think they're coming out again." Ben is married to Skye, and she won't give him a divorce to marry Vicki.

A middle-aged brunette and a pouty blond girl face off, hurling epithets at each other. Penny knows all. The brunette is Dorian, and the blonde is Vicki's daughter Jessica. Penny: "For a long time Jessica was the girlfriend of the Hispanic hunk Christian. Then she got drunk and slept with her stepbrother, and got pregnant. They decided to keep the baby. When she was nine months pregnant, Dorian hit her with a car and ran away. Dorian finally confessed, but her Mafia friend paid off the judge so she didn't have to go to jail for killing the unborn child. But ever since then she's been getting strange notes with cut-up letters calling her a baby-killer, and we think it's the baby's grandmother Vicki, or one of her alter egos." Believe it or not, my head doesn't ache—it feels light. I have become a vessel for information, completely concentrated on untangling the twisted vines of *One Life to Live*. I haven't felt this way since I crammed for the SATs.

After a commercial, Jessica phones Will, her stepbrother and the father of her baby. Will is with Jessica's grandfather, who tells him not to go: "You can't leave the cattle drive because one of the womenfolk has a burr under her saddle!" But, despite that deathless line, he does. Just then, Sam Rappaport, who looks just like Adam Chandler on *All My Children*, comes in looking for Will. Penny fills me in: "Sam is Will's father, to whom Will doesn't speak. Will has gone to the other side, the Buchanan family, and got a job with big Texas oilman Asa Buchanan—Jessica's grandpa." All clear?

Vicki dines alfresco with Ben, who turns out to be Sam Rappaport's brother. "He's the uncle of his girlfriend's daughter's lover," says Penny. Right. Vicki gets a strange look in her eye, which I wouldn't have noticed, but Penny says this is a glimpse of one of the banished alter egos. She even knows which one: "Nikki." Meanwhile, Skye (who is Ben's wife, remember) peeps around a potted palm and sees them—by sheer coincidence, they're all in the same Florida hotel! We cut to a commercial, just in time.

During the ad break, I ask Penny why she loves the soaps. "There's a gossip value," she explains. "You know, everyone loves gossiping, and I really used to be a terrible gossip. But it would always backfire, and people would talk about me, and I realized that gossip is very hurtful. So with soaps, you can sit around with your friends, and get the fun part of the gossip without actually hurting anybody's feelings or betraying anybody." Besides, it's an instant social bond with people from all walks of life. "It kind of cuts across lines," says Penny. "In a hospital waiting room, or at a bus station, with nothing to say to these people, you can talk about soaps."

Penny was a wild punk girl at Yale; we weren't friends then, because I was a film nerd and Penny's cool factor exceeded even that of our classmates Jodie Foster and Naomi Wolf. But I remember the quote under her picture in our yearbook, which was from *The World According to Garp*: "Life is an X-rated soap opera." It turns out this is still Penny's motto. "Life is more like a soap opera than not," she says, "except we've got more boring stuff, like taxes and car pools."

I tell her I'm amazed by the slow pace of the soaps—they're not only the slowest shows on television, but quite possibly the slowest things in the entire world of commercial entertainment (barring art films by directors like Jacques Rivette and Hou Hsiao-Hsien). But Penny says the slow pace is part of what makes a soap work, "because that's what enables you to come back after you've missed it for a couple of days, or a couple of weeks. The characters may be married to somebody new, but within a day or two you can catch up. And you know, I don't ever just sit and watch the soaps. I'm on the phone, I'm paying my bills, I'm running around doing things. And if it's a sex scene, or a cat fight, I'll pay attention, but it's kind of background." So if the soaps were tighter and more dramatic, they'd take up too much brain space for afternoon viewing. "With the slowness of the pace," she adds, "it's a fine line between building the suspense and just losing you because you say enough, enough, let's find out who the father is."

Back to *One Life to Live*. Vicki is reluctant to marry Ben, but he has no second thoughts. "I'm marrying the love of my life," he tells her. Vicki responds, "But what if you have new dreams—dreams I can't fulfill?" Wait a minute, that's a complete non sequitur. Did he blow his line? Was he supposed to say, "I'm marrying the girl of my dreams," which would have set up her response? "Very possible," says Penny. The actors have reams of dialogue to memorize every day, and even though the shows aren't live, nobody bothers to go back and do retakes when somebody blows a line.

"Our marriage will be our child," concludes Ben, "and we'll just enjoy the miracle we've created." "He's sort of a simp, isn't he?"

I ask Penny, who agrees. Was Vicki more fun when she was a multiple personality? "Much more fun," says Penny. "She'd put on a bad red wig and go to bars." Ben gives Vicki a ring, and they hug as bystanders applaud. Abandoned brat-wife Skye hears the applause, and watches through the slats in her hotel room, about to cry.

That's it for *One Life to Live*, and my head is beginning to ache from two hours of intense concentration on these increasingly complicated plot lines. As the credits roll, we glimpse a woman in labor on Channel 52, The Learning Channel. It's a show called *Baby Story*, and it's exactly what you think. "Oh my God," gasps Penny, "she's really having a baby!" It's not an easy event to make TV-ready, but they're doing the best they can with clever angles and strategically placed sheets. The baby is born, and wiped off far faster than seems typical. If you're interested in being on *Baby Story*, there's a website and an address. Who *are* these people who want one of the most intimate events of their life on national television? Sam recommends that we watch *Wedding Story* later: "It's the fun one that doesn't involve blood and mucus."

I'm ready to pack in the soaps, but Penny has come all the way from Montclair, New Jersey, and hired a sitter for her two-year-old, so I agree to watch *General Hospital* next. However, I soon realize that my complete ignorance of *All My Children* and *One Life to Live* may actually have made it easier for me to take everything in. By contrast, *General Hospital* is the only soap opera I've ever watched with any regularity. I had an epic case of pneumonia in high school, and when I was bedridden, my sister Eve turned me on to *General Hospital*, her favorite show. As a result, I know just enough about the show's history to ask all kinds of questions that have zilch to do with what's going on now, and within minutes I'm hopelessly confused. Penny does her best to explain the three layers of the show, which are the hospital, the rich families, and—in a novel twist predating *The Sopranos*—an organized-crime family. She tells me who's sleeping with whom, who's had amnesia, who's been kidnapped, and whose long-lost son turned up just in time to donate

CAN'T TAKE MY EYES OFF OF YOU

bone marrow to his baby brother. She gives me backstories and histories and juicy tidbits from *Soap Opera Digest*.

And yet none of it even begins to penetrate my quickly fossilizing brain. For the first time I understand the term "couch potato" from the inside. I have eyes, I feel dense, and I sit there looking lumpy. Before long, *General Hospital* is over, and not a moment too soon. Penny returns to Montclair laden with my gratitude, and my eyes start to focus again.

I decide to skip today's installment of *Oprah* to check out *The Martin Short Show*, which is still in its first few weeks on Channel 2, and therefore of more interest to me. Short is a veteran of both *Saturday Night Live* and the classic Canadian comedy series *SCTV*, and I am a genuine fan. He emerges from the back of the audience, singing "Strangers in the Night." At the finish, he tells the crowd, "Your love is like a ginkgo biloba with a wheat-grass chaser." Short has a sidekick, Michael McGrath, who asks him if he watched any of the games over the weekend. "Games?" asks Marty. To my delight, he doesn't watch sports either. "I'm very busy with my career," he says. Even more than David Letterman, Martin Short is ironic to the core—his entire existence has quotation marks around it. Is he too hip for the room? With comedy sketches and a troupe of second bananas in addition to the guests, he's clearly going for the Letterman/Conan vibe rather than emulating anything I've seen so far on daytime TV.

On Channel 4 is *Judge Judy*, the reigning queen of courtroom shows. She's a stern and snappish woman who probably makes lawyers quake in their tasseled shoes. In today's case the defendant and the plaintiff were engaged for seven years, and now he wants his ring back. After much *sturm und drang*, Judge Judy dismisses the case "because you spent two thousand dollars on the ring, but seven years together." No wonder Judge Judy is at the top of the heap; she's a TV natural who cuts to the quick. All the other courtroom shows are just trying to capture some of her lightning in a bottle.

I mute the sets for a moment and shake my head and make a

"blblblblblbl" sound. Sam hears from the next room: "That's what Cosmo does when he's trying to shake pee from his head." Shake pee? "Yeah, when he's out for a walk and he's smelled too much pee and he's trying to move on." I let this pass without comment.

After watching the very funny comedian Eddie Griffin on Martin Short's show, I check out the competition. Oprah's guest is a boring New Age self-help guy—I'm glad I passed on it today. Maria Conchita Alonso is on a Spanish channel, looking *muy caliente*. What happened to her career? Is she still a big star, but only in Spanish? And the Power Rangers still ride on Channel 5. It's nice to know that even long after a fad ends, the subject of the fad can still get a berth on afternoon TV. How long will it take for Pokémon to reach this point?

On Channel 13 it's *Wishbone*, an educational series about a cute Jack Russell terrier who imagines himself into various stories from history and literature. Today he's wearing a beret and hanging out with Joan of Arc. "Joan, don't you think you're a little bit . . . young for this?" he asks her as she prepares to fight for France. How on earth are they going to end this one for the kids?

Martin Short now features a twelve-year-old boy in a fedora, who sings "Fly Me to the Moon" à la Sinatra, and not badly at that. Marty congratulates him at the song's end—"You ring-a-ding-ding, I'm telling you, kid!"—and duets with him as they go to commercial. This show is genuinely fun, but it'll never ever make it. I'm probably the only person who would rather watch a twelve-year-old Sinatra imitator than a teen prostitute.

The commercial is for the Dean Martin celebrity roast of Frank Sinatra on video, with other roast tapes to follow. There's Ruth Buzzi. There's Dean having a drinkie. There's Foster Brooks, playing Dan Quayle to Dean's George Bush—Dino looked sober in comparison to old Foster. This is pure meta-showbiz, and it's certainly being advertised on the right show.

Still a bit shaky from my soap-opera overload today, I decide to take Cosmo for an early walk. My head is a sponge and my limbs are like granite, but going outdoors feels glorious. As I walk Cosmo through the leafy grounds of the Cathedral of St. John the Divine, every tree and bush seems beautiful to me, not least because they're not *doing* anything. It's such a pleasure to watch things that just sit there. I think of Bill McKibben's book *The Age of Missing Information*, in which he contrasted one day of television with a day spent in an Adirondack forest. The book is something of a lecture, using the programs he encounters as reasons to bemoan the evils of our industrialized world; it's an elaborate and well-written version of Mom telling you to stop ruining your eyes and go play outside. McKibben never considered the possibility that watching too much TV might make you appreciate the natural world *more* by comparison—which is certainly how I'm feeling now.

At 5:30, I dutifully return to the sets. Already in progress is the second *Ricki Lake* of the day, but this one is the sure ratings-grabber: "Before the Ring, a Same-Sex Fling!" Tommie, a chubby version of Drew Barrymore, is preparing to tell her boyfriend Mikey that she wants to be with a woman before they become formally engaged. Ricki asks whether she'll do it if he disapproves. No, she says. And would she accept it if, for instance, he wanted to sleep with *his* best friend? "Um . . . yeah," she says after a beat. The audience doesn't believe her. Out comes Mikey, who already suspects this "has something to do with another female." That's because they've been on the show once before, when she surprised him with her bisexuality. Tommie puts the proposition to Mikey, who says it's okay with him as long as he can participate. Big applause from the crowd, especially the guys. The next triangle has the same setup, except this time the girl wants to sleep with her ex-boyfriend's mother. Then a card tells us that Ricki seeks panelists for "My First Time as a Freak!" That's an easy one—just get people to talk about their experiences on *Ricki Lake.*

They're trailing a *Star Trek* movie on the Sci-Fi Channel; it's the delightful fourth movie, in which the crew of the *Enterprise* travels back in time to save the whales in San Francisco. I think about sneaking in a viewing of this old favorite instead of continuing to explore the unknown, but I don't want to cheat. I guess that means I'll never appear on a trashy talk show.

Ricki Lake returns for her scripted wrap-up: "If people feel it's better to sow their oats before saying 'I do,' maybe it's better to say 'I don't' for now." These are eminently sensible words, but of course they're spoken only after an hour of sheer absurdity. I ponder Ricki's career transformation. What happened to the bubbly fat actress who brought such subversive glee to the John Waters flick *Hairspray?* This slimmed-down, buttoned-up Ricki just isn't the same gal— her old self seems like someone she'd put on the show as a panelist now. I guess she's traded the fifteen-minute variety of fame—being famous for who you are—for the longer-lasting version, being famous for what you do. But I can't help wondering if, in the process, she's sacrificed a part of who she is.

At 6:00 P.M., I tune in to a rerun of *Due South* on TNT. This is a show about a Mountie in Chicago, which was a big hit in Canada and a flop in the States. It's like Dennis Weaver's old show *McCloud,* but with a Canadian instead of a cowboy; is that because they think no American is naïve enough anymore to make the contrast work? The main reason I'm watching *Due South* is that the square-jawed lead is named Paul Gross. I never gave this any thought when the show ran on prime time, but recently a friend told me that this is the same Paul Gross who was a member of the science-fiction club I founded in high school, the Covenant of the Hexagram. I haul out my high school yearbook, and look back and forth between the model-handsome guy onscreen and the wild-haired goofball on the page. Hmmm—it's possible.

Then I check out the headlines, as delivered by Dan Rather on CBS. The recent outbreaks of St. Louis encephalitis are actually a different strain, West Nile virus, carried by birds as well as mosquitoes. This explains why rare birds have been dying at the Bronx Zoo. What to do about it? Good question. Then Rather rehashes the controversy over the Reagan biography, using clips from last night's *60 Minutes*. Enough already!

If the NAACP is looking for minority representation on television, they need look no further than the two newest netlets, the WB and UPN. On the former is Will Smith's old show *Fresh Prince of Bel Air*, as part of a block of sitcom reruns including *The Parent 'Hood* and *The Wayans Brothers*; on the latter is an hour of *Sister, Sister*, which leads in to three full hours of comedy starring African-American performers. Of course, the NAACP is really complaining about the lack of black faces on the three original networks. They have a point, but the time has long since passed when those networks deserve to be assigned that kind of importance. This is the age of narrowcasting, not broadcasting—and that's part of the problem.

The networks once tried to make programs for everybody. That often meant the lowest common denominator, lily-white and Wonder Bread bland. But in these days of multichannel TV, they can't get everybody under the same tent, so they don't even try. It's not about ratings anymore, it's about demographics. As a result, TV in 1999 still makes programs for everybody—but not at the same time. It's like South African TV when I visited Johannesburg in the waning days of apartheid; you'd see a show in English, followed by one in Zulu, followed by one in Afrikaans. No subtitles, no expectation that anyone other than the target audience would tune in—exclusionary TV. I suspect that's what the NAACP is really upset about, and I can't blame them at all. There weren't any black people on *My Three Sons*, but the stories were so universal—and generic—that anyone could find a connection to it, however shallow. Nowadays we've traded the universal for the specific, and a show about white yuppies working at a New York magazine might as well have a Keep Out sign on the door for most of America. A number of these shows on UPN and the WB try to exclude right back, which isn't satisfying anyone, either. *The Cosby Show* was leagues better than

My Three Sons, but it was equally universal, and the whole world watched it. All it takes is a commitment to excellence, and the talent to back it up.

Seven P.M. Both *Entertainment Tonight* on 2 and *Extra!* on 4 cover the *SNL* reunion special, at one point showing the same clip (Jon Lovitz paying tribute to the late Phil Hartman) at the same time. *Jeopardy!* is on 7; I'm not watching because it's absolutely what I would be watching if I weren't doing this. Meanwhile, the Sci-Fi Channel airs an episode of the original *Star Trek*: "Let That Be Your Last Battlefield," the one where the aliens are half black and half white, but the ones who are black on the left hate the ones who are black on the right, and vice versa. Ben Stiller's production company is named after a different bit of obscure Trek trivia—it's called Red Hour, from the episode "Return of the Archons"—and he once challenged me to name the very guest stars now onscreen. (Piece of cake—Lou Antonio and Frank Gorshin.) It's at moments like these that I realize I've forgotten more about *Star Trek* and superheroes than most people besides Ben Stiller will ever know. I don't know whether to be proud or mortified.

On PBS, *Newshour* with Jim Lehrer leads with the Indonesian pullout from East Timor. And *BBC News*, on Channel 21, has an entirely different set of headlines, with names like Chechnya that are rarely heard on American TV. At times like this I miss living in London, even with four channels. Of course, since we left, they now have five terrestrial channels and cable and digital and satellite—so I miss living in London five years ago.

It's time to call David, my shrink. I don't usually do this over the telephone, but seeing him in person this week would cut too deeply into my TV watching. I've debated whether or not to cancel this session entirely—but David is a Jungian analyst, and as is traditional, he'll charge me anyway. Besides, after two days of TV immersion, I've got plenty to talk about. So I shut off all the sets, and feel better instantly.

After an hour of telephone analysis, I turn everything back on

CAN'T TAKE MY EYES OFF OF YOU

and join Sam at the dinner table. We watch the second half of *Moesha* as we eat, largely because *The New York Times* has just run a story calling it the answer to the NAACP's prayers, presenting positive black role models for viewers of all ages. Well, it's certainly positive, and star Brandy is very appealing. The problem is the writing, which is nothing special. Still, I give it points for trying.

Eight-thirty brings the new sitcom *Ladies Man* on CBS. The fine British actor Alfred Molina is doing an American accent, with Betty White as his mother. In the teaser, she catches him with a porn magazine, which is not an auspicious beginning. The news magazine *20/20* is on ABC. *Veronica's Closet*, on NBC, looks insipid. The new high school show *Get Real*, on Fox, looks like every other high school show. On the WB is *The Parkers*, a *Moesha* spinoff. On UPN it's *Seventh Heaven*, which I've missed for the second time in two nights. Meanwhile, everybody who wasn't on the *SNL* reunion has his very own profile: Tim Conway on A&E, and Truman Capote on just plain E!

"This is horrible," says Sam. She's talking about *Ladies Man*. Molina's wife, played by *NYPD Blue* veteran Sharon Lawrence, is breastfeeding their daughter. This reminds Betty White of nursing Molina—"He sucked me dry. By the time he was finished, my breast was hanging like a loaf of pita bread." I hope they're paying these actors a lot of money.

Fortunately for Sam, a potbellied pig shows up on *20/20* and she insists we pull up the sound. I pull it up higher to counterbalance the sound of Cosmo, who is snoring loudly on Sam's knee. "Many people believe their pets are more than just pets," says the host. "They're soulmates who sense our grief, and have other unexplained talents." Here's a British doctor named Rupert Sheldrake, an expert—for which read "eccentric"—who believes that dogs read their owners' thoughts. Sheldrake tells us about Pam Smart and her dog J.T., who always seemed to know when she was coming home. Over 80 percent of the time, when Pam started to come home, J.T. would take his position in the window—forty-five miles away. Wait a minute, how many times did he go to the window when she *wasn't* coming home? I look over to Cosmo, who continues to snore peacefully. My thoughts must not be very interesting to him, since they don't concern bananas or cheese popcorn.

An ad for KFC, née Kentucky Fried Chicken—God forbid they should use the word "fried"—features an animated Colonel Sanders drawling, "Folks, are you still buying chicken from those burger boys?" He sounds more like Foghorn Leghorn than like the real Colonel, who was still alive when I was a kid. This is a tiny glimpse of a larger historical process: Like Robin Hood or Kilroy, a real person is being transformed into a fictional character, a symbol. Kids today don't know Roy Rogers made movies, and I bet they think Colonel Sanders is just another advertising creation like Tony the Tiger or Mr. Clean.

At 9:00 P.M. I pass up the hit sitcom *Everybody Loves Raymond* for a show Sam really wants to watch—*Law & Order: Special Victims Unit*, the new spinoff from the long-running hit show. Unlike the original, which divides its time between cops and prosecutors, this one is all cops; to be specific, it's the Sex Crimes division. I'm mystified as to why NBC would schedule this show at 9:00 P.M. and the Monday edition of their newsmagazine *Dateline* at ten, instead of the other way around. Maybe it's to sap viewers away from *Everybody Loves Raymond*, but I suspect it's just bad judgment.

The lead cops, Elliott and Olivia, are played by a tall actor named Christopher Meloni and the fierce Mariska Hargitay, the latter of whom is not only Jayne Mansfield's daughter but a former co-worker of Sam's at a bookstore in Los Angeles. The case is an elaborate whodunit concerning a young woman who fell from her apartment window—did she jump or was she pushed? Olivia is convinced it's murder, and she pursues the case with a righteous fury. Meanwhile, as we would never see on *Law & Order* proper, Elliott has a bedroom scene with his wife. As rock critic Robert Christgau said about Steely Dan's original singer David Palmer, this fits in like a cheerleader at a crap game. I can understand why they're doing it—on *Law & Order*, we never see personal stuff, but this show is more of a regular cop show, and you see a cop's family life on regular cop shows like *NYPD Blue*. The problem is that they haven't worked it through. The rest of the show is still written in the dry *Law & Order* house style, which is basically *Dragnet* with moral complexity.

The trail is choked with suspects. It seems as if everyone the dead woman ever met was a sleazy guy who seduced her and abandoned her, including her shrink, her boyfriend, and, predictably, her father. I follow along conscientiously, guessing occasionally that the killer is one of the supporting characters who's less obvious. But in the end it turns out to be an elaborate wild-goose chase. In a twist Agatha Christie might have envied, we learn the woman killed herself, and made it look like murder to dredge up everything about the various sleazy guys. The ingenuity of this twist is weighed down by the show's thudding emphasis on the childhood abuse angle. We've had so many years of talk shows, TV movies, and news stories about real-life courtroom dramas (Menendez, McMartin, etc.) that this issue has lost its dramatic charge. Yesterday's drama is today's melodrama, and tomorrow's sitcom.

I fulminate about this, exhausted, until Sam gets up and blows a raspberry on the back of my neck. "I'm really thinking of packing it in for the night," I tell her. "I'll have plenty of time to check out late-night TV later in the week." Then I look at the 10:00 P.M. shows—the new drama *Family Law* on CBS, *Dateline* on NBC, football on ABC, and an unexceptional selection of cable offerings including wrestling, pool, and a cheerleading competition. The decision is easy. I pack it in for the night. ♉

I tend to have wild, vivid dreams. For instance, I dreamed recently that Sam and I attended a ritzy party thrown by two wealthy gay men who were lima-bean importers, where George Harrison and Eric Clapton played "While My Guitar Gently Weeps" and Cosmo turned into a human baby. That sort of thing. However, my dreams on Monday night aren't wild at all; they're mostly about watching television. When I finally wake up at 7:00 A.M., I lie in bed for a moment hoping that my TV experiment hasn't irreparably altered my brain function.*

TUESDAY

1-800-BIG-HUGS

*Of course, when I told him the following week, my analyst concluded that these dreams were *not* about watching television.

I slip out of the bedroom without waking Sam, and read the entire *New York Times*. It's heaven. I make breakfast in my bathrobe, as a tribute to Sopkin, who spent most of his TV week dressed that way. Going to bed early last night was clearly the right decision, and despite my repetitive dreams, I'm in good spirits as I power up the sets shortly after eight. After two days of skipping around the dial—not that anything has a dial anymore—I'm adopting a theme today. In addition to the usual variegated viewing, I'll keep a number of sets tuned to the twenty-four-hour news channels: CNN, Fox News Channel, and MSNBC. For the hell of it, I tune another set to the kids' channel Nickelodeon.

My mood is dampened somewhat by the first story I watch on *Today*, which is an interview with the parents of a student killed in the Columbine school shooting. The parents are fighting with their pastor, who planted trees to honor the Columbine dead—including not only their child, but the two shooters as well. When the pastor wouldn't remove the shooters' trees, the parents cut the trees down. Matt Lauer does the interview with his usual professionalism, although he's just so damn twinkly that it's hard for him to stop twinkling. I feel for the parents, but this is a thorny ethical dilemma that really deserves an entire program rather than a five-minute segment.

There's more school controversy on *CBS This Morning*. This story is about a popular teacher who changed his sex to female, and was suspended. A parent supports the teacher; a school board member opposes him/her. Wrapping up, the anchor tells the guests, "And I can assure you, gentlemen, that we will continue to—" CBS cuts abruptly to a commercial for Tagamet. This show is cursed. The hosts may retain their aplomb in the face of imminent unemployment, but clearly the technical staff doesn't give a damn anymore.

Good Morning America has set up a salad bar and asked people to make their own salads. A dietician named Elizabeth Somer goes over the salads to identify what has hidden fat and what has the most nutrients. Charlie Gibson's healthy-looking salad has 971 calories, and forty-five grams of fat; another one has the same caloric count as four cheeseburgers. Somer says to skip pasta salads, put your dressing on the side and dip lightly, and stay away from croutons. Of course, I'm eating a peanut-butter-and-jelly sandwich for breakfast, but I do usually stay away from croutons.

On Fox News Channel, consumer reporter Sally Solo is doing the same thing with packaged cereal, based on a piece in the latest *Consumer Reports*. Big news—kids like cereals with more sugar. One of the three blow-dried anchors mentions that she likes dipping broccoli in sugar.

Siegfried and Roy and the baby tiger from yesterday are on CBS, determined to make sure every man, woman, and child in America sees their IMAX film. Former Wonder Woman Lynda Carter, still uncannily gorgeous, pushes Lens Express on Channel 46. There are dueling street crowds outside *Today* and *GMA*.

I should really settle into the news, but an imp of mischief overtakes me and instead I watch *Rugrats*, the popular talking-babies cartoon on Nickelodeon. Refreshingly, it seems the parents are characters too. The premise is that the dads are getting together to watch the big game, and the moms plan to go to the mall—but can the dads be trusted to protect the babies from harm? One dad invents a protective helmet, "the Bonkomatic Baby Bumper," to keep the kids from hurting themselves while the dads ignore them. As the game begins, the unattended babies start fighting over a bottle of chocolate milk, wreaking havoc. The fight is cleverly accompanied by the play-by-play from the football game, with the bottle standing in for the ball. This is genuinely above-average stuff; at nine minutes, it's a model of concise wit that might even impress the great Warner Brothers animator Chuck Jones. I wonder if he's seen it.

Meanwhile, Diane Sawyer rides a camel in the studio, while

onlookers look through the big window. Sawyer tries to smile, but she looks as miserable as Martha Stewart with the cockatoo yesterday. I don't blame her for a moment.

Then I see a clip on *Today* from *Guinevere*, a film I worked on at Miramax, and switch over in time to hear movie critic Gene Shalit call it "vastly enjoyable and beautifully directed." "Yes!" I shout. "There's tenderness, there's bitterness, and there's ribald hilarity," says Gene, who has just made my day. Thence to the anchors. Matt: "Not too often you hear Gene rave like that." Katie: "It does look wonderful, doesn't it?" I could hug them all.

The "Sensation" exhibit is on *Today* — again. They're doing a Web survey: Should taxpayers support controversial art exhibits? Five minutes later, the story shows up on MSNBC. I can't tell if all this exposure will be good for the arts in America, or just chilling.

On to the 9:00 A.M. talk shows. Jerry Springer's topic is "Secret Lives"; Montel's is the gruesome "Dad Fathered Child Just to Kill It"; Queen Latifah's is "How to Protect Your Kids from Smut and Predators on the Internet." However, I'm irresistibly drawn to *Regis & Kathie Lee*. Kathie Lee has a completely different hairdo today, and for a moment I wonder if it's really her. Regis went to the premiere of Siegfried and Roy's IMAX movie last night. (Kathie Lee asks if he noticed the stain Siegfried and Roy—or more likely their tiger—left backstage.) When he complained about the number of ads and trailers, Walter Cronkite shushed him from the next row. Then they went to the Rainbow Room for the party. It occurs to me that Regis and Kathie Lee are the last vestige of the old broadcasting tradition of Tex McCrary and Jinx Falkenburg, or even the elegant panelists on *What's My Line?*, in which the hosts would talk about the glamorous things they did offscreen with glamorous people. The common-touch twist here is that Regis and Kathie Lee are not particularly glamorous themselves, which is why Kathie Lee should abandon those absurd hairdos ASAP.

On Channel 2, Martha Stewart keeps running her fingers through a bowl of Carolina Gold rice, as she tells us its history. It's not a brand, it's a strain. Sam steps in and watches, amused. "You're hooked on Martha?" she asks. I admit that compared to much of the competition—with a gimlet eye toward the inevitable *Barney* on PBS—it's restful. She tells me I have e-mail, and without a look back, I abandon my post and deal with it.

Six minutes later, I return. I'm scared by my developing feelings for Martha, so I decide to discover what kind of secret lives Jerry Springer is revealing. There are three generations of women on stage: a cranky, disabled grandma, a sullen granddaughter, and a sexy mother who's doing something for money at night. Is she hooking? Stripping? Proofreading? Before I can find out, Jerry cuts to a commercial.

I turn to MSNBC. I promised Penny I'd watch the channel, because her husband, Michael, works there. MSNBC is a joint venture between NBC and Microsoft, but there's a lot more of the former in evidence than the latter. The first thing I see isn't exactly up-to-the-minute news; Tom Brokaw is reporting on the fall of the Berlin Wall. I shake away my déjà vu when I realize that this is a show called *Time and Again*, which repackages old TV news footage. Someone must have gotten a raise for that idea. I'm ever more convinced that the ultimate subject of television is television itself, and *Time and Again* is the perfect expression of this. Maybe years from now there'll be a show that looks back at *Time and Again*.

There's more TV intertextuality on *Later Today*, where Elmo from *Sesame Street* is plugging his new movie. He's a better talk-show guest than Burt Reynolds. "You make a lot of people happy," says host Florence Henderson. "I love you, Florence," replies Elmo. "Can I have a kiss?" She gives him a big smackeroo, and tells the audience, "Elmo and I are running off together." But Elmo is distracted. "Do you have craft services here?" he asks, using the film-lingo term for the catering tables. It's an intricate dance—Florence treats Elmo like a peer and a real person, and Elmo stays in character while letting us know that he's in showbiz too.

A familiar face on Queen Latifah's show: It's Donna Rice

Hughes, author of *Protecting Your Children in Cyberspace*. Yes, this is the same Donna Rice whose canoodling with Gary Hart brought down his presidential campaign, but now she's born again like Chuck Colson. Ever sensible, Latifah is reluctant to endorse anything resembling censorship; after all, her career began in rap music, which is a perennial target. Donna tells Latifah she doesn't advocate censorship, just responsible parenting. Another guest is Kayla Marie St. Claire, who runs a voyeur website with nude photos of herself. Kayla is with Donna all the way, although I don't think Donna wants her help.

On 2, Martha Stewart is ironing. An ironing expert displays different fabrics and talks about how wrinkly they get. Who knew there were ironing experts in the world? Sam wanders in to check on me, and watches the ironing expert for a moment. "What's her book?" she asks. I try to remember. "*How to Iron?*" I offer limply. I have no idea. "Martha looks pained," observes Sam. In fact, Martha usually looks pained, and I think that's why I keep being drawn to her. She's the only person on TV who looks as uncomfortable as I feel.

It's 10:00 A.M. now, and I check the grids to see what to switch to. But to my relief and delight, I'm just letting 'em roll today. I may not be quite so exhausted tonight.

I pass on *Maury*, *Divorce Court*, and *Judge Mathis*, and head straight for Rosie. Doing the introductions are four women, "The Greenwich Grabettes" from Connecticut, who have lost a total of one hundred pounds since January. If I'm not mistaken, these women are a "chub club," a sort of diet version of the consciousness-raising groups of my youth. They get onstage to do a song-and-dance parody of "Walking on Sunshine," weaving in the names of Rosie's diet-related sponsors, "and don't we look good!" Rosie gives them a big Reebok bag of products from said sponsors, and a Rosie jacket each. I like Rosie, and I'm happy for the Grabettes, but I can't help feeling a twinge of sadness at the spectacle of people volunteering to push consumer products on TV. At moments like these, commercial TV starts to look like a big hamster wheel; we go round and round, waiting for treats.

At the first commercial, I think about watching *The Guiding Light* without Penny's guidance, but it's already 10:04 and I've probably missed two affairs and three cases of amnesia already. The "Sensation" exhibit is on MSNBC, including the now-familiar dung-enhanced portrait of the Virgin Mary. If Mayor Giuliani really wanted to protect the public from this painting, he should have kept his mouth shut.

The new *Family Feud* is much like the old *Family Feud*, except the host is comedian Louie Anderson rather than the smarmy but charismatic Richard Dawson. The other difference is that the survey questions on which the game is built are now put to the audience directly, through a website and a toll-free number. For instance, "What movie did everyone love that you hated?" This is one of the most natural Internet tie-ins I've seen so far—although that particular question is so subjective that I pity the family who has to match its answers.

Rosie O'Donnell talks about her problems with the *Law & Order* spinoff, which mirror my own. She got some complaints when she didn't like the first episode, but watched again last night and feels the same way. "Does television need a show about sex crimes?" she asks. I nod in agreement; after forty-eight hours of TV, I'm starting to feel a bit more sympathetic to Steve Allen's cause.

Now Rosie sings a parody of "The Candy Man," about the venerable game Candy Land: "What combines my love of candy and my desperate need to win? Candy Land . . ." She's giving the games to everyone in the audience. How can you not love this gal? She makes it look easy, and now so many other comedians with slow careers have jumped on the bandwagon—but they just can't do what she does. The difference is that there's no condescension in Rosie, and very little of the irony that dooms Martin

Short. As they say on the E! channel, she lives for this stuff. You can't fake it.

Sarah Michelle Gellar, star of *Buffy the Vampire Slayer*, bounds onto Rosie's stage and gives the host a brand-new cinnamon-flavored Altoid. Sarah Michelle, who is as undernourished as Calista Flockhart or Lara Flynn Boyle, looks as if she never eats anything *except* Altoids. Still, she's a perfect guest for Rosie, chatty chatty chatty. She talks about how "awe-inspiring" the *SNL* special was— "I've watched the show since I was born." Ouch! I feel very old all of a sudden. Sarah loved *The Sixth Sense* and *An Ideal Husband*. Rosie says she did a movie with the director of *Sixth Sense*, "but it was a Miramax movie and it wasn't very well distributed." Double ouch! Then Rosie and Sarah play with their dolls—that is, dolls of themselves, available at any toy store. "My doll can kick your doll's butt!" says Rosie, and it does.

Maury's theme today is "Help! My Girlfriend Looks Like a Guy!" Meet Patricia—everywhere she goes, people call her "sir." "What a surprise," says Sam dryly. Next to Patricia on stage, a big black woman named Roberta says people think she looks like a transvestite. Sam is startled: "That's a girl? No wonder!" Because it's television, all the women get makeovers. Roberta comes out in a dress and makeup, and *still* looks like a transvestite.

Two fitness people are on ESPN—a blond, buff woman, and a guy whose shaved head and earring give him an unfortunate resemblance to Mr. Clean. Sam gets a devilish look in her eye. "See, if you would just exercise with one of these programs, honey, it would all be worth it," she cajoles. I have to take the dare, and clamber to my feet. I try to follow Mr. Clean through a simple exercise—marching in place, then stepping forward and back. This shouldn't be difficult, but he's in superb physical condition and I'm the kind of guy who thought it would be interesting to sit in a chair watching TV for a week. Within five minutes I'm sweating like a cold beer in a hot room, and panting loudly. Sam hoots with laughter. Boy, am I out of shape. Then the phone rings. I'm saved by the bell, and I collapse onto the sofa. Sam explains to the caller that I'm attempting to exercise, but since I don't know what to do with my body, it's a hilarious sight. Still winded, I grumble that it isn't hilarious to me.

One phone call necessitates two more, and when I get back to the sets, it's 10:45. Garth Brooks is on *Rosie*, wearing a big black cowboy hat and blue denim. Does he get embarrassed wearing that stuff offstage, or is a talk-show appearance an extension of on-stage? Maybe it's just part of his image, and he doesn't get embarrassed any more than Gene Shalit gets embarrassed by his mustache. Besides, it's important for Garth to reinforce his image now that he's departing from it in his new album, which purports to be the work of an Australian rocker named Chris Gaines. Garth sings one of the new Chris Gaines songs on *Rosie*, to promote the album and his NBC special tomorrow night. It's a U2-style chanting song that occasionally breaks into the chorus of "Get Together" by the Youngbloods, and while it doesn't sound like Garth Brooks, the chorus reassures through its sheer familiarity.

I'm intrigued by the notion of stars taking on other personas. It's a showbiz equivalent of what Madison Avenue calls "brand extension"—the same principle that keeps Coca-Cola introducing variations like Cherry Coke and diet Coke and Caffeine-Free Coke. The idea is that more shelf space for you means less for your competition. But in the case of Garth Brooks, it's clearly a reaction to the narrow confines of the box he's in as a successful country star; he wants to branch out without alienating his audience. By becoming his own doppelgänger, he's blazing a trail for other celebrities, and the possibilities are limitless. Maybe Sam Donaldson could doff his toupee and start a second career as a character actor.

CNN runs a piece about *American Beauty*, my favorite film of the year so far. Here's young star Mena Suvari, then Kevin Spacey. From the look of the backdrop behind them both, these are interviews taped during the film's publicity junket a few months back, interspersed with clips from the film's EPK, or electronic press kit.

You can probably see this same exact footage on news shows all over America this week.

At 11:00 A.M., Sam leaves for work. The talk shows and channels change partners, and we start all over again. On ABC, *The View* opens with a glossy credit sequence. Barbara Walters swirls into sight: "I had this idea for a show. Different women, different points of view. Maybe a little too different. We call it *The View*." (Didn't she used to say "Be careful what you wish for"?) In the two minutes it's taken for the *View* women to assume their places on the set, Bob Barker and announcer Rod Roddy on *The Price Is Right* have gotten four people to come on down, plugged an item, solicited bids on it, and brought the winner up onstage with Bob. Their sheer efficiency is dazzling.

The View features five women—Walters, newswoman Meredith Vieira, comedian Joy Behar, attorney Star Jones, and what's-her-name who replaced what's-her-name—sitting around talking, with occasional guests. The real surprise of the show is that Vieira, formerly a buttoned-up *60 Minutes* reporter, has become its spark plug. Unleashed from the news, Vieira has gotten in touch with her inner Kathie Lee Gifford, in her willingness to say whatever she's thinking, regardless of propriety. And unlike Garth Brooks, she didn't even need to adopt another persona to do it.

Now Meredith and company are talking to actress Jennifer Grey. Grey, who's had so much plastic surgery that she's unrecognizable, is plugging her sitcom *It's Like, You Know*. She plays herself—as a former Hollywood star who's had a lot of plastic surgery. One of the women asks if even Jennifer's old friends have trouble recognizing her. "Seriously, everyone recognizes me in my life now," says Grey. "Seriously, I'm talking about another time in my life." Seriously. She is gutsy to play herself on the sitcom, and I decide to watch it tonight. A successful plug, seriously.

Sally Jessy Raphael's theme is "Sally's Odd, Odd News." I've heard about her first guest; he's Brian, a gambler who won $100,000

CAN'T TAKE MY EYES OFF OF YOU

on a bet by getting breast implants. He was supposed to have them for a year, but it's been almost three years already. Brian says he wanted something he and his friends could laugh about when he was seventy. Sally Jessy looks embarrassed—which may be a first—but she still asks to see the man-made mammaries. Brian opens his shirt, and the video engineer in the control room slaps a big CENSORED bar across his chest. (It seems breasts are taboo for TV even when they're on a guy; oh, that Lenny Bruce were still alive to riff on this.) Next we meet Dr. Felix Shiffman, the doctor who performed the operation. Dr. Shiffman prompts Brian: "Do your breasts glow?" Brian picks up two flashlights and somebody turns down the house lights—sure enough, they glow under the flashlights, which is apparently true for most implants. This is like "Hints from Heloise" for porn stars. Meanwhile, Ricki Lake seeks guests for "I Don't Care What You Say, I'm a Lesbian Until Graduation!"

It's 11:30, and I have to lie down for a moment. Battered by the whirlwind shifts of identity on this morning's shows, my stamina is decreasing rapidly. I grab my legal pad, and decide to concentrate on the news channels, to give the day some semblance of coherence before I hit the wall of soaps. On MSNBC, a familiar face—sure enough, it's Ed Meese, reacting to the Morris book. "You must understand, I haven't read the book either," says Meese. That seems to be the news-channel experience in a nutshell—people spinning the spin itself, while the substance sits somewhere in the distance. The host asks Meese what it was like to work with Ronald Reagan day-to-day. "He was not a micromanager," says Meese, choosing his words carefully, but "he brought the country out of economic chaos." Sure he did, if you don't count the deficit hole it's taken eleven years for the country to crawl out of. I'm amazed the host let that one slide.

CNN is doing the transsexual-teacher story, with a well-preserved Dr. Joyce Brothers aboard to comment. Even with Dr.

Brothers, however, they don't go over anything we didn't see on *This Morning* earlier. This is the pack mentality at work, with each channel covering the same stories over and over again until any potential interest is wrung dry. It's a repeating loop, with the occasional new segment inserted—not unlike the playlist on a radio station. Or, to adopt a more bizarre metaphor, it reminds me of my cantillation studies in Hebrew school. To read the Torah, a cantor sings the text using a limited number of "notes," which are actually little multinote riffs that repeat in different combinations. So any part of the Torah you sing sounds more or less the same—except for a couple of very significant passages marked with the rarest notes, which are like cadenzas. Similarly, twenty-four-hour TV news keeps blending the same stories—and the same *approaches* to those stories—into a cantorial drone, until you hit the news equivalent of Moses at the burning bush.

Meanwhile, the *National Enquirer*'s Mike Walker is on Fox News Channel, plugging his new show. More TV on TV. "We have to look for the story behind the story," says cheerful Mike. "Who are these people? Are they people like me?" Exactly the same question I've been asking all morning. Fox News takes live phone calls— none of that live-to-tape stuff we saw on Martha Stewart's show. The first caller asks how Phil Hartman's friends and family are doing, sparked by Jon Lovitz choking up at the *SNL* tribute to Hartman. "The death of Phil Hartman was one of the most stupid, needless deaths ever. I can't pretend to know what his children are feeling," says Mike, who's getting choked up himself. Who was it who said, "If you can fake sincerity, you've got it made"?

Next, a woman asks if Hollywood is backing off its support of the Clintons. Mike says yes. The Fox host asks if Roger Altman, the former Clinton adviser who runs the *Enquirer*, ever orders the paper to soft-pedal an item about the President. "Do you ever get a call from Rupert?" demurs Mike, referring to Fox owner Rupert Murdoch—but I notice the host doesn't answer him.

Someone has given Donny and Marie Osmond their own talk show. Is it just me, or does Marie look like a thinner Monica Lewinsky? (Of course, even Monica Lewinsky looks like a thinner Monica Lewinsky these days.) A well-dressed psychic is consoling a woman—about what? A kidnapping? "Whoever has this yellow truck, they're close," says the psychic. "They're just not telling you because they don't want to screw up the investigation. Whoever she's with—I don't want to play God with this, but I know they're watching over her." Is this about a kidnapped child? It's pretty damned irresponsible to play with a mother's emotions, and I get so angry I can't watch. When I woke up this morning, I never anticipated getting really mad at Donny and Marie. I guess anything can happen when you're watching twelve televisions. What's next, uncontrollable rage at Florence Henderson?

Then I pause on the familiar form of Richard Simmons, who used to be in the fitness racket, but has moved on. Now he's just a floating personality, attempting to moor himself to a new mast: a syndicated show called *Richard Simmons: Dream Maker.* "I can feel someone out there is dreaming!" yells Richard. "Let me catch it!" To be on the show, you can call 1-800-BIG-HUGS, or log on to www.bighugs.com. Richard reads a letter from a woman who's lost eighty pounds, and has another hundred to go. It would be her dream come true to meet Richard—short of eating a cheeseburger, probably—and so here she is in the studio, holding back the tears. She's down to 240 pounds, she's had a knee replacement and a hip replacement, but she's still optimistic: "When you've got someone like Richard Simmons on your side, you can't help but lose weight!" Did she just come out with that, or was it scripted? Either way, it gets a round of 1-800-big-applause. The woman starts to talk about how her kid was ashamed to be seen with her because she was so heavy—and she can't go on for the tears. Richard gives her a big hug dot com. "We love you just the way you are," says Richard. Then he gives her an Aladdin's-lamp necklace, and a captain's hat. Why a captain's hat? Because "You are going on my CRUISE-TO-LOSE!" In other words, we love you just the way you'll be after you lose one hundred more pounds.

Since Richard hasn't invited me on his cruise, I mute everything and go into the kitchen for a TV dinner. While I'm tearing the foil off a microwaveable pizza, my father calls. I bring him up to date on the last few days. He says I saw the least typical episode of *The Practice*; Sunday's episode was concerned with catching the audience up on last season's events, and as a result it had much less characterization than usual. Dad really loves *The Practice*; as a lawyer, he thinks it's the best legal show ever. This means a lot coming from him, because he's been known to fume for weeks when a movie or TV show is legally inaccurate. (Don't get him started on *L.A. Law.*)

I finish my lunch, which is disgusting. As my late father-in-law used to say, I've now eaten this brand of frozen pizza twice—the first time, and the last time. Now I'm poised and ready for *All My Children*. Immediately, I face a dilemma about which Penny had warned me. In the "previously" clips, I recognize only one set of people—Edmund and Alex before the latter went horseback riding. Everybody else is a stranger, and every other scene seems to be from last week. I'm in trouble now.

Fortunately, even I recognize the next person onscreen—it's the ultimate soap diva, Susan Lucci. I even know the name of her character, Erica Kane. I was so busy taking notes yesterday that it never even occurred to me to ask Penny about Erica. Erica is having lunch at a restaurant that's supposed to be in New York, with hunky Dr. David Hayward from yesterday's show. Now to Gillian, the Hungarian princess, looking at a framed photo. Is it the elusive Dmitri? No, it's Maximilian the horse! Cut to Edmund and Alex, debating about whether to shoot the horse, which belongs—er, belonged—to Dmitri. Edmund is perturbed: "I just spent all night looking for my brother, and now I have to put his horse down!"

I can't decide who looms larger as an offscreen character, Dmitri or his horse.

Back at the restaurant, Dr. David and Erica are startled by Joan Rivers, playing herself. They catch up like old friends, and Erica sends regards to Joan's daughter Melissa. This is positively surreal. Then Erica's picture is snapped by a paparazzo; what is she famous for, her multiple marriages? Meanwhile, it's easy to see the secret of Susan Lucci's success; she has the biggest eyes on television. I look over at *The Bold and the Beautiful* on Channel 2, and *Days of Our Lives* on Channel 4, but Lucci's eyes seem literally twice as big as everyone else's. Her only real competition is Bambi.

The show goes on, cutting back and forth between Erica and David, Edmund and Alex, and Princess Gillian bemoaning the loss of Dmitri. Most of it is a drawn-out lead-up to a few scant minutes of drama: Edmund shoots the horse, David reveals himself to be a cad, and Gillian agrees to live, "for Dmitri." It turns out Edmund doesn't blame Alex for the horse's death; he blames her for Dmitri's death—*and* the horse's death. "Whatever you say you love, dies," says Edmund, and on that note the show ends. How did I ever live without *All My Children*?

At 2:00 P.M., I decide on the spur of the moment not to watch *One Life to Live.* Instead, I tune to *Passions*, a new soap on NBC, which turns out to be a very different animal. For one thing, most of the characters are teenagers. It seems a girl named Charity is in a coma, and her friends are hanging out at her bedside. A Hispanic boy named Miguel wonders if Charity is dreaming of him. There's also an African-American girl; *Passions* seems to be considerably more integrated than any of the soaps I've seen so far. But this departure from soap norms is nothing compared to the next character I meet: Juliet Mills, once the star of *Nanny and the Professor*, playing a witch named Tabitha. That's right, a witch, of the peaked-hat-and-broomstick variety. It seems Tabitha killed Charity's mother and put Charity in her coma. Her sidekick is Timmy—a doll that Tabitha brought to life, played by a midget. I can hardly believe my eyes.

The first nonsupernatural adult we meet is Grace, Charity's aunt. She talks to the comatose Charity: "Twenty years ago, I was rescued from a fire and I couldn't remember who I was, who anybody was. I pray that doesn't happen to you, sweet Charity." How can a new soap have this kind of outrageous backstory already? But she keeps going. "If you opened your eyes now, you'd probably think I'm your mother—my twin sister, Faith. Your doctor thinks that would be very upsetting to you." But her cousins will be there, and so will Miguel, "that boy in your life who means so much to you." This is great; *Passions* is so new that they're loading every scene with exposition. No prior knowledge required!

I'm guessing that the creators of *Passions* are trying to incorporate some tricks from Australian soap operas like *Neighbours* and *Home and Away*, which are massively popular all over the rest of the world. Like *Passions*, they spend most of their time following attractive teenagers through everyday crises that seem almost anticlimactic after the adulteries and switched sperm samples of American soaps. To help American soap audiences go for it, the *Passions* writers have thrown in some traditional soap stuff too. But what on earth is the witchcraft doing there?

I'm glad I skipped *One Life to Live* today, because I don't recognize anybody from yesterday's show. Elsewhere, Bill Bradley is speaking on CNN—a title beneath him says it's a speech on health care. On NBC, a promo: "Tomorrow on *Today*, a new biography of Ronald Reagan mixes fiction with fact. We speak with the controversial biographer. Tomorrow on *Today*." Why didn't they just call *Time and Again* "Yesterday"? And what happens if they bring back Tom Snyder's old *Tomorrow* show? I'm sorry Abbott and Costello didn't live to see this.

My friend Jaime Wolf shows up just as *Passions* returns to Tabitha the witch. (Couldn't they come up with a more original name?) Jaime is a screenwriter and journalist who has been assigned to cover my experiment for a magazine. He's also something of a downtown hipster, and not the kind of guy who would be watching a show like this at this time of the day. I quickly fill him in on *Passions*, and I get the feeling that he wouldn't believe me if he weren't seeing it with his own eyes—especially when he gets a load of Timmy the talking doll. By the time the credits finally roll, Jaime and I are staring dumbly at the screen.

General Hospital is next, but I'm still explaining the whole Tabitha-and-Timmy bit to Jaime. By the time I turn my full attention to the show, I've lost the thread entirely—not that I remember anything from yesterday. What I do notice, however, is that not a single scene in two days takes place in a hospital, or even involves a doctor or nurse. Either *Passions* or *All My Children* seem like better candidates to be named *General Hospital* than *General Hospital* itself.

With Jaime at my side—taking notes on my taking notes, like Boswell with an unhelpfully silent Johnson—I go back to snatching at fragments, waiting for something to grab me. On *Jenny Jones*, the theme is "What's Wrong with My Family?" Do I sense a national metaphor here? The transsexual-teacher story is on MSNBC and CNN simultaneously. The teacher says the choice was easy; it was transition or die. (I wonder if Garth Brooks felt the same way before his transition to Chris Gaines?) Meanwhile, Jaime is distracted by a cartoon version of *Ace Ventura, Pet Detective*. "Did Jim Carrey do the voice?" he asks, as if two and a half days of watching TV makes me an expert on these things. I tell him I don't have the faintest idea.

I perk up when I notice Elmo on Fox News Channel. Brooke Shields and Siegfried and Roy have nothing on this monster. The interviewer asks, "Elmo, we haven't seen the movie yet, but is it safe to say this is for children?" "Well, it's *Sesame Street*," says Elmo, "so yeah, it's safe to say." They stick a card in front of Elmo, which puzzles him. "Excuse Elmo—excuse Elmo—what is that?" Interviewer: "That's my card which says when the movie opens." Elmo: "Well, Elmo can't read, but the movie opens Friday." What a pro.

Fox News returns to the studio. "We're all vomiting here," says the more serious afternoon anchor, Shepherd Smith, who's dyspeptic enough to belong on *Good Day New York*. He seems perturbed that he's introducing segments about bright red monsters instead of grilling politicians, and he can't let it go: "Why does Elmo talk about himself in the third person like Bob Dole? Did you catch that?" The next time Elmo goes to Grouchland, he should take Shepherd Smith with him.

Once again, Jaime's attention has drifted elsewhere. He's learning rapidly that it's hard to concentrate when you're faced with twelve TV sets. "Who's this teenage news announcer on MSNBC?" he asks. And once again I have no idea, although Jaime is right—the anchor does indeed seem ready for a guest shot on *Felicity*, or maybe a recurring role on *Passions*. Then she introduces Campbell Brown from NBC News, who is cut from the same cloth. They could *both* be teenage soap stars. I remember the craggy Eric Sevareids and David Brinkleys of my youth; if they came around now, they'd end up on radio, just like Daniel Schorr.

Not a moment too soon, our attention spans are saved by Oprah Winfrey, whose show today is about child prodigies. First we get a mini-documentary on Greg Smith, who could add and subtract at sixteen months. He jumped from second grade directly to eighth grade, and has just started college—at ten. His physics professor says he combines the intellectual curiosity of an older kid with the enthusiasm of a kid kid. What I really can't believe is that the college in question is my father's alma mater, Virginia's Randolph Macon. Jaime is appalled by this story: "He's going to be so poorly socialized! Stories like this can only end in tragedy."

At home, Greg plays like a kid—when he's not browsing for antiques or collecting Civil War figurines. Says Jaime, "This kid is going to hit the drugs hard the minute he reaches puberty." Now Oprah interviews Greg onstage. "My mom and dad don't believe in flash cards," says Greg. "They facilitated my needs." However, they've also given him a very unattractive bowl haircut. Greg says he has friends his own age, but how long can that last? "I can bend to what they like, as long as it doesn't run contrary to my beliefs," says Greg. Oprah asks Greg if he feels special. "I believe I've been given a gift from God," he replies. "I don't know how or why I've been given this gift, but I want to use it to help mankind." Jaime remains skeptical: "This is the kind of kid I want to track down in about five years, on whatever skid row he's living in."

Martin Short's guest is Rob Lowe, who's on the new series *The West Wing.* Lowe was friends with John F. Kennedy Jr., and says that while he's met a lot of actors, JFK Jr. had more charisma than most of them. Sincerity comes even less easily to Marty than it does to Mike Walker, and his reponse is a non sequitur: "A great tragedy. You should be very proud of it." I feel embarrassed for him. "Why does Martin Short *want* to do a talk show?" asks Jaime. I suspect we'd know the answer if we talked to his accountant.

The next child prodigy on Oprah is a tap dancer, ten-year-old Cartier Williams. And man, can he tap. For some reason I'm much less worried about this kid than about Greg the brain. The prodigies roll on, including the winner of the *Jeopardy!* kids' tournament and a disabled poet named Marshall.

Channel 2 news at five has a report on Michael J. Fox, who testified at a Senate hearing to ask for more funding for Parkinson's disease, from which he suffers. He doesn't look good when he testifies; he rocks back and forth a bit, and one hand trembles if he doesn't hold it. He says he's waiting for his medicine to kick in. "I can expect in my forties to face challenges most people won't face until their seventies and eighties," says Fox. It's astonishing to watch someone who's usually so polished when he's not in control of himself; it's an unexpectedly raw moment of television.

On PBS is an animated series called *Arthur,* of which our five-year-old goddaughter Jessica is a big fan. The theme song seems to be sung with a British accent, so I expect a British show—but the voices are American. (Or, considering the Canadian origins of much of this stuff, maybe North American.) Arthur is an ordinary suburban kid who happens to be an aardvark. Not that he looks like an aardvark; he's more of a generic funny animal. But Francine, his friend, looks like a different species of funny animal—a monkey? Does she have a tail? Nobody seems to have a tail. Plus they all have hands with five fingers, and sneakers, and Benetton-ish sweaters. It's a new wrinkle on the traditional Goofy question, as expressed memorably in the movie *Stand By Me*: "Mickey is a mouse. Donald is a duck. Pluto is a dog. So what's Goofy?"

On Channel 5, a rerun of *Unhappily Ever After*. I'm starting to identify a TV type, and here it is again, in the person of ingenue Nikki Cox. She's got that David Cassidy/Neve Campbell combination of adorable squint and pronounced eyebrows, which clearly gives aspiring TV stars a leg up. But Elmo doesn't even need that— he's still making the rounds, using the "craft services" line on CNN's Laurin Sydney. "Elmo doesn't want to be a big movie star, Elmo just wants to have fun on Sesame Street," says Elmo, who doth protest too much.

The "Sensation" exhibit rears its head again as MSNBC interviews Steven Madoff, art critic—someone who probably never expected to be on national television. They then cut to the Chris Ofili picture. Two days ago, I didn't know Chris Ofili's name, and now I toss it around casually. Once again, it's easy to see that Giuliani has done more to promote the art that offends him than the Brooklyn Museum could ever have done.

In retrospect, I can see I was mistaken to think that watching the news channels would give some coherence to the day, since the channels aren't coherent themselves. Without meaning to, I've adopted their rhythm and reduced my own viewing to bite-sized pieces and sound bites, and it's driving me quite literally to distraction. Enough, I decide. Jaime's ready to head back downtown, so I put Cosmo in his harness and leave with him, hoping a shot of the real world will restore my sense of balance—and my attention span.

I return shortly before 6:00 P.M. Christie Hefner, daughter of

Hugh and CEO of the Playboy empire, is on *Your World with Neil Cavuto* on FNC. Christie Hefner is such a media pro that she might as well be hosting rather than guesting, and she deflects any charges of sexism with ease: "Do you want a woman you can have great sex with, or a woman you can talk to? *Playboy* says you can have both." Cavuto asks how her father justifies his outrageous expenditures, since Christie runs the company and Hef sits around in his pajamas having parties. She says he's an asset to the company, in part because of the connections he makes. Everybody wants to go to the Playboy Mansion. She also says there's a major motion picture in the works. Hmm—when Harry Dean Stanton was cast as Hefner in the movie *Star 80*, Hef refused to cooperate until they replaced Stanton with the more urbane Cliff Robertson. If this whole movie is about him, he'll probably insist on Mel Gibson.

An early, early *Brady Bunch* episode airs on Nickelodeon, preserved like an all-American scarab in the amber of syndication. Interestingly, it's not on Nick at Nite, the channel's regular slot for recycled sitcoms; instead, it's in the Nickelodeon kids' block. You can tell this is an early episode because Robert Reed has straight hair. Character actor Dick Wilson shows up as a shopkeeper—is this how he got the gig as Mr. Whipple, squeezing the Charmin? At the end of the episode, Mike and Carol are in bed together, and she gives him the lucky golf club he thought he lost. He curls up with it and says good night. "Mike Brady!" she chides him. He laughs and grabs her playfully. Fade out. This is on Nickelodeon at 5:58 P.M.; it seems implied sex is acceptable on a kids' channel as long as it's between married people. That's fine with me, although I'm sure Steve Allen thinks it's leading our children down a moral sewer.

It's time for the news on most channels, and for the kids' sketch-comedy show *All That* on Nick. Two of the news shows are leading with "Sensation"—has something happened? Indeed, the board of the Brooklyn Museum is suing the city to keep Giuliani from withdrawing the museum's funding. I applaud. *All That*, by contrast, leads with a variant on the venerable gag "Is your refrigerator running?" The twist here is that it actually is running, and they actually do have to catch it. That's the way this show goes, unearthing corny jokes for an audience that's never heard them before. The commercial is a little mini-show itself: "Nickelodeon goes heart-to-heart with Melissa Joan Hart." It's a two-minute interview with clips, tied to her upcoming movie *Drive Me Crazy*, as well as the new season of *Sabrina the Teenage Witch*. I guess this is as close as Nick gets to having an equivalent of *Biography*—and for the Nick audience, Melissa is as big a star as you can get.

The graphic on MSNBC says *Decision 2000*. The guest is Senator Daniel Patrick Moynihan. I expect something about Bradley and Gore, but when I turn up the sound, he's actually talking about "Sensation." "We've had some controversial art exhibits in our time, and I think we'll survive this one," says Moynihan. This explains why he doesn't do more talk shows; perspective runs contrary to the hype mentality. The host asks what Moynihan thinks about Bill and Hillary Clinton buying an expensive house in Westchester, financed with a huge interest-free loan from a supporter. But that doesn't worry Moynihan either. He reminds her that New York voters have nothing against conspicuous consumption; they've been happy with millionaire governors like Nelson Rockefeller, and Averell Harriman before that, and FDR before that. The host is rattled by the presence of somebody who actually has a point of view, and stumbles: "Thank you very much, Sir Moynihan," she concludes.

Meanwhile, A&E is rerunning *Simon & Simon*, a show I have never watched in my life. Mustachioed star Gerald McRaney and an older guy are breaking into an office dressed as electricians. "Now, we search." "Where?" "Use your imagination. If you were a sex-starved female hiding things about your love life, what would you do?" The older guy thinks. "Never mind," says McRaney. Is he playing Simon or Simon? Within minutes, I realize why I never watched this show. The Eighties mainstream cop show has neither the nostalgic kitsch appeal of Seventies shows nor the comparative sophistication of the drama shows that followed *Hill Street Blues*. In fact, it's simply unwatchable, unless I want to fall asleep and risk missing the next few hours.

Six-thirty. Let's try *ABC News with Peter Jennings* tonight. California governor Gray Davis just signed a big health-care bill. Californians now have the right to sue their HMOs—thank God this didn't go to referendum. I can only imagine the campaign the HMOs will mount to overturn the law, if they can. When did ABC's evening news show go head-to-head against the other networks? When I was a teenager, I remember it being half an hour later. Did the affiliates complain because they didn't have room to show both *Jeopardy!* and *Wheel of Fortune* between the news and prime time?

I drift through the rest of the news, which covers the same stories I've been following all day: Michael J. Fox, West Nile virus, the shooting of the bride-to-be, the presidential race. Just as Peter Jennings winds down with "The Mayor and the Virgin Mary," my friend Doug shows up. He works in publishing, and I bet he thought watching twelve televisions would be relaxing compared to slogging through a pile of unsolicited manuscripts. But like every visitor so far, Doug is stunned by the display, and clearly unprepared for the visual cacophony of twelve TV sets in full vent. This is nobody's idea of relaxation.

As Doug settles onto the couch, we both notice a familiar-looking man in a bow tie on Channel 13. "Who is that?" I ask. "Arthur Schlesinger?" Doug thinks it might be, so we turn it up—but it isn't Schlesinger, because this guy is talking about the Federal Reserve. He seems to be an economist. "It's that guy," Doug says, "he used to be on the news all the time." I throw out names—Milton Friedman? John Kenneth Galbraith? Adam Smith?—but Doug keeps shaking his head. Finally we get an ID: the mystery man is Irving R. Levine, who used to cover the economy for NBC. I guess he's still alive.

A promo for a show about Pope John Paul II, later tonight on Channel 13. "The Pope who brought down Communism," intones an announcer. Now hold on there—that's not like saying Reagan brought us out of economic chaos, but it's still a pretty sweeping statement. "It's a journey that says as much about us as it says about him." It's a promo that says as much about the art of writing promos as it says about the Pope.

Meanwhile, *Newshour* leads with a promise to cover the violence in East Timor later in the show. The next piece seems to be about world hunger. It turns out to be an "enhanced underwriting" spot for Archer Daniels Midland, "supermarket to the world"—or, as I think of it, "money spout for politicians." The real lead is the spending bill in Congress, followed by President Clinton, for the first time today. Boy, have things changed in a year; at the height of Monicagate, you couldn't avoid him on television. Oddly, he's talking about nothing in particular, just how lucky he is to have his wife and daughter. Did he actually give a speech about this?

Since my standards of broadcast news are set by NPR, *Newshour* is clearly a lot closer to my ideal, and yet I can't imagine I'd watch it voluntarily. It's substantive, all right, but the truth is that it's kind of boring too. To be fair, my impressions of the show may have been skewed irrevocably by a certain Thanksgiving in the early Eighties. On that occasion, my father and my cousin Herbert argued at length about TV news, before agreeing that *Newshour* was the only show they both liked. They proceeded to watch it, and were subjected to a stultifying twenty-minute discussion about different methods of home insulation. But it was a matter of pride by then, and neither one could leave the couch or change channels. All they could do was fall asleep, which they both did.

I'm on the verge of following their lead when I glimpse Jerry Lewis on *Entertainment Tonight*. Sam and I are huge fans of Jerry Lewis, to the extent that we have a collection of framed posters from his movies. I race across the room to unmute the set, but get there just as Jerry's image is displaced by the prettier face of Ashley Judd, who is apparently being stalked. What happened to Jerry Lewis? "He's Ashley's stalker," cracks Doug. I refuse to believe that.

Once we're in the *ET* groove, Doug and I both have to admit it's a lot more fun than *Newshour*, and we stick to it. Here's a preview of Oliver Stone's new football movie with Al Pacino. "It's another *ET* first!" chirps Mary Hart. Does she chirp like that all day? Does she chirp to her children? Next up, Michelle Phillips threatens to sue Eddie Fisher for saying in his new memoir that they had an affair. She still looks great, if not as preternaturally beautiful as she did in the late Sixties. "Did I have a relationship with him? In his dreams," says Phillips. But Fisher sticks to his story: "I assure you I would never forget a beautiful woman like Michelle Phillips." Of course, since his memoir details his extensive drug use, he might have forgotten all kinds of things.

At the commercial, I check out *Jeopardy!* A contestant has just hit the Daily Double. "Quotations from Hell" is the category. "In *Paradise Lost*, Milton wrote 'better to do' this 'than serve in heaven.'" The answer is "rule in hell," but the contestant has no clue, which means he hasn't watched Ricardo Montalban quoting Milton and Melville in *Star Trek II: The Wrath of Khan* as many times as I have. Still, the runner-up on today's show will win a trip to Shanghai, which certainly beats the bedroom set I declined to take.

Back to *Entertainment Tonight*, where the "cover story" is the proliferation of unauthorized nude photographs of celebrities on the Internet. Now the beleaguered celebs are setting up their own sites to spin the Web their way. Apparently it costs money to log on to Cindy Crawford's website, and people actually sign up. Why on earth would anybody do that? Kathy Ireland's site has not only photos but—er, furniture designs. Ireland says she "listens to her fans, and tries to give them what they want." Short of biblical congress, of course.

Final Jeopardy is: "In April 1999, Paul Simon took center field for the dedication of a monument to this man." It's Joe DiMaggio, as in the line from Simon's song "Mrs. Robinson": "Where have you gone, Joe DiMaggio, a nation turns its lonely eyes to you . . ." All three contestants guess wrong, proffering John Lennon, Abner Doubleday, and Elvis—but as usual, one guy is so far ahead that Final Jeopardy is nearly irrelevant.

A cutesy bit on the *Newshour*, with four faces onscreen: Billy Graham, Johnny Cash, Janet Reno, and the Pope. What do they all have in common? Doug and I are stumped, until they cut to Muhammad Ali. "They all fought Muhammad Ali!" cries Doug. No, they all have Parkinson's, including Ali. I miss the follow-up because I'm entranced by the image of Janet Reno fighting Ali.

It's 7:30, and here's the recently revived *Hollywood Squares*. I smile, because Charles Sopkin watched the original show thirty-two years ago on his TV voyage. As in Sopkin's day, the show is tic-tac-toe with a bunch of celebrities who have something to promote—or who have nothing better to do. Tonight's celebrity guests are Whoopi Goldberg, Jason Alexander, Penn and Teller, Little Richard, Gilbert Gottfried, comedy writer Bruce Vilanch, Susan Sullivan and Mimi Kennedy from *Dharma and Greg*, and someone named Judy Gold. The bland host is Tom something.

Christian from Flushing won $31,535 yesterday, and is back for day two. The challenger is Dana from NYC, a restaurant manager who enjoys Rollerblading. Dana chooses Whoopi to start, and Tom asks the first question: "In Greek mythology, only a virgin can catch what?" Whoopi pauses for a beat—"Hell for getting pregnant?" As on the old show, a team of comedy writers comes up with these supposedly spontaneous answers. The correct answer is "a unicorn." Christian goes to Penn and Teller, and Tom makes the mistake of addressing Teller (the silent one) as Penn (the loud one). But they put up with it because Tom keeps plugging each square's upcoming appearances, whether on TV or on the road. It's like *The Price Is Right*, but this time the product is showbiz itself.

I am yanked away from my game-show inertia by the sight of conservative film critic Michael Medved on MSNBC. The topic is

"Is TV Too Sexy?" Medved points out that the new sitcom *Action* has gotten reams of free publicity because of the controversy about its content. He calls for the return of the Family Hour—which used to mandate unobjectionable programming from 8:00 to 9:00 P.M.— and to my amazement, I agree with him. Of course, to illustrate the point, MSNBC runs a clip from *Action*, in which Illeana Douglas has her hand down Keanu Reeves's pants. This clip is airing at 7:43 P.M.

Sam comes home. She sits down beside Doug, and the three of us stare at the sets until Sam notices that FNC has a shot of Bernhard Goetz—with a squirrel! What is the infamous subway shooter doing with a squirrel? We unmute, in time to hear the host saying "That's Bernhard Goetz and his long-in-the-tooth squirrel." Yeah, and?

Medved is back on, saying the most destructive aspect of TV is the so-called "Mean World" syndrome. Why was the story of penis-chopping Lorena Bobbitt worldwide news? Why is the killing of little JonBenet Ramsey still making headlines? Are these stories symptomatic of larger issues, or are they anomalies that are blown out of all proportion? Doug knows about this—in fact, he edited a book about it. Says Doug, "It just makes the whole world seem a lot more dangerous than it really is, so people become meaner and more violent than they would be, purely in presumed self-defense." Much as I hate to agree twice with Michael Medved in one evening, I have to say this makes a lot of sense to me, in a way that the simplistic equation of "watch violence, commit violence" never has. Crime statistics are down all over the country, but people seem more afraid than they used to be. When I was ten years old, I would take the bus into D.C. and spend the day wandering around the Smithsonian without adult supervision; not only did my parents not worry about me, but they were proud of my independence. No parents I know would allow their kids that kind of freedom now.

Doug flees back to his manuscripts and his wife at 8:00 P.M., just as the networks move into prime time. The choice is between sitcoms (*Just Shoot Me* on NBC, *Spin City* on ABC, the animated

Dilbert on UPN) and dramas (part two of the season opener of the military courtroom drama *JAG* on CBS, and a repeat of last season's finale of *Buffy the Vampire Slayer* on the WB). I've heard great things about *Buffy*, but I've also heard there's a whole complicated mythos to the show, and this doesn't seem like the time to jump in.

In the end, I decide I don't need to choose between sitcoms and dramas, because there's a middle course on Fox: It's the premiere of *Ally*, the ever-resourceful David E. Kelley's half-hour sitcom version of his hour-long drama-comedy *Ally McBeal*. Kelley has discovered that half-hour shows are much more popular in syndication than hours, so he spent the summer whittling a bunch of old *Ally McBeal*s into this new format—in between writing new episodes of that and *The Practice*, promoting his films *Lake Placid* and *Mystery, Alaska*, and being Michelle Pfeiffer's husband. Any one of these pursuits would be enough to exhaust most ordinary mortals; does the man ever sleep?

Ally starts with a gambit that is simultaneously clever and annoying, much like the hour-long show: They fast-forward through what was originally a real-time establishing pan of Boston. Then they use the fast-forward device again as Ally walks through the office—which isn't clever-annoying, just annoying. The theory seems to be that if you drop all the courtroom stuff, what's left is a workplace sitcom about a law firm. Has there been a law-firm sitcom since *The Associates*? (Which starred the young Martin Short, just to connect the dots—like the ever-popular game Six Degrees of Kevin Bacon, all roads in television lead to either *SCTV* or *Saturday Night Live*.)

The premiere is based on one of the two episodes of *Ally McBeal* I've actually seen. I can't remember the original episode's A plot—whatever Ally was doing in the courtoom—but this was certainly the B plot, in which Peter MacNicol's character, John (The Biscuit) Cage, asks Ally on a date, and is fantastically nervous about it. I can tell within minutes that Kelley's experiment is doomed.

Most well-constructed sitcoms have both an A plot *and* a B plot—and some very ambitious sitcoms, like *Seinfeld*, may have a C plot and even a D plot (as in the episodes where Jerry, George, Elaine, and Kramer are all pursuing separate interests that end up impacting on each other). By stripping a multistranded episode down to one strand, you end up with something that isn't strong enough to carry its own weight. (Imagine stripping an episode of *Seinfeld* down to an eight-minute show called *Kramer*, and you have the idea.) Nobody would have constructed a sitcom like this in the first place; scenes are jammed up against each other, and there's no real context to set things off. Another problem is that the original A plot was all about Ally, but the B plot is all about Cage. This sitcom might as well be called *Biscuit*.

Disappointed once again by Mr. Kelley, I glimpse Michael J. Fox striding down a City Hall hallway on *Spin City*, and it's the logical next choice after all those news pieces today. Fox plays the deputy mayor of New York, and his character's name is also Mike—a prerogative I thought was reserved for Tony Danza, who always plays guys named Tony. Unfortunately, the show is a bust; I watch for ten minutes straight without so much as cracking a smile, despite Michael J. Fox's considerable deftness. He's the Bob Barker of situation comedy, but even Bob Barker gets better material to work with.

So I'm not expecting much from Jennifer Grey's sitcom *It's Like, You Know*, which is about a group of friends in Los Angeles. But to my delight, it's clear from the first moment that this show has a smart, satirical point of view. We begin with a British-accented narrator telling us of the first time in L.A. history that a woman broke up with a handsome, successful, straight man—our hero, Robbie. The episode is a mockumentary about Robbie's brief relationship with this inexplicable woman, Helen. We see flashbacks of their courtship in color, while the cast members (and some guest stars) talk to the interviewer in black-and-white. Gags fly quicker than I can write them down, and most of them are actually funny. Says Evan Handler as Shrug, a millionaire with alopecia, "I'm crestfallen. I'm utterly crestfallen. My crest has fallen and it can't get up." One interviewee is a nun, speaking French. Another interview descends into chaos when the interviewee accuses the sound guy of touching her breast when he adjusted the microphone; she may sue. Robbie and Helen break up because they get into an argument about the roaming plans on their cellular phones. Says the narrator, "The moment was excruciatingly emotional. Especially for me, because I'm British." And most appropriately for my day, when Helen tells Robbie she has PMS, he replies that he's "thinking of starting a new cable network for women called PMSNBC."

I'd watch this show again. It's smarter than anything I've seen in the last few days, by leagues, and it's blissfully free of laugh track. I gather the ratings are dismal—but if I were ABC, I'd try changing the title before giving up on the show.

Before the 9:00 P.M. shows start, I check out the news channels, but there's nothing earthshaking happening. Former White House spinmeister Lanny Davis spins his own book on FNC. Bill Bradley on CNN. Eels on MSNBC. Eels? On CBS, they're rolling out the new second night of *60 Minutes*, which is imaginatively named *60 Minutes II*. (Oh, the possibilities: *Bride of 60 Minutes? 60 Minutes: The Wrath of Rather?*) On ABC, a promo for *20/20* promises singer Carnie Wilson's first interview since having stomach surgery live on the Web. We've come a long way since LBJ grossed out America by displaying his gallbladder-removal scar.

Fox is showing one of the reality-based specials that is the channel's stock-in-trade: *TV Guide's Secrets Behind the Sitcom Scandals*. This is clearly what I'd be watching if left to my own devices, with apologies to the Pope on Channel 13. But I'm determined to broaden my horizons, so I plump for the sitcom *Will & Grace*. It was either that or *Dharma & Greg* on ABC, and I should give equal sitcom time to NBC. Besides, I'm afraid my views of *Dharma & Greg* have been colored by a promo that was repeated endlessly on the *Jeopardy!* tournament of champions a few weeks ago, in which Dharma promised her mother-in-law that she'd wear a bra and bathe. Every time I look at actress Jenna Elfman now, I can't help imagining her bra-less and unwashed; I don't mind the former, but the latter is something of a turnoff.

Will & Grace is another tightass guy/spontaneous woman show—much like its competitor *Dharma & Greg*—except this time the guy is gay, so they're roommates instead of newlyweds. The premise of this episode is that Will and Grace are both campaigning to run their building's tenants committee. The problem is characterization, or lack of same. In one scene the battling roommates have to speak to the rest of the committee. Grace's overly detailed speech bores everyone, and the show commits what rhetoricians call the Fallacy of Imitative Form—the speech bores us too. Then incumbent Will's speech is two sentences long: "Change is bad. Vote for me!" The writers seem to think that being gay is all the personality Will needs. Like the cast on *Spin City*, both of these performers are attractive and spirited, and seem capable of much more than they're being given to do. I think of my friends who toil for big bucks in the sitcom vineyards writing this stuff, and of the poem "Prayer to His Bosses" by the great cynical screenwriter Ben Hecht, of which this is the least obscene stanza:

> *Oh let me grow one leaf of grass*
> *One breath of truth, one cry of man's*
> *Travail and quest, one peal of brass*
> *To drive Art from its crapping cans—*
> *One tale that doesn't kiss the ass*
> *Of ninety million movie fans.*

I bet there are a lot of well-paid sitcom writers thinking similar thoughts every day, in between breakfast at Hugo's and dinner at The Ivy.

The Fox special is still probing the sordid depths of *The Partridge Family*, so I unmute it. They're interviewing all the original cast members, who have aged remarkably well. David Cassidy still has his adorable squint. Danny Bonaduce says he always thought the show was canceled, and has only just learned that it ended because David quit. Shirley Jones says, "I began to see a burnout happening with David, and it concerned me a lot." "I call those my dark years," says Cassidy, "because my father died and my manager died." But he won't go on, because "self-pity is so unattractive."

Next up, the truth behind *Three's Company*. This is like eating a whole box of chocolates at once. We get in-depth coverage of the fights between Suzanne Somers and Joyce DeWitt, then the battles to renegotiate Somers's contract. Does anybody really care about this stuff? If *I* don't care—a man who reads *Entertainment Weekly* cover-to-cover and curls up at night with obscure showbiz biographies—it's a safe bet nobody does.

On NBC now is *The Mike O'Malley Show*, which looks like an attempt to clone *The Drew Carey Show* with a thinner lead. It's more blue-collar guys hanging around the kitchen table. Mike O'Malley, who I presume is another stand-up comic turned sitcom star, talks about taking a class at Yale. Is this show set in New Haven? I pay closer attention. Next scene, Mike is in the classroom, where Spalding Gray plays the professor. The prof asks Mike to define Heisenberg's Law of Uncertainty. (In my college days they called it the Heisenberg Uncertainty Principle, but no matter.) Mike doesn't know anything about Heisenberg, and Gray gives him a hard time as a "dabbler." This isn't like any class I ever took at Yale, but I think I'd still hate *The Mike O'Malley Show* even if it were set at Harvard. Mike and his slow-witted friends couldn't be more different from the unapologetically intelligent characters on *It's Like, You Know*. I have a sinking feeling we're supposed to identify with Mike *because* he's stupid.

Now *Sitcom Scandals* is on to *The Brady Bunch*. Barry Williams, a.k.a. Greg Brady, rehashes his entertaining book *Growing Up Brady*, talking about his date with Florence Henderson—who was playing his mother at the time. He insists the real Florence is a red-hot mama, and in home-movie footage from the time, we see he has a point. Once again, everybody is talking: Chris Knight, Eve Plumb, even producer Sherwood Schwartz, who recounts his struggles with Robert Reed. Schwartz wanted Gene Hackman for the part of genial architect Mike Brady, which leads me to imagine Robert Reed playing hard-bitten Popeye Doyle in *The French Connection*. "He hated everything" about the show, says Schwartz of Reed, "and since in his mind I represented everything, he hated me the most." If my job were to deliver Sherwood Schwartz's lines, I'd hate everything too. Coming up: Robert Reed's "scandalous private life," and the truth about Susan Olsen's post-Brady career: "I actually do have a porn credit," says the former Cindy Brady coyly as we go to commercial. I'm offended by the innuendo about Reed—he was gay, but that's not necessarily scandalous—and suspect the second bit is just a tease for the audience, taking a quote out of context. Let's see.

During the break, I check out *I Love Lucy* on Nick at Nite, in which Desi Arnaz does a number about Acapulco, with straw hat and tux. It's a little moment of pleasure.

Back on the show, Schwartz says Reed was "really reckless in terms of one-night stands and things." Meow! But Barry Williams chokes back tears as he talks about Reed, who still means a lot to him: "He was a man of great ability and talent." Even Schwartz admits that Reed, because he was such a stickler, gave the show a grounding in reality that it wouldn't have had with an actor who had a sense of humor. Talk about damning with faint praise. As for Susan Olsen, it was indeed a tease. A lookalike made a movie called *Crocodile Blondee*, and Susan did spaceship sound-effect noises for a movie called *Love Probe to a Warm Planet*.

Son of a gun—on Channel 5, they still say "It's ten P.M. Do you know where your children are?" With no children to speak of, I check on Cosmo, who is snoring in his doggie bed, as usual.

I pass up the new CBS drama *Judging Amy* with actress Amy Brenneman—I guess she couldn't avoid the Tony Danza syndrome either—the newsmagazine *Dateline* on NBC, *The Jeffersons* on Nick, and lots of news. Oh yeah, and the Pope. The choice is easy, since the new series *Once and Again* is quite possibly the only show I would have watched all week if I weren't doing this. Sam and I watched the premiere last week, and were instantly hooked by the intelligent writing and by charismatic leads Sela Ward and Billy Campbell. The premise of the show is that two divorced parents—bookseller Lily and architect Rick—fall in love, and must deal with the endless complications of their divided families. It's *The Brady Bunch* for the Nineties, with naturalism and complexity instead of one-liners and easy moral lessons.

They're continuing to use a device from the pilot, in which we frequently cut away from the action to black-and-white interviews with the characters. But unlike the similar device on *It's Like, You Know*, these interviews are used to give us a window into the characters' minds, in a way that recalls the Eugene O'Neill play *Strange Interlude*. It's easy to see that the device will be parodied on *Saturday Night Live* within weeks, and I wish the interview scenes didn't look quite so much like the old AT&T ads, with the actors' faces framed against a black background. But when it works, it gives the show a nuanced texture that's rare on television. As Emeril would put it, it kicks it up a notch. I think it also contributes to the remarkable sexual chemistry between Ward and Campbell. You really believe they're nuts about each other—not just because they're attractive and they're good actors, but because we're allowed to see their inner lives.

In this episode, Rick has to talk about sex with his son Eli. In a clever adaptation of an old *L.A. Law* trick—the lawyers on that show usually defended clients who were in the wrong—Rick keeps making mistakes as a parent. Instead of the conventional shrew, his ex-wife seems to be more on top of things than he is. And, amusingly, so is Eli: "Dad, we've been indoctrinated on sexual correctness since the eighth grade." *It's Like, You Know* took place in a stylized version of the real world, but this feels pretty close to the *real* real world, as *Thirtysomething* did. Even the teenagers on the show act like real teenagers, which is refreshing after what I've seen so far this week. (It occurs to me that both of the shows I really liked tonight are lily-white through and through. In each case, it's because they're set in a specific milieu, and not just generic TV land—but it's symptomatic of the real problem the NAACP has identified.)

Commercial. I tell Sam about my day. But then she shushes me when we see a stunning ad for the Lincoln LS, in which the camera seems to pull out from a toy train set, through a window, to a mountain road, to inside a car on the road, to back out again. How is this possible? Invisible cuts? Motion control? Morphing? We're stumped, and impressed. Meanwhile, a woman in a bikini is taking a shower on Channel 9 News. Why? The anchor helpfully explains that, according to a survey commissioned by a soap company, most men would like to shower with Pamela Anderson or Cindy Crawford, while women prefer George Clooney or Harrison Ford. This is a no-lose item; the soap company gets publicity, and the news programs get to show a woman taking a shower.

Back to *Once and Again.* I stand corrected: Lily has an African-American friend. I'm not sure a frankly token sidekick makes a real difference, but I'm glad to see that this otherwise exemplary show isn't monochrome.

After much awkwardness, Rick and Lily make love for the first time. Rick's bare butt provokes a "Yowsah!" from Sam, who would happily shower with Billy Campbell. This scene is a pleasure to watch, because it's so real. Of course, Ward and Campbell are realer than real—they're both gorgeous, and they have great dialogue—but I *believe* them. And the master stroke is the interview material. As Lily goes to bed with Rick, it's intercut with her memories of early sexual experiences with her husband, and of being pregnant. Rick remembers his ex-wife's pregnancy. Lily remembers her first clue that her ex-husband was cheating on her. ("It was my fault, you understand. Because if you know something and you don't deal with it, it becomes your responsibility.") These are three-dimensional people, and I feel as if I could watch an hour of this one scene. For a moment it's so intense that the other screens in the living room seem to express Rick's and Lily's more abstract thoughts. Is the Pope crying along with her? Is she a Madonna with a breast of elephant dung? Does he feel like a skateboarder as he explores her body? Are they crossing the line of scrimmage?

When the show finally ends, I say to Sam how brave and smart it was to have them talking about their previous marriages during a sex scene. Sam rolls her eyes at me. "I'll be talking about *my* previous marriage pretty soon," she mutters.

Flipping around at 11:00 P.M., I notice a rerun of *All in the Family* on Nick at Nite. The characters are watching TV, and to further research my TV-is-about-TV thesis, I check it out. Mike says he wants to watch Jack Lemmon and a group of scientists discussing nuclear energy on Channel 13; Archie says he wants to watch football, "and guess what's going to happen?" I had only planned to watch a few minutes of the show, but once I've started, I can't stop. I remember how by the end of the Seventies, the softer and more nuanced style of the MTM shows (*The Mary Tyler Moore Show, The Bob Newhart Show*) had made the abrasive Norman Lear style seem shrill. But now it just seems sharp, and not only because Rob Reiner has a full head of hair. Compared to the pap that was on earlier tonight, it might as well be Molière.

Besides, I find that Archie Bunker is reminding me of someone; in fact, he's like a composite of a number of powerful men I've met in Hollywood. I recognize the way he belittles and humiliates everyone around him, and the way he doesn't listen to anyone else, his sense of his own rightness unshakable even when he's dead wrong. It's not intrinsically funny stuff, but the writing is strong, and the brilliant Carroll O'Connor *makes* it funny because his details are so precise.

At this point Sam orders me to shut down for the night. I'm of two minds about this. Part of me is revitalized by the excellence of *Once and Again* and *All in the Family*, and that part of me is ready to dive into the waters of late-night TV, where Leno and Letterman and Conan and Craig await. But another part of me is exhausted to a degree I can't remember feeling in my life, and that part of me clicks off the sets before the first part knows what's going on. ⊟

I wake up in the middle of the night, around 4:15, to find my fingers twitching. To my horror, I realize that I've been taking notes in my dreams. I finally get back to sleep when Cosmo moves from the foot of the bed to my pillow, and starts snoring in my ear. This would keep many people awake, but it's always a sure-fire soporific for me.

Then I wake up for real at 6:45, five minutes before the alarm would have gone off. I throw on clothes and get the car and drive downtown for an unavoidable doctor's appointment. I've scheduled it early so as not to interrupt my TV watching any more than necessary. Driving through Central

WEDNESDAY

Act Like the Porn Star That You Are

Park, I listen with almost physical pleasure to National Public Radio's *Morning Edition*. NPR has its own version of enhanced underwriting, but the lack of actual commercials still leaves a lot more room for stories to find their proper length. As a result, when *Morning Edition* covers the same topics I've been watching on TV, it does so with more depth—as well as with a wry wit that even PBS's *Newshour* sorely lacks. NPR is also covering stories the rest of the pack hasn't attacked, which is even more pleasurable.

Of course, there's a more important difference between television and radio, which is that I'm driving a car while I listen, and doing both with a fair degree of concentration. If on some level I prefer the medium of radio, that's precisely why; it's more efficient for multiprocessors like me. To be fair to TV, Sam knits while she watches, and it works just fine for her. But you can't drive a car and watch television; I shudder at recent news reports that some 2000-model sport utility vehicles are equipped with TVs and even satellite dishes.

After seeing the doctor, I drive straight home, sort of. I have a craving for an Egg McMuffin—perhaps it's the subliminal result of all those commercials—so I go to the McDonald's drive-through on 125th Street. Once I've got the food, I eat it in the parking lot while listening to oldies radio. Could I be malingering? Then when I get home, it's time to walk Cosmo, and for some unimaginable reason I take him for a longer walk than usual. As we approach 108th Street, we see a cluster of trucks and lights up ahead. It turns out they're shooting an episode of *Law & Order*, and Cosmo and I stop for a moment to watch the bustle. There's no escape from TV, even two blocks from home. Finally, when I can delay no longer, I walk Cosmo back to the apartment, give him a dog biscuit, and settle down to the overstim gallery around 10:00 A.M.

I've missed a lot—but in a twenty-four-hour television universe, you can say that about any day. You're always missing something before you turn it on, and something else after you turn it off. In fact, this is the exact sensation I always enjoy when I go to Las

Vegas; any time, day or night, someone is standing at a table ready to play blackjack with me. And now, since the advent of the VCR, there's no need to miss anything, ever. TV is already beginning to morph into the shape it will take once the broadband revolution is complete, when TV and the Internet and the video store will all be one big menu of channels, goods, and services waiting for your click. It'll take a while to get to that place, but we've already come a long way from the immutable and evanescent broadcast of six channels that Charles Sopkin received in 1967.

My theme today is to tune six of the sets to Sopkin's original terrestrial stations—ABC, CBS, NBC, and the local stations that now carry Fox, UPN, and the WB—while setting the other six on channels I've almost never watched before. Those are Court TV, C-SPAN, home-shopping networks HSN and QVC, and two premium services—The Disney Channel and The Playboy Channel. I can't deny that my primary interest is in the last two, and that I'm hoping the juxtaposition of these two extremes of content will reveal . . . something.

Maury's theme today is "I Was a Nerd . . . Now I'm Hot, Hot, Hot!" There are fat people on *Divorce Court*, and thin people on *Judge Mathis*. There's a marquise sapphire-and-diamond 14-karat gold ring for $294.75 on QVC. *The Little Mermaid*—the series, based on the movie—is on Disney. And then there's C-SPAN, which spends most of its time relaying events in Congress (whether taped or live, I don't know). Right now, Rep. David Dreier (R.-Cal.) is protesting religious persecution in China. I have no argument with that, if religion is what it takes to get Republicans concerned about human rights. Next is an amendment to an agriculture bill— the new fiscal year starts Friday, and Clinton has signed a one-month extension to allow Congress to finish the appropriations package. I know that because I listened to NPR.

And on Playboy, surprising as this may be, a naked woman is lying in bed. Dissolve to a hunky farmboy walking through a field. Back to the woman. Back to the farmboy, and now the woman is dressed like Kelly McGillis in *Witness* and lounging against an antique car. Is she Amish, or does she just like the fashions? Clearly this is meant to be her fantasy, although once the lovers get together, he just swings her around until her dress opens. It's all pretty surreal when accompanied by the narration of Rep. Pete Sessions (R.-Tex.) talking about the Agriculture Risk Protection Act. "This bill provides greater protection at a lower cost for our nation's farmers," says Sessions, and I'm sure the farm couple on Playboy will appreciate that. They're going to need protection pretty soon.

I turn to Court TV. A very helpful card tells us, "Interracial Engagement Ends in Killing. Trial of man accused of fatally shooting another man." On the stand is a burly guy with a short haircut, in tie and white shirt. He could be a cop. "We'll be back with more, don't go away," says a host. Improbably, the host looks like a gigolo in an early-Thirties Jean Harlow movie, with thin mustache, red tie, and what looks like brilliantined hair.

Back on Playboy, two Scandinavian blondes frolic. No, it's not what you're thinking—they're fully dressed, and are running around what might be the streets of Stockholm. We keep cutting back and forth to a middle-aged couple sitting in a living room, talking to the camera—what gives? Are they related to the gals? Are they fantasizing about being Scandinavian blondes? Is this one of those *Sexual Freedom in Denmark*–type documentaries, where the couple are sexologists telling us it's healthy to run around Stockholm in a raincoat and boots? I could turn up the sound and find out, but it's more fun to speculate.

Raymond Brown is back—that's the faux-gigolo on Court TV—with two legal experts. They're impossibly dull, and I don't think it's just because I'm distracted by the blondes on Playboy, although I can't discount the possibility. The girls are unclothed now, and posing prettily—one brushes her hair languorously, then the other's hair. Morning on the Playboy Channel seems to be more about exhibition than exertion, shall we say. There's no suggestion that these are two people living their lives; these women are just a cool spectacle for undemanding viewers. Maybe that's why I'd rather read *Celebrity Sleuth* than *Playboy* the magazine. The kick of voyeurism is spying on someone, and seeing something that would be going on even if you weren't watching. It's the defeat of the Heisenberg Uncertainty Principle (the act of observation affects what is observed) that stumped Mike O'Malley last night.

Now the blondes are taking a shower together. I can only imagine the director giving the same instructions that *Premiere* magazine's Libby Gelman-Waxner suggests Stanley Kubrick gave his actors after every take on *Eyes Wide Shut*: "No, slower. Really, really, really slow." Then the credits run, and I see I'm wrong about Stockholm; the title of the piece was "Dutch Twins." I can understand why I didn't know they were Dutch, but how could I not have noticed they were twins? Maybe it's because they look just like however many other women on the same channel, or on the soaps, or on any nighttime show produced by Aaron Spelling.

On Disney, it's *The New Adventures of Winnie the Pooh*—and boy, are they new. It starts with Pooh, Tigger, and Piglet breaking out of prison, where they board a train engineered by Christopher Robin. (*The Poohgitive?*) Just as the train jumps the tracks and crashes down the side of a canyon, everybody snaps out of the fantasy when Christopher Robin's babysitter sends him back to bed. Disney's Winnie cartoons from the Sixties and Seventies were respectful of the original stories' English setting, but this Christopher Robin has an American accent, and seems to live in the same suburb as Arthur the anteater. Does Christopher Robin's suburban house still sit on the edge of the Hundred-Acre Wood, or can we anticipate visits to the Hundred-Acre Mall? And where are Rabbit, Owl, Kanga, Roo, and Eeyore? When did a star system emerge in Pooh country? The whole enterprise depresses me. Without the specifics that permeate the A. A. Milne stories, Christopher Robin has lost his personality and become Everychild, and Pooh is just a hungry teddy bear.

Meanwhile, *Ricki Lake* seeks guests for an upcoming show: "I Want a Threesome with My New Mate and My Ex!" This is the fourth threesome on *Ricki* this week; I detect a theme here. Is the show's producer a wee bit obsessed? Or is it that the ratings spike when the theme is threesomes? The charitable explanation is that this is just the latest manifestation of the eternal triangle, but I suspect no charitable explanations are needed.

In a similar vein, Playboy features a show called *Night Calls*, in which two semiclad, bleached, and enhanced ladies take phone calls from viewers while demurely stroking each other. (The third woman who sometimes joins them on the couch is a "fax girl." As my grandmother would say, "This is a profession?") Just as the latest caller hangs up, a little person dressed as a leprechaun appears inexplicably in the studio, waggling a large foam penis. "Erin Go Bragh!" he cries, and the ladies all laugh. One of the women sticks out her behind, and the leprechaun whacks it with the penis. There's something pagan about this—or is it a reference to the famously well-endowed Toulouse-Lautrec?—but the surrealism is more than I can take right now. According to the credits, every woman on the show has her own website.

I hurry back to Disney, where Christopher Robin has finally gone to bed with Pooh, Tigger, and Piglet. (Next on *Ricki Lake*: "I Want a Foursome with a Bear, a Pig, and a Hyperactive Tiger!") Mom peeps in and asks if this well-behaved child can really be Christopher Robin. Barf. I might have expected to see a rape on the Playboy Channel, but I never expected the Disney Channel to feature the rape of A. A. Milne.

I wonder if *Jerry Springer* will look good by comparison, but Jerry lives down to expectations, as usual. Today's theme is the relatively tame "Back-stabbing Best Friends!" There's a huge woman on stage talking cheerfully about how she slept with her roommate's boyfriend: "You know how you keep telling me to stop sleeping around and get a real boyfriend? Well, now I got one!" Then they bring out the guy, and it's a free-for-all.

I flee to *The Price Is Right*, where Bob Barker looks after the pet population and everyone comes away a winner, even though some win more than others. Once again, Sam hears the show's peppy music—unchanged for at least twenty years—and comes running. On today's Showcase Showdown, however, nobody wins—both bids are too high. "That almost never happens," says a disappointed Sam, whose attention is quickly drawn elsewhere. "These women on the Playboy Channel are not attractive," she declares, pointing to several particularly artificial-looking specimens. "Is it just me? They're so hard-looking. Who are these women who want fake breasts? They're like rocks on her chest—it's so sad. What a way to make a living."

Fortunately, we are rescued by the Dream Maker. Richard Simmons emerges from a huge fog of dry ice, before a backdrop of fluffy clouds and blue sky. "Hello, dreamers!" he shouts. "I love him!" says Sam. "He's so terrible, you have to love him." Then she's distracted again: "This is hilarious. On the Playboy Channel, the Burger King woman just dove into the window of the car to kiss the woman at the drive-through."

Richard's guest today is B.J. McCombs, a kid who was horribly burned in a house fire. B.J. is onstage in a wheelchair, his face sadly disfigured, with his whole family alongside him. His mother wants to thank a Mr. and Mrs. Wolf for their support—they're strangers who have been sending money since the fire. And heeere they are, in a tearful meeting. Richard gives the Wolfs a solid gold Aladdin's-lamp necklace and bracelet, with each presentation accompanied by a glissando on the chimes. Little B.J. gets an RX Rocker wheelchair, with black leatherette padding. Then Richard reads a poem by B.J.'s cousin, picturing B.J. as a lone warrior on the battlefield, which stuns me to the point that I can't even transcribe it. This is a level of blatant sentimentality no TV show has attained since the halcyon era of *Queen for a Day*, and it soon drives Sam out of the room.

On to the wholesome family entertainment of Donny and Marie, who are bantering with each other in the style of Regis and

Kathie Lee. Marie says her kids made her watch MTV's *Celebrity Deathmatch*, which pits animated versions of celebrities against each other. In this episode, Julia and Eric Roberts were fighting against—Donny and Marie. They show a clip, but I'm still trying to get my head around these clean-living Mormons watching a show in which clay puppets decapitate each other.

As Donny and Marie go to a commercial, I turn up QVC. There are Crock-Pots on screen—so why are the hosts talking about crop insurance? Do they grow their own crops to make soup with? Then I realize I've unmuted C-SPAN by mistake. These damn remotes!

The person who's really talking about crop insurance is Rep. Sheila Jackson Lee (D.-Tex.), the one black face on any of the twelve screens. Then another one pops up—cookie king Wally "Famous" Amos, explaining the difference between "concrete" and "abstract" on a show called *G.E.D.* These two examples really point out the paucity of minorities in similar contexts in prime time. If a member of Congress figures in a sitcom or drama show, it isn't usually in the form of a black woman; nor is a businessman/entrepreneur likely to be played by a black man (unless it's Amos playing himself, as he did on a memorable episode of *Taxi*). It's a useful reminder that the America I glimpse through my TV window is often quite different from the unmediated reality.

It's time for *All My Children*, on which I am rapidly getting hooked. But today I'm really in for it; I recognize absolutely none of the characters on the "previously." No Alex and Edmund, no Marian and Stuart, not even Erica Kane. And this turns out to be fair warning for the rest of the hour. I'm starting to understand the structure of these shows, which is to set up five long scenes at the beginning, then to rotate from one to the next until the hour is over. But with big ensemble casts and only five scenes a day, the writers need to feature different characters on different days just to keep all the story lines afloat. Nothing is duller than a recap of soap-opera plot lines, so I'll spare you the details—except to note that most of the characters on *All My Children* are still deeply upset about Dmitri and his horse.

On Channel 11, I notice a courtoom show hosted by Judge Mills Lane, the squeaky-voiced boxing referee who called the fight in which Mike Tyson bit Evander Holyfield's ear. The case today is an unpaid loan, which seems to be to courtroom shows as sexual triangles are to daytime talk shows. Judge Mills finds quickly for the plaintiff, quipping, "I'm a lot of things, but stupid is not one of them." Then we see a promo for the season premiere of *Dawson's Creek* tonight, in which a young woman takes off her shirt, but stops short of Playboy territory. Meanwhile, on Playboy itself, a couple ruts endlessly on a bed, changing positions every few minutes. Someone once compared this kind of pornography to watching people chewing, and that's not far off.

On HSN, a Sterling Silver Fancy Diamond-Cut Bracelet is $36.75. On QVC, a Beautiful Impressions 36-Piece Paint Pad Kit is $43.57. What's a Paint Pad Kit? "Well, you can use it to spruce up a birdhouse, kitchen wallpaper, or even a toilet, with an attractive pattern of brightly colored leaves," says the perky host. This is just what my toilet needs, not to mention my birdhouse.

There's an ad that seems to run every twenty minutes on various channels, for the new album by Hispanic singer Marc Anthony. Ricky Martin's breakthrough album is starting to fall off the charts, and the record company is clearly trying to push Marc Anthony into the Ricky Martin slot. This reminds me of my friend Jaime Wolf's Theory of Demographic Place-holders.* Jaime's theory is that some actors attain popularity not necessarily because of their talent, but because they stand in for a segment of the audience. For instance, Ernest Borgnine was a place-holder for blue-collar white

---

*Confusingly, this is a different Jaime Wolf from the one who visited yesterday. Yesterday's Jaime was a writer, while this Jaime is a lawyer. Yesterday's Jaime went to Harvard; this Jaime went to Yale with me, and was my roommate in Hoboken after we graduated. I once introduced the two Jaimes to see if the world would explode, but it didn't—instead, they became friends and proceeded to confuse everybody else.

men in the Fifties and Sixties; when he left television, Tony Danza filled his slot. Now that Danza has returned to the stage, Drew Carey is flying the blue-collar white-guy flag. If Jaime's theory is correct, the departure of Angela Lansbury and *Murder, She Wrote* has left a slot for someone to fill; if I were Ann-Margret's manager, I'd whip up a TV series for her, pronto.

Sam departs for lunch, to preserve her own sanity—the constant TV sound leaking in from the next room is driving her nuts. After she leaves, I prepare today's TV dinner. It's meant to be fried chicken with mashed potatoes, and on some other planet, maybe it is.

It's 2:00 P.M., and the choice between *Passions* and *One Life to Live* is no choice. *One Life to Live* is a soap opera, but *Passions* is a phenomenon. First, we meet a wealthy couple in an ostentatiously decorated house. They're arguing about whether or not to attend the police benefit—she's the co-chair—and he mentions that "Grace Bennett and her husband Sam, our chief of police," will be there. I love the expositional way people talk on *Passions*, and I determine to start adopting this mode around the house. I'll say, "Wife of mine, will you please take our three-year-old pug Cosmo for a walk on 110th Street?" And Sam will reply, "Of course, just as soon as I get off the phone with my mother, Sallie, the Philadelphia landscape designer." No one who enters our apartment will ever be confused again.

It goes on from there. *Passions* seems to be built on a simple dramatic device. Every character has exactly one goal, which he or she pursues with singleminded determination in scene after scene. That pursuit is usually good old-fashioned unrequited love—for instance, the scheming Kay loves the ingenuous Miguel, who loves the comatose Charity—but it also includes things like witchy Tabitha's determination to kill Charity once and for all. The characters are all wind-up cars who just keep going in the same direction until their motors run down—so of course they crash into each other all the time, which creates conflict. While nobody is remotely complex, they're all as active as hell. It isn't subtle, but it is effective, basic dramaturgy. These actors *never* have to ask their director for a motivation.

At 3:00 P.M., *General Hospital* starts with a tough chick in a Mexican prison, trying to cry convincingly for the guards. Her cellmate laughs off her attempts: "Who you gonna call? 1-800-JAILBREAK?" Frankly, I've lost the thread of this show entirely. I consider myself lucky to be following the ins and outs of two soaps, and now officially declare my window for new soaps closed.

Sam returns from lunch at about this point. She takes one look at the circus in her living room and retires to the bedroom to work.

On Disney, it's *Timon and Pumbaa*, a spinoff from *The Lion King*; on Channel 11, it's *Tiny Toon Adventures*, which features pint-sized versions of the Looney Tunes characters. This is more brand extension, TV-style. If Orson Welles were doing those Paul Masson commercials now, he'd have to change the slogan to "We will sell no wine until we've squeezed every last drop out of every grape."

On *Dr. Joy Browne*, another really fat couple. (And I say this as someone who is no sylph.) The topic: "Will This Marriage Survive?" The guy is clearly such a misogynist that only a few minutes should lead Dr. Joy or anyone else to conclude in the negative—but then how would we fill up the hour?

HSN is pushing Christie's "Personal Property of Marilyn Monroe" catalog, with over 1,500 objects for sale, for $84.95. That's how much it costs for the *catalog*, before you even buy anything. The hosts/saleswomen/spokesmodels dwell on the dress Marilyn wore to sing "Happy Birthday" for JFK: "It appeared at first that she was covered in a spiderweb of glittering beads, and nothing else." By contrast, QVC's Carved Lapis Leverback Earrings, 14K, seem underwhelming even at $75. "To get carved lapis is next to impossible," says the host. "I've never seen carved lapis, except here on QVC." Something tells me there's a reason for that.

Meanwhile, another couple is going at it on Playboy, carefully framed so we see a maximum of her and a minimum of him. It's funny, because when we lived in London, every once in a while Sam would shriek happily, "Penises on television!" The rule there is that you can't show male frontal nudity before 9:00 P.M., and the organ in question must be at an angle less than the Mull of Kintyre, which is a peninsula off the coast of Scotland. (I am not making this up.) But on the Playboy Channel, we never, ever, ever see a penis, regardless of angle or time of day.

I must admit that a day of watching people having sex, even out of the corner of my eye, is starting to wear on me. On one hand, there's a certain automatic reaction that a heterosexual male can't help having to this stuff. On the other hand, the more I see, the less effect it has on me, and the stranger it feels to be watching it on a TV set in between *Wimzie's House* and Court TV. It might not feel as strange to a European, but I'm not European. I realize that for me, what makes something sexy is context—and without context, even The Playboy Channel's vast sexual smorgasbord seems meaningless and dull.

On Court TV, the afternoon host—who looks much more like a traditional silver-haired anchorman than this morning's louche specimen—talks with Charles Barron, who is identified alternately as "Former Black Panther" and "Community Activist." Barron talks skeptically about "people who say they don't see race, they just see a heart." The host says, "Some people who say that may actually mean it." Barron responds, "That may be, but I find it hard to believe that most people don't see a black face and a white face." He's smiling, and seems without rancor—just a bit weary.

On *The People's Court*, the defendant has a brilliantly hued red-and-green parrot on her shoulder. She sold another bird to the plaintiff, Mr. Farricelli, who wants his money back because it died. It occurs to me that I'm paying much more attention to the syndicated courtroom shows than I am to the real trials on Court TV, but that's because the courtroom shows are paced at the rhythm of multichannel television. This experiment may have ruined me for the kind of extended concentration needed to follow one long trial through its ins and outs—and there's no suggestion yet that the proceedings on Court TV are anywhere near their conclusion.

Multiple synergy: a commercial on The Disney Channel for *Disney's One Saturday Morning* on ABC, with a mention of www.disney1.com as well. Disney is way ahead of the other studios in trying to make all its component parts work together, with Warner Bros. a distant second. So on ESPN, you'll see a jump-rope competition taking place at Disney/MGM Studios in Orlando; on Disney shows, lots of cross-promotional ads like these; and on ABC, the wholesale handing over of Saturday morning to Disney programs. One way or another, your mind belongs to the mouse. I'm startled out of this reverie by the announcer: "We now return to *Aladdin*, here on Disney!" What, the feature? No, it seems to be yet another half-hour spin-off series from the movie.

Meanwhile, on Playboy, a woman with the ultimate rocklike breasts. No matter how she wiggles, her breasts remain perfectly still—they're like gyroscopes. The irony is that her face is genuinely pretty, far more so than most of the bimbos we've seen today; so why has she stuck these cannonballs on her chest? I'm convinced that, years from now, people will look back on this age of breast implants the way we look back on bound feet and clitoridectomy.

Martin Short's show begins, and his sidekick, Michael, asks him about the *SNL* reunion. "It was absolutely surreal, seeing some of those old faces," says Marty. "And some of them are *old* faces—wheeled out from Shangri-La, some of them." The sidekick makes a Foster Brooks joke, which gets no laughs. Short then mentions former *SNL* cast member Terry Sweeney, as if to one-up Michael on the obscurity quotient. Marty's too hip even for his own room, and proud of it. Michael congratulates him on being a part of the *SNL* heritage, and at this the audience dutifully applauds. We pan across the bleachers, and the crowd doesn't look particularly American; they may in fact be foreign tourists visiting Los Angeles. No wonder they don't get the jokes.

Why do the *SCTV* alumni bother? Not one of them has the

career he or she deserves, or is doing the caliber of work they did together. Consider Rick Moranis's years on *SCTV*, which demonstrate that he can do absolutely anything—and consider his film credits, in which he plays nerds and only nerds. If *SCTV* were a rock group, they would have reunited years ago and resigned themselves to being *SCTV* for the rest of their lives, like the Eagles or Pink Floyd or Yes. For God's sake, even Crosby, Stills, Nash, and Young are reuniting! And I'm not talking about a single appearance at the Aspen Comedy Arts Festival, either. With this lineup of talent—even minus the late, great John Candy—any network would order a full season of a new *SCTV* show, sight unseen. As with the rock reunions, this would also boost the value of the back catalog, and maybe get the reruns back on the air.

On Lifetime, it's a pre-outing episode of Ellen DeGeneres's sitcom. I never saw the point of this show before Ellen came out of the closet, much as I don't see the point of a lot of the interchangeable workplace sitcoms on the air nowadays. ("She's adorable, her friends are goofy, and they all work together!" This does not a sitcom make.) But after Ellen came out, the media brouhaha completely eclipsed the fact that her show got a lot funnier. What scared ABC about the show—that Ellen's sexuality was central to the comedy, and that she even began an onscreen relationship—was what made the last season of *Ellen* endlessly more amusing and provocative than last night's toothless and sexless episode of *Will & Grace*. I still think the gamble might have paid off if ABC hadn't changed the time slot every week out of sheer terror. (And this is the downside of synergy. *Ellen* was a Disney-produced show airing on Disney-owned ABC, and it made the company a target for the religious right.)

At this moment, however, the closest thing to lesbians onscreen are three augmented babes on Playboy. I wonder if the channel features so much "girl-girl action," as they call it, because it's popular with the viewers, or because it's one time they don't have to worry about how to shoot around those pesky penises.

WEDNESDAY

These women look as if they're having much more fun than the women in the overstrenuous straight scenes; they're even smiling. When the background music ends, the women suddenly laugh and relax, as if they've just heard "Cut!" Oddly, a number of Playboy Channel segments end with this card: "Custodian of Records, Myron Dubow." Is this some obscure cable regulation? If I tracked down Mr. Dubow, could he produce an index of every sex act on the channel?

The 5:00 P.M. news shows all lead with the same story: An elderly Canadian tourist has died of West Nile virus while visiting New York. The Centers for Disease Control will conduct house-to-house questioning and testing in the relevant neighborhoods. Channel 2 is the first to cut away to the latest wrinkle on "Sensation"—with a shot of the now-familiar Chris Ofili painting, plus a few of the other works in the exhibit. By the time this story is burned out, we'll see every piece on TV news. Channel 7 has found a new twist on the story by interviewing artist Chuck Close, or at least purporting to—but as soon as he opens his mouth, they cut away.

Judge Judy has ended on Channel 4, but there's yet another courtroom show on the air. On the Playboy Channel, Z-movie queen Julie Strain poses and preens before mounting a throne in a stylized courtroom. It's the inevitable *Sex Court,* a further example of the cross-pollination of genres that rules TV. These days, every channel needs its own version of A&E's hit series *Biography;* VH1 has *Behind the Music,* E! has *True Hollywood Story,* American Movie Classics has *Hollywood Real to Reel.* (What will they do on the Weather Channel?) And now every channel is going to need its own courtroom show; besides *Sex Court,* there's also one on Animal Planet (which our cable system doesn't carry, to Sam's dismay).

First up on *Sex Court* is "The Case of the Porn Star Who Sucked in Bed." It seems the star in question has married a guy who thought he would get all the bells and whistles, but isn't even getting a joy buzzer. "Why won't you perform for him like you do in the movies?" asks Judge Julie. "Because I think it's perverted, and

I love my husband," says the defendant unconvincingly. This is clearly a throwback to the staged trials of the old *Divorce Court;* there must not be enough real sex-related cases to fill a docket. Judge Julie's verdict is that the couple should have sex right there in the courtroom, "and act like the porn star that you are!" I've heard enough—show dismissed.

At this point, something snaps. I stare at the sets, trying to decide which one to watch, and not one of them beckons me. Not *Designing Women*, not the adorable squint and pronounced eyebrows of Nikki Cox on *Unhappily Ever After*, not the Franco Franchi Calf Leather Handbags (Leopard or Zebra) for $105 on HSN. Not *The Torkelsons*, a family sitcom on Disney. And certainly not *Sex Court*. I think of a line from Nietzsche that Jaime-the-journalist quoted yesterday: "When you look long into an abyss, the abyss also looks into you." For once, I am in complete agreement with Nietzsche. To save myself from the gaze of the abyss, I make a radical move—I mute 'em all and retire to the bedroom for a nap. Sopkin started napping on his second day, and this is my fourth, so I figure I've earned it. Just before I go, the news gets interesting for a moment— Al Gore has moved his campaign from D.C. to Nashville, and challenged Bill Bradley to a series of debates—but it's too little, too late. I'm gone.

For almost two blissful hours I sleep the sleep of the dead, undisturbed by dreams or even pug. When I return to the living room around 7:00 P.M., Sam and our friend Caroline are sitting on the couch. Caroline, who went to college with Sam, is Chair of Liberal Studies at Parsons School of Design; she came right over after work to check out the TV fiesta. Sam looks up at me, somewhat sheepishly: "We're mesmerized by the Playboy Channel. Is this erotic for men?" "Men with very short attention spans," I reply.

Fortunately, our attention spans are diverted by *Extra!* on Channel 4, which seems to be a low-rent version of *Entertainment Tonight.* (This isn't saying a lot.) Dudley Moore has been diagnosed with an incurable brain disorder. "I've known that for years!" says

Caroline, a proud reader of the *National Enquirer.* The next story is "Sabrina Strips," referring not to some porn star on Playboy but to Melissa Joan Hart, the star of *Sabrina the Teenage Witch,* who posed for some mildly racy pictures in *Maxim* magazine. Archie Comics still controls the character of Sabrina, and they're demanding an apology from Hart, since "her contract stipulates that her character be depicted as a virgin." At first I think Archie executive Michael Silberkleit must be complaining for the publicity—but no, he really seems angry. This makes more sense when I remember what a cartoonist friend once told me about his visit to the headquarters of Archie Comics. What stunned him was that the middle-aged writers and artists had absolutely no sense of irony about their work, no matter how distant the world of Betty and Veronica might be from the lives of actual teenagers. He said the staff pointed proudly to a story in which Archie defended a black friend against prejudice at Pop's Chocklit Shop—a character who appeared exactly once, and in the mid-Seventies at that. The NAACP has never launched a protest about *Archie,* but that's probably because no African-American youngster would ever think of picking up an *Archie* comic in the first place.

Sam and Caroline are reacting to the photographs of Ms. Hart rather than to the Archie executive. "Wow, she looks great," says Sam. Caroline agrees, but thinks her makeup is overdone. I get the sense that for women—at least the women in my living room—TV is one big fashion show that happens to have content as an added bonus. It's like flipping through a live-action issue of *Vogue.*

The gals head out to a restaurant, leaving me alone with Cosmo, who is snoring on the couch as is his wont. In honor of my faithful animal companion, I turn to a show about tracking crocodiles on The Discovery Channel, which looks like fun. Besides, I'm irresistibly drawn to the only trees on any screen, even though in my everyday life I tend to regard the outdoors much as the writer Fran Lebowitz does—as something you pass through between your front door and the taxicab. The host is the wide-eyed Australian bloke who also does a program on Animal Planet that's more like *Zoboomafoo*. He takes us through a series of tidal pools, and hoists up a four-foot-long baby croc. Then we see a different lizard, a goanna, which eats crocodile eggs. This one is five feet long, "one of the largest lizards in Australia. That forked tongue tastes the air, picking up any traces of a potential meal—or a potential problem." Our late tabby cat, Flora, used to do the same thing.

At the commercial I switch to *Extra!*, which is interviewing Jacquie Stallone, mother of Sylvester. Jacquie, who looks remarkably like Michael Jackson—hair, plastic face, shiny red jacket—has an odd hobby: "I am a rumpologist." She claims to be able to read patterns in a rump-print. (Would this work with the surgically identical rumps on the Playboy Channel?) "Jacquie insists that rumpology is an ancient art that's been practiced for centuries," says the reporter with a straight face. Of course, the reporter makes his own rump-print, in tasteful silhouette, to strip music. Jacquie reads it, and she predicts he'll make big money by January. The kicker, of course, is that Sly won't sit for his mom; he's smarter than he looks.

The Playboy Channel is showing a movie called *Angels in the Attic*. Putting aside that these women don't look particularly angelic, I'm more confused by the absence of attics. The angel currently on display is pleasuring a young man on a patio, in front of a replica of the Venus De Milo. Then a different couple takes the screen, perhaps in the same house—but only marginally closer to the attic. These two are in a big paneled living room, perched precariously on a couch that may not take too much more of this.

Meanwhile, the selling continues on the shopping channels. Of course, the selling continues on all the channels, including PBS with its enhanced underwriting, but at least on the shopping channels it's up front. There's a Maggie Sweet Floral Print Blazer for $45 on HSN, and a Northern Nights European Tri-Channel Featherbed for between $57 and $109 on QVC. What exactly are they selling? The frame? The feathers? It turns out I don't know what a featherbed is. I thought it was a bed stuffed with feathers, but in fact it seems to be a kind of padding that goes on top of the mattress. Rather conveniently, a woman calls in to say that she can't sleep without it.

On *Angels in the Attic*, we're back to the couple on the patio, who have moved away from the statuary and are colonizing the lawn furniture. The woman has remarkable nipples that stick out like pencil erasers—or perhaps like pencils. The guy has a very hairy butt, and the camera lingers on it in a rare show of equal opportunity. Then it's back to the living room, now on a mat above the shag carpeting. My guess is that both couples will go up to the attic for the grand finale.

I need a refuge, and seek it in *Newshour*. Guest host Margaret Warner is talking to three pundits about Warren Beatty, who may run for President. This may not be TV about TV, but it's certainly showbiz about showbiz. Former Carter aide Gerald Rafshoon points out that Beatty and John McCain are the only two potential candidates talking about campaign finance reform, because they're the only two who can position themselves as being above the fray of politics—McCain as a war hero, Beatty as a movie star. Still, I find this earnest discussion about the possibility of President Beatty absurd, despite his genuine intelligence and political commitment. If the press is in a frenzy because George W. Bush might or might not have snorted cocaine, I can't imagine how they'd go after one of the most famously promiscuous men on the planet.

Next, David Gergen talks with Ken Dychtwald, author of *Age Power*, against a black backdrop, which looks much like the one on *Charlie Rose*, which looks much like the one on *Once and Again*. Dychtwald says that because the baby boomers are aging, "we're headed for a train wreck." The average American lives to be seventy-six, but then we fall prey to diseases like cancer and Alzheimer's. Also, "Twenty-five million boomers have less than $25,000 in their household assets. That's a large number of people barreling toward their later years unprepared." This is actually interesting—but again, why would I want to sit here and watch it?

Is it just because I'm used to doing the dishes or driving when I hear a substantive discussion? In the Golden Age of radio, people sat around the console; maybe it's a form of patience to do the same with TV, but if so, it's a patience I don't have. The example is apposite because *Newshour* is, in fact, illustrated radio. To explore this, I close my eyes for a few minutes and listen. I open them again and look at the earnest face of Ken Dychtwald, and while there's nothing unpleasant about it, I don't know what additional information I'm getting. If I were producing *Newshour*, I might at least illustrate the talk with clips, or even stills. On many cable channels, like the ones I watched yesterday, they'd have a little box onscreen with relevant facts. But that's part of why this show seems so dull—it's *visually* dull, and the first rule of television is to go for the eyes.

However, the show ends by noting that regular host Jim Lehrer was honored by the President. We see Clinton presenting the medal: "Author, journalist, moderator of presidential debates . . . Jim Lehrer is a modern man of letters who has left us a gift of professionalism and civility." So *somebody* appreciates this show, and I feel a bit churlish for resisting its charms.

No wonder there was no attic in *Angels in the Attic*. When I check my grid, I realize that the show by that title was on Disney— which I clearly wasn't watching for a while. The movie on Playboy that never left the ground floor was called *Another Man's Wife*.

Eight P.M. A tough choice. Bill Cosby reunites with his old *I Spy* partner Robert Culp on CBS; the Garth Brooks special is on NBC; a sitcom called *Two Guys and a Girl* is on ABC (it used to be called *Two Guys, a Girl, and a Pizza Place*; will it eventually be called *Two Guys*, and then just *Two*?). Fox has the aged *Beverly Hills 90210*, which I've never seen but suspect is too late in its life to bother with now. There's something called *Seven Days* on UPN, and the teen drama *Dawson's Creek* on the WB. Despite my rocky experience with *Felicity* earlier this week, I decide for *Dawson's Creek*, which is the only one of these shows that has a passionate following. As with any show on the WB, its ratings are negligible, but its demographics give advertisers a direct pipeline to teenage America. The show was created by *Scream* screenwriter Kevin Williamson, who has attained almost guru-like status in Hollywood for depicting wiseass, pop-culture-savvy teens in a way that real teens eat up.

"*Dawson's Creek* is brought to you in part by WB's *Three Kings.*" Warner Bros. is trying to close the synergy gap with Disney here. Then that annoying, robotic Gap ad again, followed by an animated ad for something called Juice Bar. Is it juice or perfume? It turns out to be a "refreshing body spray," which puzzles me. How many teenagers want to smell like a fruit market? (According to Sam, plenty. She says most scents marketed to teenage girls are fruit-based, because fruit isn't as overtly sexual as something like musk. This makes perfect sense; it's the same reason teenage girls go wild for androgynous, nonthreatening teen idols like Leonardo DiCaprio and, of course, David Cassidy.)

The show itself starts with a disclaimer: "Tonight's WB premiere is recommended for older viewers," etcetera. I can see why. *Dawson's Creek* has not only a "previously" but a "coming-up" montage, and the first line we hear in the latter is, "This year, Dawson, you are going to get laid." As for the "previously," it contains a lot of scenes that don't mean anything to me as a nonviewer. I know the basic dynamic of the show, though, from reading *TV Guide:* high-school student Dawson grew up with a girl named Joey, whose feelings for him have developed beyond food fights and Monopoly.

So why, with all this momentum, do I end up watching only the first half of *Dawson's Creek*? Here's a multiple-choice quiz:

1. I'm poleaxed by what I think of as the Hill Street Blues Effect. Most dramatic shows since Steven Bochco's breakthrough have adopted ever-more-byzantine continuing story lines, and this one is no exception. If you don't get in on the ground floor, each episode puts you farther behind.

2. I'm astonished by the gulf between teenage life on *Dawson's Creek* and teenage life anywhere on Planet Earth. I don't expect every show to be as truthful and naturalistic as *Once and Again,* or as snappily written and performed as *It's Like, You Know,* but it does strain my credulity when Dawson and his best friend Pacey celebrate their first day of senior year—at a strip club. *Dawson's Creek* is so far removed from anything resembling reality that I can only assume that's the point. This is what teenagers wish their lives were like—glamorous, picturesque, full of sex (for the boys) and romance (for the girls)—with all the boring stuff left out. The end result, with my apologies to the attractive cast, is a wised-up, sexed-up Archie comic for the millennium.

3. Katie Holmes, who plays Joey, is so adorable that Dawson is a complete idiot not to reciprocate her attentions.

4. I can't wait to watch the new sitcom *Work with Me* at 8:30 on CBS.

5. Much to my chagrin, my TV experiment has shrunk my attention span to roughly that of a gerbil.

If you guessed "all of the above," you're wrong; I don't really want to watch *Work with Me,* but it seems like the logical alternative after burning out on *Dawson's Creek* for reasons 1, 2, 3, and 5. So, after heating up another barely edible TV dinner, I unmute CBS and hope for the best.

I should have remembered the theme song from the Mel Brooks movie *The Twelve Chairs*: "Hope for the Best, Expect the Worst." *Work with Me* stars Nancy Travis and Kevin Pollak as married lawyers who go into practice together. It's full of schtick and slapstick (slapschtick?); once again, a bunch of talented performers are stuck with material that isn't remotely funny. After twenty minutes of this, I glance over to *Dawson's Creek,* ready to forgive and forget, but it's commercial time. The ad is for *American Beauty,* and it's aimed specifically at teens: "Your parents don't get it. Your friends can't help it. Life doesn't cut it. How long can you take it?" This is an R-rated movie, kids, so don't forget to bring your parent or guardian. Or your fake ID.

Sam and Caroline come back from dinner in a giddy mood, and they immediately launch into a running commentary on what I'm watching. I take notes as fast as I can. Caroline is particularly scathing on the subject of *Work with Me*: "This is like the Island of Misfit Toys for people whose other shows didn't work out. CBS is relentless with Nancy Travis." Indeed, this is her second or third sitcom in as many years. I prefer to think she just hasn't found the right show yet, but Caroline thinks she may be jinxed. Then we go to a commercial, and the ladies turn their attention to the Playboy Channel. "The thing that makes me nuts," says Caroline, "is that people watch this and think that's what people look like." Sam says she feels that way about most actresses on TV, "but I don't think most men think all women have big boobs and take their clothes off." I keep my mouth shut.

Caroline says her husband Ned's favorite show is *Norm*, the sitcom starring former *Saturday Night Live* cast member Norm MacDonald. In honor of the absent Ned, I decide to check out the show's last ten minutes. The wonderful actress Laurie Metcalf, formerly of *Roseanne* and even more formerly of the Steppenwolf Theatre Company, is a regular, which gives me hope. Then former *Murphy Brown* regular Faith Ford shows up, which sets Caroline off again: "It's another Island of Misfit Toys! Once you're on one sitcom, they'll never let you off!"

Norm—who's been given a Robert Reed–style perm, possibly to soften his characteristic aggression—is carrying a dachshund. What is the premise of this show? They're all in some kind of office. A bald guy has kitted out another dachshund with fake poodle fur. Then Norm sells his old sports equipment, but the sports-memorabilia guy doesn't give him much for it. Is there any thread to this show at all, or is it just a collection of dadaist scenes? Caroline's husband is a poet, so he may appreciate the surreal, random aura that just leaves me stumped. Before I know it, the show is over, and I haven't deciphered a thing. I'm starting to feel stupid. What kind of moron can't enjoy a sitcom, perhaps the least demanding form of entertainment? Have all those Krzysztof Kieslowski and Ingmar Bergman movies ruined me for everything else?

Sam and Caroline are now commenting on absolutely everything, faster than I can take it down—it's like a real-life version of *Mystery Science Theater 3000*, the cable show in which the hosts annotate old movies with wisecracks. Tori Spelling shows up on *Beverly Hills 90210*, and Caroline quotes comedian Janeane Garofalo: "Beverly Hills, a place where everyone is beautiful except Aaron Spelling's daughter." I can't help feeling sorry for poor Tori, who is trying to gain credibility by acting in independent films like *Trick* and *The House of Yes*—but her every appearance onscreen must be a slap in the face to any genuinely talented actress waiting for her big break. Meanwhile, Sam points to the latest babe on the Playboy Channel: "Those are real breasts," she says. She invents a drinking game: Watch Playboy all day, and drink every time you see a woman with real breasts. Unlike traditional drinking games, you'll never get very drunk.

Caroline leaves at 9:00 P.M., which is when *The West Wing* starts on NBC. It's the second episode of this new drama series by Aaron Sorkin, who wrote *A Few Good Men*, created the sitcom *Sports Night*, and was once very rude to Sam. This show is set at the White House, and I'm especially interested because I just toured the real White House for the first time last month. The cast is amazing: Moira Kelly, former *L.A. Law* regular John Spencer, the fine character actors Richard Schiff and Allison Janney, Rob Lowe as a character based on George Stephanopoulos, and Martin Sheen as the President. I can testify that the sets are completely convincing. Did they buy the expensive White House sets that were used in *The American President*—also written by Sorkin—and reused in *Independence Day*?

As for the show ... well, it's mildly entertaining, and mildly frustrating as well. I have a problem with Sorkin that goes beyond his past behavior toward my wife (which he probably doesn't even remember): he loooves the sound of his own voice. Every scene is longer and talkier than anything else on television, including shows like *Once and Again* that aren't exactly terse. Sorkin still thinks like a playwright, revealing character through dialogue rather than action. (By contrast, think of what writer-producer David Milch does on *NYPD Blue*; the dialogue is pungent, but many of the most telling moments are unspoken.) Still, professional TV critics seem to adore this stuff. I remember this effect from my days at HBO, where the critics were always more forgiving of our shows than we were. On TV you get points just for trying—whereas in movies or on Broadway you actually have to succeed. On an episodic series there's always hope that later episodes will deliver on the promise. Or maybe it's just that TV critics expect so little that anything halfway intelligent seems like a bonanza. And that's what *The West Wing* is—it's halfway intelligent.

At the first commercial, Sam calls my attention to a friend of ours, writer and professional sexpert Lisa Palac, who's on the Playboy Channel. Mercifully, she's not *in flagrante delicto*; she's a host on *Sexcetera*, a magazine show. Lisa introduces and narrates a piece about a series of porn videos called *Shane's World*, which "blows away the old stereotypes about women in porn." *Shane's World* seems to be an X-rated version of the MTV series *Road Rules*, in which the cast goes on a road trip and videotapes everything that happens. "Shane doesn't direct," says Lisa. "She throws a party, and everyone does their own thing." Shane herself looks like the kind of cute California blonde who'd show up on *Dawson's Creek* or *Felicity* as the nasty cheerleader. "I just want everyone to have a good time," says Shane. Lisa gives her the full bio treatment: "Her story begins seven years ago, when she looked through her dad's porn collection and stumbled on a Seymour Butts video." Apparently, Seymour Butts is a real person. "She sent him a tape of herself masturbating, and before long she was a porn star." As showbiz discovery stories go, this sure beats Lana Turner sitting at the lunch counter at Schwab's.

Lisa then introduces Josh and Liz, fans who feature in Shane's latest video. Josh was thinking of getting into the business when he met Shane at a club. She invited him to come along on the next road trip, and his girlfriend Liz decided to join in. This disturbs me, on a deeper level than I might have expected. On the one hand, Shane's free-for-all seems much livelier than the grim calisthenics we saw earlier today. On the other, I worry about Josh and Liz, who don't look like hard-bitten porno commandos, and about Shane herself. I don't know the details, but this interview makes it look as if Josh and Liz decided to have sex on camera the way I might decide to visit a friend for the weekend. This seems like the flip side of the Mean World Syndrome—call it the Nothing Matters Syndrome. Sam doesn't share my concern. Unlike me, she finds Josh and Liz easier to understand than professional porn stars. She thinks it's my own control issues that are at work here—my characteristic fear that one wrong move will tumble the world into chaos—and that it's simply a lark for them, albeit one that may come back to haunt them.

And maybe that's true. Maybe Josh and Liz are just having a good time, and they'd think I was old-fashioned and uptight to be worried about their future. But I still wonder if the omnipresence of sexual content on TV might be most harmful to young people not because it may affect them strongly, as Steve Allen fears, but because it may cease to affect them at all. The devaluation of sex is what depresses me most about the Playboy Channel. Sure, the Food Network also devotes twenty-four hours a day to one particular human pleasure—but it *celebrates* food, in a way that not even the "real people" on *Sexcetera* manage to do for sex. The Playboy Channel is actually closer in spirit to the Sci-Fi Channel, since most of the programming takes place in a fantastic world that bears only a surface resemblance to our own. On Sci-Fi, supernatural beings and inter-galactic portals lurk around every corner; on Playboy, any encounter can turn sexual at any time, and usually does. By contrast, *Once and Again* is genuinely sexy, because it's about real sexuality—how it makes you feel, how it defines you, how it can betray you. Real sex has consequences, while porn sex has none. That doesn't make it evil, any more than *Spin City* is evil, or *Wheel of Fortune* is evil. Pornography is just a specific form of escapist entertainment, like most of what I've seen on television this week, and as such it's better enjoyed in small doses.

In fact, the extreme escapism of Playboy is almost a microcosm for all of TV, in its concentration on physical beauty and sensation at the expense of all else. It's that lack of consequence that's wearing me down as I reach the midpoint of my TV week. Again and again, TV brings up strong emotions only to toss them aside—and perhaps more than any other reason, that's why I'm feeling exhausted and depressed.

I return to *The West Wing*, determined to find something to enjoy in it. I find it in a scene that revolves around the Latin phrase *post hoc, ergo propter hoc*—the logical fallacy of assuming that because one thing follows another, there's a connection. This is the second bit of Latin on television in four days, and I hope somewhere my high-school Latin teacher, Mr. Bell, is smiling.

Meanwhile, Rob Lowe's character is obsessed with a call girl. This is a classic case of truth being stranger than fiction, considering the goings-on in the real White House over the last few years—I'm thinking of Dick Morris's indiscretions as well as the President's—and in Rob Lowe's own life. The call girl is also a law student, and she makes long speeches just like everybody else on the show. (This must be how Aaron Sorkin talks.) Why has it taken this long for Rob Lowe to get a TV series? Despite his lack of squint, he's got that David Cassidy thing going strong. He used to skid off the big screen in a pool of slickness, but he's fine on TV. With the exception of occasional cameos like his hilarious turn as the young Robert Wagner in the *Austin Powers* sequel, I suspect he'll spend the rest of his career on the small screen, where he truly belongs.

At the halftime break, there's a fantastic commercial for Monster.com, which seems to be a jobs website. In a black-and-white parody of the Nike ads, kids say things like "When I grow up, I want to be underappreciated." "I want to be a brown-noser." "I want to climb my way up to middle management." "Anything for a raise." Dot-com commercials (dot-commercials?) are proliferating these days like rabbits in Australia. They all share the same snarky tone, although this is a much more successful example than most. Frankly, I have a hard time keeping them all straight in my head.

On Channel 13 a mariachi band is playing on a special called *Americanos.* According to *TV Guide,* it's "a celebration of the evolution and diversity of Latin music." This is something I might actually enjoy, but you can't dip in and out of music. Sound demands mental concentration as vision does not; I can watch more than one show at a time, but I can only listen to one. This experiment would be impossible to do with twelve radios.

The new sitcom *Oh, Grow Up* on ABC has my number. Every time the dog on the show barks, the barks are subtitled (e.g., "I am the alpha dog! I can take you!"). It's created by Alan Ball, who wrote *American Beauty,* and I think about changing over, but I'm determined to stick with *The West Wing,* in part to make up for my half-assed attempt to watch *Dawson's Creek* earlier. I'm not watching *Star Trek: Voyager* either, or the new WB teen show *Popular,* or the new Fox teen show *Get Real.* I'm also not watching *The Paper Brigade* on Disney, an original movie. I'm not even watching any more of *Sexcetera.* I thought my nap would leave me better prepared to deal with the overstim, but instead it feels as if I've lost my momentum—I'm out of synch now.

The West Wing ends with a military crisis that gets the White House awake and buzzing with people at 3:35 A.M. John Spencer's character, Leo, the White House chief of staff, tells the President that—in an improbable twist—his kindly black military physician has been killed in a terrorist attack. Either boldly or foolishly, Sorkin names names; the terrorists are backed by Syria. Leo turns to leave, and the President stops him. "I am not frightened," says the previously pacifistic Commander-in-Chief. "I'm going to blow them off the face of the earth with God's own thunder." We pull out of the Oval Office window onto the lawn as he picks up the phone, a lonely man in an impossible job with overwritten dialogue.

Despite the Latin and the swell acting, I'm not likely to watch *The West Wing* again. But why do I keep saying that? I'm not likely to watch most of this stuff again. Some people like to watch a lot of TV, and this week has reconfirmed for me that I am not one of those people. I lean my head into my hands. Why did I do this to myself? Why did I think a Martian would make more sense of this planet than its inhabitants? I haven't felt this bad since Monday afternoon. I don't even blame Aaron Sorkin; mostly I blame myself—and perhaps Hugh Hefner. Then I straighten up, remembering David Cassidy's warning that self-pity is so unattractive.

I decide to do something about my life, or at least this particular half hour of it. I turn off the Playboy Channel entirely, leaving the sets free of augmented breasts for the first time all day, and depart from my grid to watch the animated phenomenon *South Park* on Comedy Central. I'm in awe of creator-performers Trey Parker and Matt Stone, who are among the funniest people working in TV right now. In fact, this is a rerun of one of my favorite episodes, in which the foulmouthed kids from Colorado have to write a school report with a highly overcaffeinated boy named Tweek. Tweek spends most of the episode twitching, emitting strangled "Awk!" sounds, and occasionally screaming, "I can't take that kind of pressure! Oh, sweet Jesus, please!" Watching him, I begin to feel better by comparison.

Tweek's parents run the local coffee emporium, which is being threatened by the arrival in town of a coffee chain called Harbucks. They're a lovely couple, except that they keep giving the kids coffee and ignoring their son's nervous twitches. Every time Mr. Tweek speaks, soft guitar music starts playing and he drones on about blends of coffee in a soothing baritone: "Country fresh, like the morning after a rainstorm. . ." But if Harbucks comes to town, says Mr. Tweek, "I may have to shut down and sell my boy Tweek into slavery." "Slavery?" gasps little Tweek. "Yes, slavery," says Mr. Tweek pleasantly. "They really have my balls in a salad shooter."

Tweek suggests the report should be about the underpants gnomes. They come into your bedroom at 3:30 in the morning and steal your underpants, and only Tweek knows about it because he can't sleep. It's all that coffee. Over the course of the episode, the other kids get as caffeinated as Tweek, and they see the gnomes too. The kids track the gnomes to a cavern where they've amassed a giant underground mountain of underpants. The kids ask them why, so the underpants gnomes unveil their business plan. Phase One is "collect underpants," Phase Two is a big question mark, and Phase Three is "profit." This strikes me as a perfect description of the strategy of most Internet companies in 1999. Just replace "collect underpants" with "sell books," and the underpants gnomes could be on the cover of *Time* magazine too.

Despite its crude animation, *South Park* has the charge of savage iconoclasm that *Saturday Night Live* had twenty-five years ago, although a great episode like this one (and I've left out literally hundreds of very funny gags) is more on a par with the best of Monty Python. I feel better for having seen something this good—but then I feel worse, when I think of how much smarter *South Park* is than almost everything else I've watched. I walk into the next room, where Sam is checking her e-mail, and vent my frustration. She's sympathetic, but only up to a point. "You have to admit, you brought this on yourself," says Sam. "Remember, most people don't watch the Playboy Channel all day long."

At this point I am left with only one course of action, and I take it. I walk the dog, which has its usual bracing, head-clearing effect. When we return home, I ignore the sets for a while and cuddle with Sam and Cosmo on the bed. Only when my sense of duty overwhelms my sense of comfort do I wrench myself away and prepare to brave the waters of late-night TV for the first time this week.

Before the 11:30 talk shows start, I catch some of Howard Stern's show on E! This may well be the cheapest show on TV that isn't public-access programming; they just stick cameras in the studio where Howard does his regular daily radio show, and edit the proceedings down to thirty minutes. Stern can be genuinely funny, and I don't think he's the Neanderthal his more rabid fans sometimes wish he were. However, his guest tonight is a guy for whom the word "Neanderthal" is too evolved. The guest is critiquing the getup of an anxious transsexual, in the jaded tones of a fashion-business pro: "Middle too thick, makeup looks good, but hair should be darker, more natural. Soften the lipstick a bit, it's a little tacky. You're great to bang one night, but to trot you around you'd be a little embarrassing." "Could she be in *Playboy*?" asks one of Stern's sidekicks. "I don't think so," says the fashion guy. "On a scale of one to ten? She'd be a nine to pick up for the night, a six for a girlfriend."

Interestingly, the three networks now end their local news and start their late shows at 11:35. Why? To hold the audience so they're already too late for the other 11:30 shows? But if all three nets are doing it, it's only a matter of time before someone realizes there's now an advantage to starting at 11:30 and getting a jump on the competition.

In the eternal war between David Letterman and Jay Leno, I'm an instinctive Letterman loyalist. During the almost twenty years that he's been on the air, I've gone through periods of watching his show every night—most memorably, in the summer of 1994, when I returned to New York after three years in London. Sam was programming the London Jewish Film Festival and couldn't join me until November, so I tended to stay up late out of loneliness and anxiety. Reconnecting with Dave's brand of sarcasm was a surprisingly important part of my reconnecting to America, along with wallowing in NPR, luxuriating in the culinary joys of New York delis, and catching up with the proliferation of Snapple flavors. Letterman had only recently made his move from NBC to CBS, and I identified with him as someone going through a risky transition. Besides, his show is based in my adopted city of New York, while Leno's is based in my abandoned city of Los Angeles. (Specifically, it's taped in Burbank, where I used to work.) Finally, there's the essential difference between the two hosts. Jay Leno is a likable and professional joke machine, and he'd probably be a lot more fun to have lunch with than morose, self-hating David Letterman. But Letterman has a point of view in everything he does—an attitude, a style, an amused recognition that his show is a performance in which the audience is playing the role of the audience just as he is playing the role of the host.

This comes through clearly in his monologue. His opening salvo is, "We have the least caring studio audience in the history of television." It seems that during the warm-up, Dave told the audience an anecdote "from my own personal life," and was met with dead silence. He seems amused by this, as Leno would not be. Then he launches into a riff on autumn in New York City: "Ah, autumn, the browns and the golds. The browns and the golds. Weren't those the two families victimized by O.J.?" This tasteless and weirdly dated joke meets with more silence, until Dave counters, "I thought a heartless audience like you would enjoy that!" This, of course, gets big applause. Like Carson before him, Letterman is actually funnier when his jokes die.

At the commercial break, I am startled to glimpse *Village Voice* columnist and Bill of Rights expert Nat Hentoff on ABC's *Nightline*, talking about the "Sensation" exhibit and Giuliani. When I wrote for my college newspaper, Hentoff was a big influence on me, and it's great to see him on TV. Besides, as a rabbinical-looking Jew myself, I'm pleased that someone is acting as a place-holder for my own demographic. Hentoff thinks the Mayor will lose the court battle, because while there's no requirement for government to fund art, the Supreme Court has ruled that you can't pull existing funding just because you don't like something. This is confirmed by Kate O'Beirne from *National Review*, although she thinks the Court's decision was "ludicrous." Prodded by O'Beirne, host Ted Koppel asks the panel why "we're prohibited from displaying religious artifacts in public buildings, unless they're in a jar of urine?" Kurt Andersen from *The New Yorker* points out that there's one law for art, whether religious or controversial, and another law for religious artifacts. This substantive conversation is doing wonders for my state of mind; it's like cool water to a man with heatstroke.

Up comes a commercial for the Mitsubishi Galant, which has been irritating me all week. I don't remember how it starts—I never notice it until it gets to the singsong punchline, "Deep down inside, we're saying, *I'm* better than *you* are . . ." Why would anybody want to buy this car after watching this ad? Is this really what consumer culture has come to? Why not just use the slogan "Big cars equal big penises"? But, of course, this *is* what consumer culture has come to. Commercials now aim for demographics just as keenly as TV programs do. This ad is targeted directly at the kind of smug yuppie who's happy to flaunt his earnings through conspicuous consumption and conspicuous transportation. I find it hard to believe there are enough of these people to make the Galant into a success—but I have a history of overestimating the intelligence of the American public, as evidenced by the low grosses of many movies I've worked on.

Back on Letterman, there's more postmodern fun. A bunch of children play the carnival water-pistol game, with balloons that inflate to reveal the face of Dave's bandleader, Paul Shaffer. Then Dave introduces the Top Ten list, "The least intimidating things to say to your opponent before a prizefight," which is read by boxers Evander Holyfield and Lennox Lewis. The funniest are "You look great—have you been working out?" and "I've been very very bad. Punish me."

The Disney Channel has won my personal playoff. It's outlasted the Playboy Channel in my living room—and unlike the latter, Disney isn't just rerunning its afternoon lineup to fill out the nighttime schedule. Here's a black-and-white episode of *Zorro*, which I haven't seen since I was knee-high to a Mexican revolutionary. I listen for a while, but it's pretty stiff.

It's midnight, and the measured conversation of *Nightline* has given way on ABC to the wilder *Politically Incorrect*, in which an eclectic group debates the government's lawsuit against the tobacco companies. The panelists are the comedian Margaret Cho, whom I adore; Darlene Kennedy, a black conservative law professor; actor Michael Monks, who plays the decapitating psycho on *The Practice*; and rapper-filmmaker-entrepreneur Master P. Host Bill Maher agrees with Darlene Kennedy that the suit is another example of government hypocrisy, because of the money the government makes off cigarette taxes. Cho, an ex-smoker, disagrees: "You're talking about advertising that they're directing at kids. That slogan, 'Alive with pleasure' should be 'Dead with disease.'" Maher: "You're saying a company that has a legal product should advertise it with words that should discourage people from buying it. What other product can you name where we might do that?" "Rap music," says Master P dryly, to general hilarity. Before long, the lines are drawn—bizarrely, it's Monks and Kennedy and Maher defending the tobacco companies against Cho, who's outnumbered but keeps swinging. I can't tell how Master P feels, because he can't get another word in. I find this show—and Bill Maher himself—both amusing and annoying. It feels more like a wrestling match than the more genteel discussion on *Nightline*, probably because there's no live audience whooping it up on *Nightline*.

I am starting to droop, and I flit from set to set to stay awake. There's an ad for the new movie *The Story of Us* on Channel 45, focusing on Bruce Willis. He looks as if he's looser in this one; after

CAN'T TAKE MY EYES OFF OF YOU

all those grim action roles, it's hard to remember that he started out on *Moonlighting* as a jokester. I would kill for a rerun of *Moonlighting* right now.

It's 12:24, and both Leno and Letterman only have time left for their musical guests. Letterman has the talented singer Paula Cole, but Leno has one of my all-time heroes, Elvis Costello, promoting his new CD and tour. Elvis looks good—no beard, no stupid hat. (I say this as a guy who has a beard and often wears a hat. Trust me, they look better on me.) He performs a strong new song about turning forty-five, pulling a lot of resonance out of the number 45, including 45 r.p.m. and .45 caliber. He's still singing with the new clarity he gained on his Burt Bacharach collaboration, *Painted from Memory*. Did he quit smoking? Start taking voice lessons? Both?

On Disney, a rerun of the ancient black-and-white *Mickey Mouse Club*. It's Talent Roundup Day, and the Mouseketeers are walking around a painted Wild West backdrop. Karen, the littlest Mouseketeer, sings a song, "Gee, But It's Hard to Be Eight." She's clearly drilled and rehearsed, but still sounds kind of real; she doesn't nail every note, and she'th got a thlight lithp. Then Cubby, who went on to drum for the Carpenters, introduces the adventures of dude-ranch kids Spin and Marty. This is where I came in— twenty-seven years ago—and even then it was a rerun.

On CBS and NBC, Letterman and Leno are succeeded by Craig Kilborn and Conan O'Brien respectively. Craig and Conan seem to be wearing the same outfit: dark single-breasted suit, blue shirt, blue-and-white polka-dotted tie. This must be the late-night TV equivalent of *Time* and *Newsweek* running the same cover. In the past, I've enjoyed the loopy O'Brien and disliked Kilborn's frat-boy smugness; deep down inside, he's saying, "*I'm* better than *you* are . . ." I consider ignoring Kilborn entirely, but this week he's broadcasting from Las Vegas, and I love Las Vegas. His material, however, is typical: "When I woke up this morning, I was getting a lap dance from Cirque du Soleil." Kilborn has no band and no sidekick, which is at least different, but I can't help feeling it's because he is his own admiring sidekick.

It's almost 1:00 A.M., and I'm running on fumes. Late-night TV isn't the magical underworld it was when I was a kid—there's ballroom dancing on Channel 13, for heaven's sake!—so there's really no point in going on. Still, I know I'm missing some cool infomercials and bizarre public-access shows, and I promise myself that I'll stay up later tomorrow night. The last thing I see before clicking off the last set is the familiar *Mickey Mouse Club* sign-off: "Now it's time to say good-bye..." ᗡ

I sleep fitfully on Wednesday night, my dreams inchoate and inscrutable. One of the phone calls I took yesterday was from my friend Steve Shainberg, who directs commercials. To get away from everything, Steve goes on frequent retreats to a monastery, where external stimulation is reduced to almost nothing. "It's like the diametric opposite of the experience you're having," Steve said, "but the brain has more than twelve channels going." Lying awake at 4:00 A.M., I can't seem to switch off my brain channels as easily as I could switch off the Zeniths. Eventually, Cosmo moves from my feet to my head, and the white noise of a snoring pug has its usual effect on me.

THURSDAY

The Promised God-Man Is Here

At 8:20, Cosmo reacts to a noise and leaps off both my head and the bed, abruptly awakening me. Sam is doing the dishes, because she is a saint. Cosmo thinks she's making him breakfast, which becomes a self-fulfilling prophecy once he appears in the kitchen. While Sam deals with the dog, I prepare reluctantly to return to my mission. "What are your plans for the day?" asks Sam before she leaves for work. "I'm going to watch television," I reply with a straight face. "You know what I mean," she says. So I tell her: In addition to the usual channels, I'm going to watch Manhattan public access all day.

Every cable system is legally required to reserve a number of channels for public use. Anyone can book the studio time and broadcast just about anything. In Manhattan there are five public-access channels, one of which broadcasts almost entirely in Spanish during the day, and almost entirely in porn during the night. Sam and I have seen astonishing things on public access, like an informational show on penis enlargement that rendered my usually talkative wife absolutely dumbstruck; and a show about tarot cards, which consisted of a thirty-minute lesson on shuffling.

When I turn on the sets at 9:50 A.M., I'm plunged right back into the rhythms of daytime TV, just as the fanfare and crawl at the beginning of a *Star Wars* movie plunges you into that galaxy far, far away. Queen Latifah is talking to gang-bangers again, telling them, "You can represent for your hood on a positive level." On *Jerry Springer*, an audience member asks the woman onstage, "What makes you think he wants to be with you when you're sleeping with everybody else?" Martha Stewart poaches eggs, and the Teletubbies play with stuffed lambs mounted on what look like airport luggage trolleys. The only bit of real novelty is on *Montel*, who talks with a cheating couple onstage. As usual, they don't look as if they have any interest in staying together—but for once, Montel seems to agree that this marriage is toast.

For a moment, all twelve screens are showing commercials. The funniest, inadvertently, has actor Robert Vaughn pushing the law firm Jacoby & Meyers. We see a fat-cat corporate lawyer trembling in his $300 shoes: "Jacoby & Meyers? Let's settle right now." I laugh out loud at the thought of anyone being frightened by a law firm that advertises on television.

Now on public access is a show called *Audrey's Whirl*, which features a group of African-American women talking about jewelry. On another channel is a show on jazz, with a white-suited host interviewing two sharply dressed young players. I like jazz, but I can't pay attention, for two reasons. The first is that they're speaking Spanish. The second is that the sound recording is awful. This is a far cry from the professionalism of *Audrey's Whirl*, which wouldn't be out of place on any "real" channel. With the jazz show, even if I understood Spanish, I couldn't make out a thing anyway.

Meanwhile, on New York One—the local twenty-four-hour news channel—Mayor Giuliani is investigating whether the city can evict the Brooklyn Museum. The camera lingers over the Ofili painting. After all the airtime this painting has gotten, the heavens have not rained down blood and frogs. Does the mayor plan to sue all the local TV stations for broadcasting shots of the painting to the public?

Maury's theme today is "Outrageous Secrets Revealed." He has a guest named Sheila, who wants to reveal a secret to her sister. Sheila looks like a suburban matron, and I assume it's another cheating story, but no—it turns out Sheila was in a maximum-security prison for six months, for reasons I never learn. Then a woman reveals to her fiancé that she cheated on him with a woman. There must be some mistake here; I think these people belong on *Ricki Lake*. Coming up, a young man will discover his mother is a dominatrix.

I run to Rosie. Her guest is an elderly black woman named Freddie Mae Baxter, who's written a book about her experiences as a young woman in the Harlem Renaissance, called *The Seventh Child*. I heard about it on NPR last month. In a remote, we see her delight when she's picked up by a long stretch limo. Then, onstage, she tells

Rosie how she came to forgive her father for leaving her as a kid. "That word you call hate, it really"—she shakes her fist—"it will kill you. And when I gave it up, boy, I got going. And I kept going." She's a delight, and I resolve to read her book. Ms. Baxter goes on: "We were poor. When I say poor, we were *under* poor. You can't go lower than under poor."

Rosie says she's heard that Ms. Baxter usually watches *The Guiding Light* instead of her show. "They are telling an untruth!" declares Ms. Baxter. "I have two televisions in my house! I like *Guiding Light*, but I like *Rosie* too." No wonder I like her; she's a fellow multiprocessor. Then Rosie and Freddie Mae are off on a discussion of *The Guiding Light*, about which Rosie seems surprisingly *au courant*. Does she tape it? I only wish Penny were watching this. They argue about a recent plot point, until Rosie brings out a *Guiding Light* actress named Kim Zimmer to settle it. Freddie Mae Baxter is in heaven—"I don't believe this! I don't believe this!"—and there are big hugs all around. "You must go back to Josh!" insists Ms. Baxter, talking to the actress and her character simultaneously. "I believe your sister's going to get your man." Freddie Mae Baxter is one of the only people I've seen on television all week—besides game-show contestants—who's not in showbiz or politics, but isn't severely dysfunctional either. She seems to have no place in the Mean World Syndrome, for which I'm grateful.

Former heavyweight champion George Foreman does a commercial for Meineke mufflers. I'm amazed at how he and Muhammad Ali have traded personas since their fight in Zaire twenty-five years ago, when Ali was the outgoing one and Foreman was a quiet brooder. Now Ali has the stone face, courtesy of Parkinson's disease, and Foreman is such a confident and loquacious showbiz pro that it's a wonder he doesn't have his own sitcom.

A boy is bar mitzvahed on Channel 13, complete with yarmulke and prayer shawl. Ever astonished to see my own culture on TV, I quickly unmute. It's a kids' show called *Puzzle Place*, which is populated mostly by puppets. The bar mitzvah footage leads a puppet named Leon to an epiphany: "Wait a minute! I could have my own ceremony! I mean, I'm not Jewish, so I can't have a bar mitzvah, but —" He goes into a fantasy song-and-dance number about how he can't wait to be a grownup. This is some distance from Karen's song on *The Mickey Mouse Club* last night, in which getting older brought more responsibility and more problems. Of course, both songs were written by adults. I don't think I'm reading too much in to see adults in the Fifties wishing to prolong childhood as long as possible, versus adults in the Nineties impatient for the kids to grow up already.

While Sting promotes his new CD on *Rosie*, I check out the public-access shows again. On Channel 56 a bearded guy named Salvador Gomez speaks Spanish in front of a giant picture of Jesus, complete with crown of thorns and dripping blood. On Channel 34 a Black Muslim in bejeweled white robes and hat preaches in a mosque. It's better-quality video than the competition. "And I read once that when Jesus went down into hell, that's where he found the key that Satan had dropped. And Jesus picked the key up. And when he came up he had the key, because the key was for him." It's Louis Farrakhan himself, and despite my loathing of his politics, I find myself extending to him the same instinctive respect I extend to Bob Barker and Emeril Lagasse—he's a natural showman. And of course, that's the problem with using showbiz as a yardstick. Every demagogue is a natural showman. It's part of the job description.

Now it's 11:00 A.M. On the *National Enquirer* show, Mike Walker introduces a segment on "Beatle Babies." Leading off is Stella McCartney, who is now designer-in-chief at the fashion house Chloe. Other than Stella, however, the Beatle kids aren't very interesting, and the segment is over in a flash. The celebrity gossip rolls on. Tori Spelling is hooked on MTV's *The Real World*. "Tori Spelling and the Real World," snickers Walker. "For us, it's entertainment; for her, it's education." Ann-Margret scattered the ashes of the late producer Allan Carr. Al Pacino loves chop suey.

But lest we think celebrity gossip has become reduced to a

collection of colorless factoids, the show then proceeds to a full profile of Farrah Fawcett. *Enquirer* reporter Suzanne Ely, who looks to be somewhere in her twenties, talks about the days of *Charlie's Angels* as if they were ancient history: "It was something called jiggle TV . . ." This makes me feel equally ancient.

Numbed by gossip, I turn to *The View*, only to discover the gals deep in a discussion of global importance—whether men or women are "nastier in their bathrooms." Says Star Jones, "If you sprinkle when you tinkle, please be neat and wipe the seat."

That does it. I take Cosmo for his morning walk. The sun is shining, and the sky is a startling Pepsi blue with clouds the color of Charmin. Halfway around the cathedral, I realize that I'm really losing it. Not only am I beginning to see the world through a filter of TV commercials, but Sam already walked Cosmo two hours ago. I'm enough of a Jungian to believe this is significant; I must have needed to get out and move my body. This is unusual for me, and despite my mental lapse, I decide it's a sign of health. Somewhere, a part of me may be resilient enough to resist the assault of twelve TVs.

Grudgingly, I return to the apartment and give Cosmo his second biscuit of the morning. Bereft of anything interesting on public access, I surf aimlessly for the rest of the hour, through *The Price Is Right, The View, Mister Rogers*, and *Jerry Springer*. There's William Schallert on an ad for Globe Life and Accident Insurance. I'm glad to see he's still getting work. "No waiting periods, no physical exams," says Schallert. This reminds me of a commercial we used to see when we lived in L.A., for a service called 1-800-NO-BILLS, which was supposed to banish collection agencies from your life. Sam and I were always tickled by the idea that someone was marketing directly to deadbeats. What happened when, inevitably, the deadbeats couldn't pay the generous folks at 1-800-NO-BILLS?

At noon I glimpse the face of Danny Glover on Channel 9, and unmute what turns out to be the *Leeza* show. Leeza Gibbons has assembled a genuinely diverse panel to debate minority representation on TV; by daytime talk-show standards, this is pretty substantive. Much of the discussion is driven by an actress named Anne-Marie Johnson, who's on the board of the Screen Actors Guild and is clearly a real firebrand. "The makeup of the country isn't the same as the makeup of TV," says Johnson. Leeza asks whether that's because white guys own Hollywood. I think back to my own Hollywood years, and remember an insular world in which a successful white executive could go from home to work to restaurants to screenings, and never once meet a person of color who wasn't serving him in some way—as a secretary, a waiter, a maid, a parking attendant. The entertainment industry is no longer as uniformly Jewish as it used to be, but white? You betcha. It's appalling.

A dark-skinned black woman with head scarf, pierced nose, and big African earrings stands up in the audience and says, "with no disrespect," that the only black women on TV look like Anne-Marie Johnson—straight hair, light skin—and not like herself. Leeza brings up Oprah Winfrey, but the woman isn't appeased. When you're talking about minorities on television, the exception really does prove the rule.

At the commercial I check out an odd-looking public-access show on Channel 57, hosted by one Victoria Looseleaf. Victoria is your classic New York bohemian eccentric, who plays Erik Satie on the harp and changes her hair color frequently. I'm not generalizing; these are things she does right here on the show. She's interviewing the Lounge-O-Leers, who perform various kitsch and near-kitsch classics. Victoria tries to decipher her own notes: "It says—you *played* at Carnegie Hall, or you were *in* Carnegie Hall?" The guys say they played, as part of a benefit. "This was *après* renovation?" asks Victoria. *Oui*, and *au revoir*.

Back on "Hollywood Blackout," actor Edward James Olmos walks up to Leeza and kisses her on the lips. "Right now," he says, "there are millions of white people all over America who are offended." This causes an uproar in the audience, and Leeza looks kind of rattled herself. "Wait a minute," she sputters. "On *ER* we had the interracial love affair." "But how long does it last?" says

Anne-Marie Johnson. Then a black guy in the audience points out that while white people get upset if they see a black man kissing a white woman, "nobody gets more upset than black women!" Johnson responds that black women aren't pulling the strings. The guy says the interracial affair on *Ally McBeal* (between Ally and a character played by black actor Jesse L. Martin) ended prematurely, presumably because of pressure from the network. "No, it didn't," insists Johnson, pointing out that Martin got a regular gig on NBC's *Law & Order.* Wait a minute, which side is she arguing? This is starting to feel like the cartoon where Bugs Bunny tricks Daffy Duck into saying it's duck season. Now it's a complete shouting match between the two of them. Leeza interjects, "I have two words for this discussion before we take a break: Will Smith." She smiles as if this will answer everything.

During the commercial, I turn to *Donny and Marie*, whose guest is actress Markie Post. She used to be on *Night Court*, a show I always liked, and she has a new sitcom called *Odd Man Out.* As if to prove my theory that TV is ultimately about TV, Marie says she's heard that Markie doesn't let her kids watch her own show. Markie replies that it isn't on the air yet, but she's very judicious about what her kids watch: "They're the only kids who haven't seen *Titanic* or *There's Something About Mary.* I don't want the networks telling my kids what to watch." Big applause. "It's really worked out well, because my kids love Shakespeare." While I'm all for parental guidance, this attitude makes me a bit nervous—not just because I watched scads of TV as a kid and love Shakespeare as well, but also because I remember the social difficulties encountered by my friends in college who hadn't grown up watching television. You don't want your kids blindly following the herd, but you don't want them to be outcasts either. Of course, I only have a pug and three goddaughters, so what the hell do I know about parenting?

Back on *Leeza*, it's a verbal melee. Danny Glover is talking, and so is Anne-Marie Johnson, and so is a Hispanic woman in the audience who says, "I don't care who you are. If you're funny or you're good, I'll watch you!" Then a modest-seeming white producer named Peter Engel is trotted out. He's the guy behind a raft of bland teen TV shows, of which the best-known is *Saved by the Bell*. They may not be much creatively, but they're all multiethnic from the git-go. "There are not enough Peter Engels in the industry," says Johnson. Engel says it's just good business, "and it's better storytelling. Diverse characters are more interesting." And so are diverse talk shows. Hats off to Leeza! "I hope we turn off television for good," says Olmos, whose *Miami Vice* residuals must have dried up by now. "No!" shrieks Leeza. "It's my livelihood!"

In closing, Danny Glover calls for a different kind of television—not shock television, but television that illuminates. Remarkably, this hour has been illuminating indeed, although here at Overstim Central it's hard for me to imagine a TV schedule in which every show had this much bite. I wonder if Leeza will take courage from this, and do more explorations of social issues instead of same-sex threesomes. Her show is comparatively new, and she should know you can't outschlock Jerry Springer. But would enough people watch a show like that? As is typical of these questions, I have no answers, because nobody has tried it, and nobody is likely to, either.

It's 1:00 P.M., and I quickly heat up last night's leftovers so as not to miss a moment of *All My Children*. Erica Kane, back from New York already, goes to pick up Maximilian the horse, "for Bianca." I rack my brains and my notes for any mention of Bianca, but I'm pretty sure I've never heard of her. Gillian and Edmund explain to Erica that they shoot horses, don't they, and Susan Lucci has a feast of a scene: "How did this happen? This horse was healthy! And gorgeous! And strong!" Who knew a horse could be such a major character on a soap opera, and without even appearing on camera?

After the commercial we're right back in the same scene, to my delight—I could watch Susan Lucci grieving for Maximilian all day. Edmund tells Erica, "I believe that—AHEM!—this was a senseless accident that could have been prevented." I know these actors have a punishing schedule to get through, but I can't believe the director didn't make Edmund do another take on that line. Unfazed by the loudest throat-clearing ever emitted by a nonpolitician on daytime TV, Erica rages not only about Dmitri's horse but about the missing-and-presumed-dead Dmitri as well. Here's where my lack of knowledge is a problem, and I consider calling Penny for help when the show is over. Why is Erica so troubled? Was Dmitri her husband? Her lover? Her riding instructor?

This segues to an ad for the Pledge Grab-It sweeper, electrostatically charged to attract dustballs. This sounds good to me, especially since Cosmo is sleeping in the sunbeams at my feet, shedding hair on the floor with every twitch. *All My Children* isn't the only place where the fur is flying.

After several scenes involving less entertaining characters, *All My Children* returns to Susan Lucci's big scene. "Why wasn't someone watching Dmitri?" she rails at Dr. Alex. "How dare you doubt my husband's love for me?" asks Alex, who's clearly outmatched. Erica delivers the coup de grace: "Because he was my husband too!" That clears that up. "You were divorced from him twice!" says Alex. "But I was married to him twice!" responds the indignant Erica, and I laugh out loud. This is better than *South Park*! They talk over each other until Princess Gillian breaks it up. Erica takes a deep breath before delivering her exit line: "Gillian, you have a very forgiving nature, but I have no intention to forgive." She storms out of the house, confident that the Academy of Television Arts and Sciences will have to pay attention this year.

None of the subsequent scenes on *All My Children* can top that one, although at one point talk-show host Tad and his brother Jake depart from the usual topics of conversation—affairs, amnesia, and switched sperm samples—to discuss heart disease with the same expositional fervor that Erica and Alex expended on poor Dmitri. "It's the number-one killer in America," says Tad, adding that only half of the women who go to hospitals feel they're taken seriously.

This must be some sort of public-service segment. I hope this idea catches on; I look forward to hearing Detective Sipowicz on *NYPD Blue* telling a perp to get a prostate exam.

As I await the arrival of *Passions*, I glance over to *Charlie Rose* on Channel 13. His guests today are First Amendment attorney Floyd Abrams, the Catholic League's William Donohue, and some guy named Michael. At this point I'm a "Sensation" coverage completist, so I unmute it. Abrams says the cure of censorship is worse than the disease of offensive art, and Michael says that if Veronese had been condemned by the Inquisition, his paintings would have been painted over and we wouldn't have his work now. It sounds as if Donohue is outnumbered this time, and I can't say I'm sorry. He infuriates me—not least because, as a recent *Village Voice* article pointed out, his wrath is mostly directed not at genuine anti-Catholic prejudice but at Catholic artists like Chris Ofili, Kevin Smith, and Martin Scorsese. It's as if B'nai Brith's Anti-Defamation League spent most of its time protesting Philip Roth and Jackie Mason.

At 2:00 P.M., it's time for *Passions*. To my chagrin, Tabitha the witch and Timmy the talking doll aren't in evidence today, and most of the show is taken up by the teenage characters. Since every first-rate teen actor is making a fortune on prime time these days, *Passions* is left with the second-rate—they're all attractive, but none of them seem likely to follow in the footsteps of soap-opera graduates like Julianne Moore and Kathleen Turner.

At the first commercial, I surf the public-access channels. There's a doozy on 34: a large bald man wearing a long necklace and not much else. "There's an overriding impulse in you which you are only now beginning to understand," he says enigmatically. He sounds a lot like Christopher Walken. We pull back and see a row of white-robed acolytes sitting before him. He hands them something out of a wooden bowl—wafers? mushrooms? campaign buttons? Playing over this is a bad Broadway-type ballad that seems to be called "I Am Who You Are." The singer sounds suspiciously like Christopher Walken too. Who on earth is this guy, Guru Merman?

According to a card, he's written a book, modestly titled *The Promised God-Man Is Here*. His name is Adidam, and the card urges us to visit his website. I can't wait.

The Promised God-Man then gives way to a cooking show. This guy is an even more unlikely chef than Emeril; he looks like a Hell's Angel, with dark glasses, a ZZ Top beard, a black T-shirt, and a surprisingly high voice. The name of his show is *Biker Billy Cooks with Fire*. I love him. Meanwhile, *Reading Rainbow* on Channel 13 features an early Arthur book, when Arthur still had a snout and looked more like an anteater. My knowledge of Arthurology has increased substantially this week.

Passions finally comes to an end, and I learn that the show was directed by one Phideaux Xavier. Can this be anybody's real name, or is the director so embarrassed about this gig that he's adopted a pseudonym?

Rather than endure another day of courtroom shows, I check out *Wimzie's House* on PBS. It's "brought to you by Pediasure," which makes me think ruefully of when "brought to you by the letter P and the number 8" was only a joke on *Sesame Street*. This show is the most obvious attempt I've seen yet to design Muppets who aren't technically Muppets. Dad seems to be a dragon—and a firefighter. (It's whimsy's house, all right.) The kids also have a mother with a yellow beehive tall enough to rival Marge Simpson's, and a grandmother. Which one is Wimzie? According to the opening song, *Wimzie's House* is "a place where your imagination is free— where you can be you, and I can be me." This sounds distressingly like the philosophy of the Promised God-Man. If Wimzie turns out to be a bald puppet with a necklace, I'll know something's up.

It's not terribly engaging, so I go to the kitchen for a glass of water and some pretzels. When I get back, Dr. Joy Browne is hosting a couple who—for once—don't look miserable. A title onscreen says that "Nehla's low sex drive is ruining their marriage," but there's a twinkle in their eyes that makes me wonder if they just thought it would be a hoot to go on a talk show.

Despite my vow to avoid courtroom shows, I end up right back at *The People's Court,* for the utter lack of anything else absorbing enough to watch. Judge Jerry Sheindlin—I no longer think of him as Judge Mr. Judge Judy—is eviscerating a plaintiff: "It doesn't make sense. It doesn't sit well with me. I'm sure it doesn't sit well with you, sir. And it wouldn't sit well with anyone else who had a brain in their head." It seems the plaintiff was robbed, and he's over-reported the value of his lost belongings; he's asking the defendant (his landlord) for a lot more than he told the police was missing. "Have you ever had a drug problem?" asks the judge. The now cowed guy shakes his head. "Maybe you didn't hear me. I repeat: Have—you—ever—had—a—drug—problem?" "I experimented with drugs," says the guy sheepishly, "but I never had a problem, sir." "What drugs?" asks the relentless Judge Jerry. "Marijuana." "What else?" "Acid, back in the days when I was young." While I admire Judge Jerry's persistence, I can't figure out what this has to do with the case. Apparently, neither can Judge Jerry, because he drops the line of questioning and never returns to it. I can only imagine what kind of verdicts Judge Jerry dished out to real criminals when he was on the bench.

At first I thought the courtroom shows were like trashy talk shows with sterner moderators, but now I see there's something else going on. If anything, they're like a repudiation of the anything-goes ethics of Jerry Springer. Judge Jerry and Judge Judy are here to put the lid on the can of worms opened by Springer and Jenny Jones. It's the same wish-fulfillment that once produced *The Brady Bunch* and *The Cosby Show;* the TV judges enact our fantasy of the strong, wise parents who will set limits for us and protect us from ourselves.

As *Wimzie's House* ends, I clear up the titular mystery: Wimzie is neither the mother nor the grandmother, but the oldest girl monster. Next up is *Zoboomafoo,* and for the first time, I watch the opening, which lays out the backstory like the opening of *Gilligan's Island.* Chris and Martin Kratt—they're brothers, and the show's executive producers—were out in the woods one day when they met Zoboo, and they hopped after him to discover his wacky world of animals. Another mystery cleared up: Zoboo is indeed a lemur. (When I tell Sam, the repository of all animal knowledge, she just rolls her eyes at me—she knew all along. "I can't believe I married somebody who would mistake a lemur for a skunk!" she says.) In fact, I can see now that Zoboo is played in some shots by a real lemur.

There are more Jews on Channel 34. When I was a kid, you never saw anyone wearing a yarmulke outside of the occasional Sunday-morning religious show, or the obligatory Passover and Yom Kippur news stories. It turns out things haven't changed that much; this is a rabbi talking about Hanukkah at his synagogue, although it's months away. "We have the largest program for retarded people in the borough," says the rabbi. He used the *R* word! My sister-in-law, who's been known to refer to blind people as "visually impaired," would have his head.

I unmute *Beast Wars* on the Fox Kids block on Channel 5. It's a computer-animated show that seems to consist entirely of robots morphing into animals and vice versa. The computer animation is impressive. Only three or four years ago this sort of thing cost an untold fortune, and now it's cheap enough that they can do five episodes a week. A computer-animated rat named Rattrap surfs a branch down a river of lava. Just before he goes over a flaming waterfall, he yells, "Rattrap—maximize!" and turns into a flying robot. Why did he wait so long? And here's a dinosaur robot, unimaginatively named Dinobot. It's Cartoon Plot #659, in which the good guy—in this case, Dinobot—has an evil clone who impersonates him to infiltrate the headquarters. The best moment comes when Dinobot confronts the clone in a doorway, and they do the mirror routine from *Duck Soup* for a full minute before whaling the tar out of each other. When it comes to fighting, Dinobot and the rest of his team, including Rattrap and noble leader Optimus, have awesome abilities for violence. The most disturbing is Optimus, whose arms turn into machine guns. The title character in the great animated film *The Iron Giant* had the same ability, and it was *supposed* to be disturbing—but here it's just supposed to be cool. There's a fun tag, though, in which Optimus asks what happened to the evil clone. The question is answered when Dinobot burps, picking his teeth with one of the clone's claws. "You're disgusting," concludes Optimus.

It's the time of the day for cereal commercials. The leprechaun pitchman for Lucky Charms chants the names of the marshmallow shapes in every box: "Hearts, stars, and horseshoes, clovers and half moons, pots of gold and rainbows, and red balloons!" When I was a kid, there were only four goodies—hearts, stars, moons, and clovers. Now it's become a marshmallow cereal with little bits of toasted oat.

Next, there's a free trial pack of Life Savers fruit chews in every specially marked package of Trix. The cartoon rabbit is still chasing Trix after all these years, but I'm startled to see that nowadays he actually succeeds. As a result, they can't use the classic line, "Silly rabbit, Trix are for kids!" Then I remember dimly that some years ago General Mills had a national referendum, and it was decided the rabbit should get the Trix—which negates the whole point of the rabbit's existence. You can't leave this stuff to the public, because they're too fixated on the short term. The public wanted David and Maddie to get together on *Moonlighting*, and they wanted to find out who killed Laura Palmer on *Twin Peaks*—but when the long-awaited resolutions happened, the shows had nowhere left to go. Does Wile E. Coyote ever catch the Road Runner? Of course not, and the result is that the Coyote's struggle is timeless, while the mystique of Laura Palmer has evaporated. As Hitchcock knew, suspense is an end in itself. Sure, we want it to resolve, just as we desire happy endings for characters we care about. But *Gone With the Wind* wouldn't be as resonant if Scarlett and Rhett lived happily ever after. That's what we want, but it's not what we need. By the same token, we're satisfied momentarily when supense is resolved—

but then the story is over, which is disastrous for an episodic series (or even a series of cereal commercials). I think one of the reasons *The X-Files* is so successful is that the producers understand this principle. Mulder and Scully don't actually solve mysteries; they merely uncover them, and many episodes end with more questions than answers.

At 4:00 P.M. I forgo *Martin Short* and stick with Fox Kids to watch a show called *Digimon*. I get a bad feeling when I see that it starts with a "previously." Sure enough, I can't make head or tail of it, except that a group of kids and monsters have encountered some ghosts who want to eat them. Just as I'm about to resign myself to half an hour of bewilderment, I remember that Aretha Franklin is on *Oprah* today, plugging her new autobiography. My admiration of Aretha borders on idolatry, so I can't miss this.

Oprah seems genuinely excited, and does a full Ed McMahon of an introduction: "Ladies and gentlemen, please welcome ARETHA FRANKLINNN!" "Think" starts up on the piano, and Aretha strides onstage, in a sequined turquoise dress-and-wrap combo and a hairdo that looks like a cloverleaf on an L.A. freeway. Four backup singers materialize with percussion instruments, and Aretha launches into an extended version of the song. Her voice isn't at its full Arethiosity, but half-strength Aretha is still enough to melt the walls.

When they sit down, the usually even-keeled Oprah seems awed by her guest. "Everyone calls Aretha Diva Supreme," says Oprah. "I call her Diva Omnipotent." But they have something in common—Aretha says losing weight is the hardest thing she's ever had to do. Oprah says she's a carbohydrate addict. Aretha says, with some hesitation, that she has what she calls a "singing weight" of 160 pounds. "It does change the tones," she says. This may be a little disingenuous, considering that in the last twenty years I doubt Aretha Franklin has come any closer to 160 pounds than I have. Then we cut to an ad for Stouffer Lean Cuisine. "It's not just lean—it's cuisine!" Well, in fact, it isn't, and that's how I feel about Aretha too. There are plenty of slinky divas, but there's only one Aretha

Franklin. As long as she can sing, she shouldn't be obsessing about poundage. But why should I expect her to be different from anyone else in America?

Back to Aretha, doing a medley of fairly obscure songs with the four backup singers, one of whom is her sister Erma. Aretha's voice is still on cruise control, which makes me wonder if she smokes. At the end of the concert segment, Oprah asks Aretha if she ever plays her own music when she does romantic things. But Aretha isn't going there; she'd rather make banana pudding, with Nilla wafers, Jell-O banana pudding mix, and banana slices.

My attention drifts over to public access, where Channel 34 displays mariachi musicians in the kind of shifting multiple-screen format last used in the original *Thomas Crown Affair.* Then the mariachis are replaced by little Latino girls doing a pretty spiffy dance routine, with an entirely different set of multiscreen effects. This reminds me of a USC student film I saw years ago. I can't remember the actual title, but I've always thought of it as *We've Got an Optical Printer and We're Gonna Use It.*

Oprah's final minutes today are introduced by new-agey graphics—"The child in you," and "Spirit"—over gauzy shots of wildflowers and a white woman sitting in a meadow. "For today's 'Remembering Your Spirit' segment," says Oprah, "here's Aretha singing 'We Need Power.'" The backup musicians have multiplied, and singing gospel has the same revivifying effect on Aretha that it always does. Suddenly that voice is at full strength, and how; it's as if she yelled, "Aretha—maximize!" Like every good Jewish boy, I love gospel music and Chinese food. Oprah thanks Aretha, and she launches back into the song as the credits roll. Then, right in the middle of the joyous Aretha explosion I've been waiting for, the anchor for Channel 7's 5:00 P.M. news appears onscreen to tease the headlines for a full minute. He finally disappears, and we get ten more seconds of Aretha before it's over.

I'm so pissed off that I watch the news on Channel 4 instead. "An unprecedented nuclear accident in Japan" is the terrifying headline—but this is America, so the actual lead item is the mosquito-borne virus in New York. First comes the scary part, in the form of new estimates that instead of one in one thousand mosquitos infected, it might be one in one hundred. Then a doctor tells us that the number of virus cases is dropping fast, and might even have been declining before the city started spraying malathion to kill the mosquitos. In other words, it's not such a big deal after all, so why lead with this story when there's been a nuclear accident? The next item is less parochial: a major earthquake in Mexico, registering 7.5 on the Richter scale. Then, finally, the nuclear accident. No one knows what went wrong, and it's still going on—a reactor is out of control. "Two workers got a huge dose and were rushed to a hospital in critical condition." It may be more serious than Three Mile Island, but not as serious as Chernobyl.

And here's the dilemma. I finally get the news, it's troubling, and now what do I do about it? For lack of anything better, I walk the dog. It's a lovely afternoon in Manhattan, far from any nuclear reactors, and once again I glory in my momentary freedom from TV prison. As we round the cathedral grounds, I'm still thinking about the way Channel 4 teased us with the headline about the nuclear accident. I'm reminded of the first book about music videos, *Rocking Around the Clock,* in which author E. Ann Kaplan suggested that the "coming-up-next" mechanism of television is intended to keep the viewer in a perpetual state of anticipation. Her theory was that every time we relax, we're told there's something more to come, and this denial of fulfillment keeps us from turning off the set. I still think this is a fundamental misreading of television, despite the fact that I just turned off the set when I got what I was waiting for. The coming-up mechanism isn't intended to keep you from turning off the set; it's to keep you from changing channels. It's like what salesmen call "closing on a minor point." TV takes as a given that you're going to keep watching, and the only thing to determine is which channel you'll watch. Right now I'm an exception to this rule, because I'm simply sick of watching TV.

Back before the sets, I decide to pamper myself, and to give equal time to good television—by which I mean something smart, entertaining, and memorable. The logical choice is a rerun of *The Simpsons* on Channel 5. It's an episode I haven't seen, in which Homer becomes a professional boxer, managed by Moe the bartender. As usual, there are five gags for every one on a live-action sitcom, and many of them make me laugh out loud. Homer asks Moe why he stopped boxing himself, and Moe replies, "I lost forty fights in a row. Plus politics. It's all politics." "Lousy Democrats," agrees Homer. This is followed by a beautifully executed parody of *Raging Bull*, in black and white. (You can't be a self-respecting animated show these days if you don't do a segment in black and white.) Moe advises Homer to visualize how he's going to beat the reigning champion, and Homer imagines the champ keeling over from a congenital heart defect just before the bout. Perhaps the funniest thing in the whole episode is the simple sight gag of Marge Simpson's blue beehive hairdo moving through the crowd toward the boxing ring.

The huge success of *Seinfeld* proved it's not impossible to be this funny in live action—it's hard, but not impossible. So how on earth does a show like *Mike O'Malley* or *Work with Me* ever get past the drawing board? Being funny should be a minimum requirement for a sitcom, not a special bonus. It's no easier for animated sitcoms to be funny, as various cartoon stinkers of the past might indicate. But it is remarkable how high the standard is for today's animated shows, and that standard was set by *The Simpsons*, which continues to be funny and incisive in its zillionth year. Matt Groening and his team have taken unique advantage of animation's strengths. The story can move at cinematic speed, with far more scenes per episode than you'd find on a live-action show with sets and extras; on *The Simpsons*, five minutes of World War III costs no more to animate than five minutes of Bart Simpson in the school cafeteria. The voice actors are superb, but they record their lines and go home instead of jockeying for creative control to the detriment of the series. And, most notably, the writers consistently get away with some of the edgiest and sharpest satire on television. Just as the contours of the Stealth bomber allow it to fly past radar undetected, the unthreatening surface of an animated cartoon allows it to evade the bluenoses. The only significant exception to this rule has been Fox's series *The Family Guy*—but the protests against that show turned out to be a vendetta by the show-runner's former prep-school headmaster. (This makes William Donohue and the Catholic League look like the Ford Foundation.)

Now it's 6:00 P.M. There's more local news on the network affiliates. I decide to watch *Ready Set Cook*, a competitive cooking show on the Food Network. I hope it's good, because otherwise I may fall asleep, and I don't want to nap two days in a row.

Today's cooking challenge is to use ingredients you would take if you were going camping. I don't catch the host's name; she's extremely perky, with a smile that seems nailed into place, and she reminds me of Nicole Kidman's character in the movie *To Die For*. The contestants are a tall African-American guy named Joe and a New York chef named Mina. The host admits that the fully stocked kitchen set has a lot more pans and burners than any campsite, "but it's *Ready Set Cook*, so what the hey!" For some reason the action is interrupted every few minutes by sirens. Is the Food Network so underfunded that their studio isn't soundproofed? As the cooking clock ticks down, the chefs prepare what look like actual meals. I get a phone call and miss Joe's dish; Mina makes potato-wrapped brook trout with zucchini spaghetti, and the panel of three tasters finds two to one for Mina. This was pleasant and innocuous, but not very memorable. Perhaps it would have registered more thoroughly with me if I cared more about cooking—as opposed to eating, about which I care a great deal.

At 6:30, all three network newscasts lead with the nuclear accident, which is still unresolved. We see the exact same shots of bodies on stretchers on NBC and ABC simultaneously; a minute later they show up on CBS as well. On the spur of the moment,

I decide to watch all three network news shows with the sound up, and compare. I take notes frantically, recording each news item and its duration, and conclude the following:

1. They're all pretty similar—not just in approach, but in the stories they cover. All three networks cover the nuclear accident, the Mexican earthquake, and the inevitable Dow Jones Industrial Average. Two nets each cover Jesse Ventura's controversial interview in *Playboy* (Quote: "Organized religion is a sham and a crutch for weak-minded people who need strength in numbers"), the NASA spacecraft that burned up in the atmosphere of Mars, congressional dithering on the budget, and the comparative fund-raising tallies of Bill Bradley and Al Gore. Single-net stories include Günter Grass winning the Nobel Prize for Literature (ABC); Nile fever (CBS); anthropological grave-robbing (ABC); the boom in cellular phones (CBS); and ambulances that don't arrive on time (NBC). ABC covers more stories than the other two, because its pieces are all a bit shorter.

2. Except for NBC's five-minute-long piece on a hitherto unreported massacre in the Korean War, and CBS's four-minute piece on the fiftieth anniversary of the People's Republic of China, every other segment is one to three minutes in length, and usually on the shorter end. Boy, am I spoiled by National Public Radio; only the Korea and China stories are remotely of the length and depth I expect as a matter of course on *All Things Considered* or *Morning Edition*. Otherwise, it's like watching CNN's Headline News, or like skimming the front page of *The New York Times* really fast. Of course I want to know what happened today, but I'd also like some suggestion of *why* it happened, and of any possible ramifications, and of what people think about it.

3. Between Dan Rather, Tom Brokaw, and Peter Jennings, it really is a beauty contest and nothing more. They're all smooth, professional, middle-aged white men who read copy well and bring no visible trace of personality to the enterprise. Yes, I know they all *have* personalities, as evidenced in their books and interviews, and I'm sure they do a lot behind the scenes. Nevertheless, the job of a network news anchor at the end of the century is still primarily about looking good on camera and not tripping over your lines.

4. Watching three network newscasts at once is not something I'd recommend to anyone.

For a somewhat different perspective, I check out *BBC World News* on Channel 21. Of course, it's not a fair comparison, because the BBC news has no commercials—but, as the host of *Ready Set Cook* put it, what the hey. Four of the stories are the same. The nuclear accident is now under control; it seems workers put four times the normal amount of uranium-nitric-acid solution in a tank. Interestingly, this is not only the lead but the longest story in the show, running a full five minutes. Also familiar are the Mexican earthquake, the celebrations in China, and Günter Grass. Sam comes home just in time to hear that Grass won the Nobel, and she resolves to call the used-book store where we recently found his novel *The Flounder* in the cooking section.

But it's striking how many of the other stories are global; not only are they not about America, they're not even about Britain. The second lead story, after the nuclear accident and before the Mexican earthquake, is political unrest in Serbia, which none of the American nets even mentioned. The BBC also covers left-wing protests in Turkey, a Palestinian leader's return to Israel, and debates in the Indonesian parliament about political reform and East Timor. I remember this approach from my days in London. It's not just that America is a remarkably xenophobic country; it's also that Britain is remarkably self-effacing. Except for some unreconstructed Tories, Britons are more likely to accept that their country is one among many—in part because they know it's never going to recapture the inflated importance it once had in the world.

Just as the BBC signs off, I realize that I was so absorbed I forgot to feed Cosmo, which explains why he's whimpering at Sam's feet. She's pissed off, and I can't blame her. I may be absent-minded—okay, I *am* absent-minded—but I have never forgotten to feed the dog before.

Emboldened by my revivifying experience with *The Simpsons* earlier, I decide to devote the next half hour to *Wheel of Fortune*, another show I genuinely enjoy and watch when I can. It's nearly as much of a plug-a-thon as *The Price Is Right*, but the game itself—a variant on Hangman—is endlessly playable, and Pat Sajak and Vanna White are a class act as far as this stuff goes. There are die-hard Alex Trebek fans who think Pat Sajak is smarmy, but I think very highly of his abilities as a host. Like the underrated Dick Clark on *The $25,000 Pyramid* years ago, Sajak is always very conscious that it's just a game. His attitude puts everyone at ease, including the viewer.

I also regard the saga of Pat Sajak's career as a sort of show-biz Pilgrim's Progress. When *Wheel of Fortune* hit it big after Pat succeeded original host Chuck Woolery, the world opened up for him, and with much fanfare he launched a late-night talk show on CBS, opposite the still-reigning king Johnny Carson. Like every challenger to Carson's throne, Pat's show went down to humiliating defeat. But unlike every other challenger, Pat didn't reinvent himself (think of Alan Thicke exchanging hosting for acting, or Dick Cavett moving to PBS); he went right back to his original gig, where he has prospered anew. He's the Prodigal Son of game shows, and his acceptance of his lot is remarkable in an industry where frustrated ambition is the norm—where "What I really want to do is direct" is such a familiar joke that it's become a cliché.

The final puzzle is _ _ _ _ R _ E N _. A brother-and-sister

team named Joel and Jonalyn get only a D, but it's enough for them to get BOYFRIEND. They win a Dodge Durango, worth $33,505 and big enough for Barney. Their total is $73,505, not bad for half an hour's work. "I don't think I've ever seen anyone win that much money," says Sam in wonderment as Joel and Jonalyn and their significant others whoop it up in and around the Durango. And of course, that's why *Wheel of Fortune* is so irresistible. Who doesn't like to see people winning money? Who doesn't like to imagine winning money themselves? And who doesn't prefer the fantasy of winning money in a flash to the reality of eking it out bit by bit through hard work? Like any great game, *Wheel* has a balance of luck and skill, combining the thrill of gambling with the exculpatory satisfaction of feeling that you've earned your winnings.

As I microwave the leftover Chinese food, I review my toughest viewing choice of the week: Thursday at 8:00 P.M. There's an argument to be made on behalf of each channel, but of course I can't pay attention to all of them; my experience of multiprocessing three newscasts proved that. My old hero Dick Van Dyke is playing to the *Murder, She Wrote* audience with his doctor-detective series *Diagnosis Murder* on CBS, and tonight is something of a historic occasion because Dick's brother Jerry guest-stars. Fox has one of its tried-and-true reality specials, *World's Wildest Police Videos*, following in the distinguished tradition of *Secrets of Magic Revealed* and *When Good Pets Go Bad*. ABC has the American adaptation of the British improvisational comedy show *Whose Line Is It Anyway*, which I loved on Channel Four and I love here as well. There's wrestling on UPN, and yet another new teen series, *Popular*, on the WB, plus every manner of entertainment on seventy cable channels.

But I finally plump for the long-running sitcom *Friends* on NBC, because I'm convinced every single person in America has watched it except me. However, while I've never seen the show, I'm familiar with most of the cast members through their movie appearances—and with David Schwimmer, who plays Ross, through personal experience. I'm probably the only person—including Schwimmer himself—who thinks of Schwimmer first as the director of *Since You've Been Gone* (a doomed Miramax movie that ended up on ABC instead of playing in theaters), second as the star of *The Pallbearer* (a movie that Miramax released the week I joined the company), and third because he's on that sitcom I never watch.

I can tell that *Friends* is written, directed, and performed to a higher standard than most of the crappy sitcoms I've watched so far this week—and yet I don't find it very funny. You probably have to know these characters pretty well to laugh at the nuances of their behavior, and I don't know them at all. At moments like this, I can't take pride in my TV ignorance, as Sopkin did in his; I feel as if I'm outside the window, staring in at people having fun I'm not having myself.

At 8:30, I realize to my chagrin that I've missed a show on public access with the funniest title of the day: *Perfidy Exposed*. Meanwhile, as I switch over to the second half of *World's Wildest Police Videos*, Fox runs a highly appropriate commercial in which the Taco Bell Chihuahua accompanies a group of policemen on a raid, imploring the perp to "Drop the chalupa!" I've seen this ad literally dozens of times this week, to the point where it occasionally gets stuck in my head like a catchy song: "Drop the chalupa!" "Drop the chalupa!" "Drop the chalupa!"

Within minutes, the police-video show is already funnier to me than *Friends* was. Our host seems to have permanently clenched teeth; he's a bizarre throwback to the era of the great clenchers like Burt Lancaster and Kirk Douglas. He emerges from a police cruiser and stalks toward the camera, virtually spitting out his lines: "Chases are terrifying, but even when the chase ends, the danger isn't over until the subject is in custody." This sets up real police footage of a chase that seems to be over in moments—but then the suspect's car rams the police car, knocks it sideways, and takes off again. It's a dirt road, and the suspect's car sends up a tremendous cloud of dust as it drives, nearly obscuring the cop's vision. It must obscure the suspect's vision too, because he runs directly into a snowplow, and the cop blocks him in. But now there's a new problem, according to the narrator: "The suspect could be armed, and backup units cannot find them. The officers have to handle this on their own." After this buildup, I'm expecting fireworks—but the cops cuff the suspect in no time flat. The narrator's hype has turned what would have been a satisfying capture into an anticlimax, by raising our expectations too high.

When we go to a commercial, Sam and I learn that the official title of the show is *World's Most Dangerous Crashes, Chases and Busts.* It's that old devil hype again; nothing we've seen so far has been particularly dangerous, and neither is the next segment. Quoth the narrator, "In Los Angeles, a driver in a stolen Toyota does something he's never done before—running from the police. Unfortunately, he's not very good at it." In fact, this is probably what it would look like if *I* ran from the police. The suspect hesitates at every red light, and drives through three gas stations for no good reason. The narrator points out that the police could catch him at any time, but he doesn't pose an immediate threat and they don't want to make things worse. It's also possible that they're laughing too hard to get out of their cruiser. Then, still clenching, the host asks viewers to send in home-video footage of police chases. "So many people have that just sitting around," says Sam dryly. "Oh, honey, let's look through our archive of wacky police action and send some in!"

It's 9:00 P.M. I decide to pass on *Frasier* on NBC, as well as the new sitcom *Stark Raving Mad,* which follows it. Instead, my plan is to conduct a playoff of hospital dramas by watching *Chicago Hope* on CBS, then *ER* on NBC at 10.

Sam and I used to watch *Chicago Hope* in its first season, when the flamboyant Mandy Patinkin became the star of what was intended to be an ensemble show. As an arrogant surgeon named

Jeffrey Geiger, Patinkin pulled out all the stops, and Patinkin without stops is the biggest ham you'll ever see without "Boar's Head" stamped on its tush. The show's writers, headed by the ubiquitous David E. Kelley, gave him considerable ammunition. Geiger was raising his daughter by himself because his wife was confined to a mental institution, and when he got upset (which was often), he would sing. And sing. *Chicago Hope* in the Patinkin era often resembled Al Jolson's Broadway musicals of the Twenties, when during the second act Jolie might step to the footlights and say, "Folks, you know what happens—the guy gets the girl. Now do you want to go through all that, or would you rather hear me sing?" As a result, *Chicago Hope* was rarely believable, but very entertaining nonetheless for people like me who really would rather hear Mandy Patinkin sing.

Then came several years during which Kelley left, Patinkin left, and Sam and I stopped watching, along with most of the rest of the audience. I didn't see the final episode of last season, when Patinkin and Kelley finally returned, but I gather that Jeffrey Geiger fired most of the regular characters, while Kelley fired the actors who portrayed them. Tonight's episode is the second one of the new season, and now Geiger is running a hospital whose staff is composed of a few holdovers like Hector Elizondo and Adam Arkin, and a bunch of newcomers including Barbara Hershey and Lauren Holly. I can't remember whether Mark Harmon is new or old. My secret hope is that Patinkin will lead them all in a rousing chorus of "Everything's Coming Up Roses"—who needs medicine?

Unfortunately, Kelley and Patinkin seem determined to beat *ER* at its own game. The premise is that two patients are waiting for heart transplants—a rich guy named Henry Strauss, whom Geiger hopes will donate a wing to the hospital, and a poor but saintly hospital employee named Stanley. Just before the opening credits, Adam Arkin as Dr. Aaron Shutt encounters a traffic accident on his way to work, and quickly ascertains that the driver isn't going to make it. "Is this guy a donor?" he asks. It's going to be a race for the guy's heart. Sam turns to me with a smile. "I just had a premonition about how this show is going to end," she says. "Shall I tell you what I think?" I shake my head, because Sam is usually right about this stuff—she deduced the big twist in *The Sixth Sense* simply from watching the trailer—and I'd rather figure it out myself. Instead, she writes it on a piece of paper and folds it up.

The doctors call a meeting to decide what to do with the donor's heart, and Patinkin and Elizondo argue the relative merits of Strauss versus Stanley. Stanley is younger, says Elizondo, whose character is a caring, dedicated doctor who also wants to stick it to Patinkin. Strauss has a family who can help him through post-op, counters Patinkin. Barbara Hershey flips a coin, and Elizondo calls heads. It's tails. (If this were a soap opera, we wouldn't know the outcome until *after* the commercial.) Elizondo explains to Stanley that he didn't get the heart. But Stanley's failing heart is made of gold, and he trusts that everything is for the best. You almost expect him to conclude with "God bless us, every one." Then Geiger apologizes to Stanley, telling him, "When your heart comes, I'm doing the surgery." If this were a first-season episode, here's where Patinkin would sing Stanley a lullaby. It's a lot less fun this way.

Barbara Hershey performs the heart transplant on Strauss. "It's completely unbelievable," says Sam. "What?" I ask, thinking she means the dramaturgy. "That they can do this to people," she replies, amazed by the very existence of heart transplants and thinking of a mutual friend who just had one. After the operation, Hershey tells Geiger she wishes Stanley had gotten the heart. He starts to argue, but then they hear there's a problem with Strauss, and they run back to the operating room. "She hasn't even washed her hands," says Sam indignantly, "and she was drinking coffee." "I think she must have washed her hands between shots," I say. We're the kind of viewers no hospital show wants—the kind who watch a tense drama and worry about sepsis.

Sure enough, Strauss is a goner, and Geiger determines to "get Stanley in here"—the heart's still good. But just as he gets permission from Strauss's family, Elizondo walks in to say Stanley is dead. Now Geiger is miserable. At the fancy kindergarten that his daughter has applied to, he completely breaks down. I raise my hopes once again, but instead of an *a capella* rendition of "My Heart Stood Still," Patinkin delivers an impassioned speech about how the system shouldn't distinguish between rich and poor. I can't help thinking of the song parody in the satirical revue *Forbidden Broadway*—I think it was "Hyperactive, Narcissistic, Self-Indulgent Mandy," to the tune of "Supercalifragilisticexpialidocious." For my money, the problem with the latest incarnation of Jeffrey Geiger is that he isn't self-indulgent *enough*. Sing, baby, sing!

I look at the piece of paper on which Sam wrote her prediction. It reads, "Rich guy won't survive surgery. Stanley will end up with the heart." I give points to the writers of *Chicago Hope* for surprising my usually clairvoyant wife even halfway. Still, this is yet another show that I am not remotely tempted to watch again—unless I hear that Broadway diva Bernadette Peters is doing a guest shot.

On to the season premiere of *ER*, the other Chicago-set hospital show. I've never sat down to watch a whole episode, but Sam is a devoted viewer. I realize quickly that I know a lot more about *ER* than I thought, just from years of listening with one ear while playing computer games in the next room. Julianna Margulies, heavily pregnant, rides the subway. A snotty slacker-dude won't stand up to let her sit. Then she goes to a coffee shop. The snotty guy is there too, along with a nice but invasive old black woman who wants to touch her belly. A little girl's balloon pops, and Julianna jumps. Then she walks out, just as a truck goes barreling into the store, presumably injuring or killing everybody. It's a total surprise, effectively delivered—albeit utterly contrived.

As the credits run, Sam asks me, "What's the show with the cow on Channel 21?" I look it up in *TV Guide*. *"When Good Cows Go Bad,"* I tell her. "You're kidding," says Sam, incredulous but willing to believe it after everything we've seen this week. Actually, I am kidding. It's the science program *Nova*, which is covering mad cow disease.

Back on *ER*, we're now in the ER itself as the doctors deal with the survivors of the coffee-shop accident. Things haven't changed since both shows premiered on the same night; *Chicago Hope* does a steady fifty-five miles per hour, while *ER* rockets out of the gate at eighty. In short order, we meet regulars like Anthony Edwards, Eriq LaSalle, and the actor Sam refers to with a sigh as "the adorable, pug-owning Noah Wyle," all of whom are trying frantically to save patients' lives, and none of whom would even consider taking a break to sing show tunes. The snotty guy is on a stretcher, yelling, "I want to talk to the manager! You sons of bitches, give me something for the pain!" Then he recognizes Margulies, and knows fear.

Actors keep turning up, most of whom seem to be regular characters. I haven't seen this crowded a TV workplace since the glory days of *Hill Street Blues.* One of the new regulars—replacing the departed George Clooney—is Goran Visnjic, a darkly handsome European actor who was in the Miramax film *Welcome to Sarajevo*, as well as the big-budget *Practical Magic.* Sam saw both of those movies, but clearly Visnjic has a different impact on her when he's an idealistic doctor. "He's gorgeous!" she says. "He's giving me goosebumps—who needs Clooney?" Julianna Margulies sees Visnjic being tender and adorable with a little kid, just the way Clooney used to before he left the show, and they have a moment. You can hear the writers laying pipe for future episodes, clank clank clank.

Unlike *Chicago Hope*, *ER* doesn't have one main story line; it's crammed full of story threads of different lengths and emphases, some of which are mere whispers, like the promised connection between Visnjic and Margulies. The most prominent thread of this episode is that nobody wants the obnoxious Romano to become chief of staff. Romano, played by the wonderful actor Paul McCrane, is *ER*'s equivalent of Jeffrey Geiger without the vulnerability or the singing voice. Gentle, bespectacled Mark Greene (Anthony Edwards) sticks his neck out to oppose the appointment, but ambitious Carrie Weaver (Laura Innes) realizes it's inevitable and sells Mark out. "Whaaat?" cries Sam, taken aback. "She's got her own careerist agenda," I say, grateful that a character on a TV show has done something unpredictable.

At the commercial there's a promo for the eleven o'clock news, referring to the "encephalitis outbreak." "I thought it wasn't encephalitis," says Sam. "It's West Nile virus," I tell her. "So why did they call it encephalitis?" she asks. I feel like an expert on this topic by now. "Sometimes they call it a virus resembling encephalitis, sometimes they call it 'the mosquito-borne virus...'" Then an ad for the upcoming Harrison Ford movie *Random Hearts* distracts us both. "My God, there's like seven movies I want to see," sighs Sam. "What are we going to do, see a movie every night?" I smile more broadly than I have in a while. "That sounds good," I say.

Back to *ER*. The adorable, pug-owning Noah Wyle treats a beautiful patient who's clad in a slip. "That actress looks familiar," says Sam. "It's Rebecca DeMornay," says me. "That's Rebecca DeMornay? That's a terrible haircut for her," Sam exclaims, once again appraising beauty on the TV catwalk. I must admit that with her big eyes—which could outstare Susan Lucci's—and other parts visible, I hadn't noticed her haircut.

There are more patients and more crises, until the episode finally ends (rather abruptly, in fact). The show is never boring, and it's a technical marvel. But when I think of the series that first plowed this furrow—*Hill Street Blues* and *St. Elsewhere* in particular—I can't help thinking there's something missing here. *Hill Street Blues* had not only riveting plot lines and colorful characters, but also a portrait of society that at its best was worthy of Dickens or Thackeray; *St. Elsewhere* had a streak of sheer absurdism that could turn either comic or tragic, not unlike the work of John Irving. I like *ER*, but if

I had to compare its world to that of a novelist, I'd probably have to go with the show's creator, the techno-wizard Michael Crichton— and despite Crichton's skill and success, that's a different league. I don't get the sense that the writers on *ER* are busting their asses to push at the envelope of TV drama, the way Bochco's gang continues to do on shows like *NYPD Blue*.

I am beaten, drained, incapable of thought. It's the perfect condition in which to watch a show called *Blind Date* on Channel 9. To retain some semblance of responsibility, I decide to watch it without sound, while listening to the 11:00 P.M. news. The premise is that a woman and a man are interviewed separately, then thrown together on a blind date. We see their date, while a pop-up video device (clearly inspired by VH1's seminal show of the same name) keeps telling us what's really going on. Soon after the date begins, we've learned that the gal has named her breasts Patti and Melanie. This piece of information is so distracting that I immediately forget what the lady's name actually is. The guy, Tomas, wants his next lover to be his wife. She wants her next lover to be Tomas. They're both very attractive, and her low-cut top says she's ready to play. They stop at the Hollywood lingerie store Playmates, where she tries on sexy outfits in front of him, including a thong bikini. Tomas is tempted between lust and virtue, and his feelings are continually charted by a "Temptation Meter." Then they go to a spa with private hot tubs, where she throws herself playfully into his arms. Tomas's Temptation Meter is now at 10 out of a possible 10, and I suspect that if the cameras weren't there, events might take quite a different course. (It's yet another demonstration of the Heisenberg Uncertainty Principle.) But the cameras *are* there, so they go to a restaurant instead. She's about to say something, and an onscreen countdown begins: "She loses Tomas in 3 . . . 2 . . . 1 . . ." I think about getting off the couch to unmute, but it's too late to find out what she said to lose him—whatever it was, she sure did. They end the date by shaking hands. She leans in for more, but he ducks. We see his thought bubble: "I've got to get to bed." Hers: "I hope I still have batteries." *Blind Date* is impossibly cheesy, but I find myself enjoying it. I might even watch it again. The future for the pop-up format is limitless. How about pop-up news? Pop-up soap operas? Pop-up C-SPAN?

I finally walk the dog. When I return, I take a deep breath and prepare to watch as much late-night TV as I can handle. I think of the sheer bliss I experienced as a kid on those rare nights when my parents would let me stay up late enough to see Johnny Carson's monologue. Or when I was eleven years old, at the height of my obsession with the Marx Brothers, and I actually stayed up past midnight to catch a rare showing of *A Night in Casablanca*. Late-night TV was like an unexplored paradise to me then, and I longed to be old enough to enjoy it at my leisure.

I couldn't have imagined that someday I'd be watching the strangeness afoot on Manhattan public access. *Fairyland Tonight* on Channel 67 is a fairy variety show, hosted by a fairy queen who talks like Glinda the Good Witch. I use the word "fairy" advisedly; the folks on this show aren't gay men, or even transvestites. Rather, they're self-proclaimed fairies, and most of them seem to have XX chromosomes. The queen and her puppet sidekick introduce their first guest, a folk singer. She sings "A Pretty Maid Milking Her Cow," which clears my wife out of the room in seconds flat.

Suddenly I see something on another screen. I yell to Sam, "Pug!" She comes running back in, but just misses the sight of a pug being picked up and swung around in Central Park on 56, another public-access channel. Instead, she sees a naked woman jumping up and down on a trampoline. "That's not a pug," says Sam with obvious disappointment, and she retires to the bedroom. Next we cut to some well-lit and well-composed nude stills of the same woman. Refreshingly, she has a mischievous smile and real breasts. After the plasticized specimens on The Playboy Channel yesterday, it's startling to see a naked woman on TV who's attractive and real-looking.

David Letterman is doing his monologue: "I hope tonight's show goes better than last night's. What a lousy show. Last night's show went over like an art exhibit at the Brooklyn Museum." Big laugh. "The Academy called, they want their Emmy back." He turns to the subject of Warren Beatty: "This country will *never* elect a womanizer. So far, Warren has only one campaign promise: better-looking interns." Dave is indeed much looser tonight, dancing and singing "It Had to Be You" between quips.

At the commercial, I take a look around. George Clooney is on *The Tonight Show,* plugging his new movie *Three Kings.* The ancient British sitcom *Are You Being Served?* is on PBS, whose Anglophilic viewers can pride themselves on enjoying a bit of culture from the mother country. But the joke's on them, because in Britain the show is thought of as a sniggering embarrassment when it's thought of at all. Whenever Britons hear about its place in the American cultural firmament, they laugh and laugh. On Channel 9, it's a rerun of *Star Trek Voyager.* Where would UPN be without this show? They might as well cancel the rest of the schedule and just turn the network into an endless *Voyager* marathon; the ratings would actually go up.

Something's happening to the public-access channels at Time Warner Cable; both 56 and 67 go on the fritz at the same moment. Then 35 joins them. When they straighten out, Channel 35 has switched over from Spanish programming to its late-night incarnation. Here's the notorious *Robin Byrd Show,* in which a middle-aged ex-hippie in a crocheted bikini interviews strippers whose cup size exceeds their hat size. An electric guitar plays the blues as we see two legs shakin' it in front of the show's neon logo. Cut to an ad for 550-BODS, complete with a penis that would flunk the Mull of Kintyre test. After more ads for similar services, we cut to Robin herself, in close-up. She looks harried. "This is *The Robin Byrd Show,*" she says, "and what would *The Robin Byrd Show* be if I wasn't putting my makeup on while we're doing the show?" She tells us she used to have one or two guests per show, but tonight she has seven, which is why her makeup isn't on yet. "You all got hungry for television. Hungry for television."

Politically Incorrect appears on ABC. Bill Maher talks about the earthquake in Mexico: "Robert Downey Jr. is lucky he's in jail, because drugs are going to cost a fortune this year." Then on to the Republican presidential race—Gary Bauer called a press conference to deny he had an affair. "He blamed the rumors on Steve Forbes, his rival," says Maher. "Apparently, Forbes is also behind the rumors that Buchanan's a Nazi, Bush is an empty suit, Quayle's a moron, and Liddy Dole's husband has to take drugs just to bang her." This is what passes for sophisticated political satire in 1999.

The Robin Byrd Show features a stripper named Heather Hunter, who may still have her own Byrd-type show on public access. More energetic than most of Robin's guests, she doesn't even seem to be stoned. Heather is the new face of the business, stripper as sex-industry entrepreneur.

A world away from Heather's gyrations is the current segment on *The Tonight Show*, in which Jay is interviewing identically dressed five- or six-year-old quadruplets Kendra, Kelly, Megan, and Sarah. "Who's the boss?" asks Jay. "Mommy!" responds Kendra, without a moment's pause. The quads are red-haired, freckly, and losing teeth—the Tooth Fairy is busy in this household, although the quads can't seem to agree on the going rate for teeth. Jay asks about boyfriends, and all hell breaks loose, five-year-old style. One of the quads says Sarah has a boyfriend named Aaron. Sarah disagrees, letting loose a sirenlike "Nooooooo!" that could break glass. What do they want to be when they grow up? The answer is unanimous: "Police!" Is Aaron going to marry Sarah? "Nooooooo!" she wails.

After watching him with the quads, I begin to understand the appeal of Jay Leno at last. Letterman wouldn't have been able to pull this off—he would have put quotes around it, and it would have been about him interviewing the girls rather than about the girls themselves. Like Dave, Jay is able to keep things entertaining; but unlike Dave, he can function as a straight man for the girls and let them shine. However, I feel a strange sense of sadness at the sight of the quads, so happy and sparkly and full of innocent joy. Maybe it's because I've seen so much adult sordidness over the last few days.

At around 12:30 A.M., there's a rerun of *Oprah* on Channel 7. Her guest is one of my all-time crushes, Cybill Shepherd. It's not just that Shepherd is gorgeous, and in that perfect-blond-cheerleader way that quickens the pulse of any heterosexual American Jewish boy. It's her genuine wit and smarts, the naughty twinkle in her eye, the way she wears Reeboks with an evening gown. Cybill has just turned fifty, and she makes fifty look awfully good. Oprah starts right in on menopause. Cybill doesn't like the term: "Isn't there something so awful about *men*-o-pause? We don't want the men to pause!" Cybill says she's "still getting my period, if it's okay to say that." Oprah laughs, "On a show about menopause, yes it is." This is a whole show about menopause? Cybill says CBS censors wouldn't let her say "period" on her sitcom; "What should I say, my monthly visit from Aunt Flo?"

Oprah leads a true-or-false quiz on menopause, and I start to wonder what I've gotten myself into. I thought I was just going to admire Cybill during an hour-long celebration of her Cybillness. But instead, she's being used merely as a vehicle to explore something else—and something for which I, as a thirty-seven-year-old man, may not be the ideal audience. Okay, I was the projectionist for the Feminist Film Society in college, but I'm still a guy. I ponder this during the commercial, and before I know it, the show is back with clips from the classic menopause episode of *All in the Family*. Archie yells at Edith, "If you're going to have a change of life, you've gotta do it right now!" He points to his watch.

It seems Cybill did two episodes about menopause on her own show, which is why she's here as the spokeswoman for—uh—what? For menopause itself? I dimly remember something from earlier in the week (it seems like months ago now), in which somebody called Cybill "the new face of menopause." Has she simply appointed herself to the position, despite the fact she's still receiving monthly visits from Aunt Flo? Should Leonardo DiCaprio take over from

CAN'T TAKE MY EYES OFF OF YOU

Bob Dole as the spokesman for Viagra? I don't think it's just the lateness of the hour and my lack of remaining brain space, but I can't quite follow this concept.

As Oprah brings out a gynecologist to provide expert advice, my eyes begin to glaze over. With apologies to menopausal women everywhere, I start to channel-surf. John Travolta and David Spade are on yet another rerun of *Saturday Night Live*. There's Clooney again, on Craig Kilborn's show—two networks, two shows, two hours! Robin Byrd buries her face between a stripper's enormous boobs, as all her guests dance to her theme song, "Baby, Let Me Bang Your Box." Moving on, Robin waggles a male stripper's penis in her face and pretends to put out her eye with it. I guess the show isn't over until she's mimed sexual activity with each guest.

I surf on. My earlier exhaustion has evaporated. Either I've got my second wind, or I'm so tired that I don't even notice it, like an intern at a hospital. On Disney is an old *Walt Disney Presents* from the Sixties. It's a special on Disneyland's "Pirates of the Caribbean" ride, which had just opened. A boatload of tourists float through as the robotic buccaneers sing "Yo-ho, yo-ho, a pirate's life for me." I made this particular trip in 1973, and suddenly all the details come back to me, as if I'm regressing through some sort of advanced hypnotic therapy. The amazing thing is that somebody thought this was a TV program. It's a common criticism of trashy action movies to say they resemble theme-park rides—but this show really is a theme-park ride, and even at the time it must have seemed strange. There's no story and no characters. There's no narration about how the figures work. There's not even a celebrity in the boat. Just the ride, ma'am.

Cut to a promo for the forty-fourth anniversary of the *Mickey Mouse Club*. Forty-four? Who celebrates forty-four? They couldn't wait one more year?

We're back. Now a smiling woman who might as well be animatronic herself explains that the present has caught up with Tomorrowland, and so Disneyland has pushed Tomorrowland farther into the future. We see documentary footage of the grand reopening, attended by Walt himself, along with a space-suited Mickey Mouse and a guy who takes off from the podium in a jet pack. This segues nicely to a helicopter panorama of the Magic Kingdom.

Deep in Disney, I've almost forgotten the other channels— no, really!—until I notice out of the corner of one eye that Cybill is singing on *Oprah*. I turn it up, but the song isn't "I Told Ya I Love Ya, Now Get Out," which she once sang on *Moonlighting*; it's "I Got Those Menopause Blues." I hurry back to Disneyland.

The People Mover is also new to the park. A stentorian announcer declares, "Someday, a conveyance like this may travel through your community." Yeah, we all thought that. He continues, "From the People Mover, you can view each of the attractions in Tomorrowland." For instance, Flight to the Moon, which "takes place sometime in the future, when travel to outer space is common-place." Oh, the ache of it—nothing is more poignant to me than people in the past imagining a future that never came to be. Now, once again, we see the attraction in real time, as if we were there on the ride. Here's the announcer, who's wearing a space suit: "They're the latest thing in moon fashions." He must be one of those stiff leading men like Marshall Thompson or Rex Reason who never quite made it in features.

Next up, the Carnival of Progress, in which the audience revolves around the exhibits, or is it the other way around? It's accompanied by a song that makes "It's a Small World" seem like Cole Porter: "There's a great, big, beautiful tomorrow, shining at the end of every day. There's a great, big, beautiful tomorrow, and tomorrow's just a dream away." I thought this stuff was creaky when I was ten years old, and now only my intense nostalgia keeps it from being agonizing. Then we see an animated model of EPCOT—not what they finally built in Florida, and not even what has recently opened as the town of Celebration, but Walt Disney's original vision of an entire metropolitan city where everything is Imagineered to within an inch of its life. Walt never lived to see it through, and it was the first thing to hit the scrap heap after his death. For some reason, I find this unbearably touching. What becomes of a crackpot dream deferred?

It's nighttime in the park now, and time for Fantasy on Parade, featuring all the costumed characters. I'm figuring this special dates back to about 1964 or '65; the latest characters I recognize are from *Babes in Toyland*, which came out in 1961. A hydraulic bandstand lifts up, revealing a bunch of performers who split the difference between the Rat Pack and the Association. We finish up with Fantasy in the Sky, which is fireworks, of course. The fireworks were just getting started when my family and I left Disneyland in '73; I remember seeing them in the distance as we drove away. As the screen settles into colorful abstraction, the announcer cries out, "Here comes Tinker Bell now, through the happiest land of all!" Is Tinker Bell animated? Animatronic? A skydiver? We'll never know, because the show is over, on a literally suspended note that is sadder than just about anything I've seen all week. This kind of strenuously achieved innocence breaks my heart in a way real innocence can't, because I see the effort and I know it's a patch job. Some of those clean-cut youngsters riding the Rocket Jets in Tomorrowland will soon be riding Hueys over Khe Sanh.

And yet, this stuff is mesmerizing, not least because it hasn't been repackaged in any way. Cable television's desperate hunger for product means that anything ever filmed or taped might show up at any time. Our local cable system doesn't feature Turner Classic Movies, but my mother-in-law's does; I've spent hours at her house watching all manner of video detritus, like old MGM product reels that were originally shown to conventions of theater owners. I'm tempted to stay up until 5:00 A.M. to watch *The Ink and Paint Club*, which seems to be a catch-all for more relics from the Disney vault, but now I feel my exhaustion, and I'm more than ready for bed.

Still, this is my last chance to see whether there's more on late-night TV that you can't get earlier in the schedule, and my sense of duty keeps me awake. It's shortly after 2:00 A.M. There's an old *Kojak* on Lifetime. (This is "TV for women"? Who loves ya, baby?) *The 700 Club* is railing against the work of Chris Ofili. The host announces that the Catholic League will be marching outside the museum at 11:00 A.M. on Saturday morning. I'd go to the counter-protest if I didn't plan to be watching *Pokémon*.

Round and round I go, and where I stop is the History Channel, arrested by the words "Men in tuxedos and women in evening gowns came to gamble away their riches." Now you're talking! It's the history of Las Vegas on a show called *Modern Marvels*. Most of this footage hearkens back to the Vegas I first knew, rather than the unrecognizable corporate resort it's become. (I still love it, but in a different way.) A tour of the vintage signs, at which I stare in sheer pleasure. The old Sands. The giant sign for the Dunes, where Sam and I stayed the first time we went to Vegas together; it was a dilapidated place with cigarette burns on the bedspread, and they dynamited it soon after. The show pays special attention to the original sign for the Stardust, as well it should. On that first trip to Vegas, Sam and I must have sat in front of it for a full twenty minutes, just watching it go through its sparkly paces. A Vegas expert calls it "a purely decorative piece of architecture, totally made out of light." Of course, they tore that down too, auctioning off each letter individually. Sam still kicks herself for not buying an S.

It's 2:21, and I really am fading. At some point while I was lost in Vegas, *Inside Edition* gave over to *Entertainment Tonight*, which seems to be featuring—William S. Burroughs? What's next, Hubert Selby Jr. on *Hollywood Squares*?

As I turn off the sets and head for the bedroom, I hear a horrible grinding noise from 110th Street through the open window. I go to the window, and look down to where a gigantic hydraulic truck is either picking up or dislodging a Dumpster. I can't tell if this is what the driver wanted to do; he keeps getting out of the truck and looking at the situation. It occurs to me that late-late-night TV is a kind of landfill for the contents of every channel's Dumpster. You've got this useless stuff to discard, you have to put it somewhere out of the way, and if you're lucky you can build on it eventually. But in the meantime, much of it smells. ♉

"Paging Dr. Timmy! Stat!"

After my late-night marathon, I sleep as soundly as Cosmo. Sam wakes up first and departs for her office downtown, leaving me to my slumbers. It's only when Cosmo stands on my chest and licks my face that I finally join him in the world of the living. I glance at the paper, throw on my bathrobe, and stagger groggily to the sets. I have become Charles Sopkin.

I decide to reward myself for getting this far—and to give myself an incentive to keep going—by setting my five utility sets to the channels I watch most when I'm not watching twelve TVs at once: VH1, MTV, American Movie Classics, Comedy Central, and Cartoon

Network. Tomorrow I'll go back to the kind of rigorous channel-switching I haven't done since Sunday.

It's 10:00 A.M. On American Movie Classics, I notice Barbra Streisand in Gay Nineties regalia, descending that famous movie staircase. It turns out to be *Hollywood Real To Reel*, the channel's equivalent of *Biography*, with a piece on the making of *Hello, Dolly!* While *Hello, Dolly!* is far from my favorite musical (I'm a *Singin' in the Rain* man myself), this is the kind of very specialized programming that justifies the existence of multichannel cable television. The probable audience for a show like this is pretty damn small: a diminishing number of women my mother's age, gay men of the Stonewall generation, and the occasional heterosexual movie buff like *moi*.

But musical fever seems to be raging across the sets this morning. On Channel 7, an ad for Roma Furnishings features a toga-clad woman who materializes in the middle of the store and shows off the merchandise, with more than a nod to the classic Kurt Weill–Ogden Nash musical *One Touch of Venus*. I half expect her to start singing, "Speak low, when you sell love seats . . ." Then, on *The Rosie O'Donnell Show*, the TV audience is introduced to Kristin Chenoweth, whose performance in a recent revival of *You're a Good Man, Charlie Brown* has made her the toast of Broadway. Chenoweth sings "Taylor the Latte Boy," one of those new-cabaret songs that isn't bad, but isn't especially memorable once you get the idea. But Kristin! She's tiny, blond, and bursting with talent. At the end, Rosie comes rushing out to hug her. "How good is she?" cries Rosie. Damn good, I agree. As Rosie thanks Kristin, she pops a sacred TV bubble in the process: she mentions that while this is the Friday *Rosie O'Donnell Show*, it's actually taping on Thursday at 3:30, and Kristin opens in a new play called *Epic Proportions* tonight, i.e., last night.

Meanwhile, AMC has another piece of video flotsam, similar to the stuff I enjoyed last night—a visit to the set of the 1965 comedy *How to Murder Your Wife*. Studio prop men are constructing a cake large enough to conceal Virna Lisi, who wears "a bikini-type costume consisting of nothing but whipped cream." Did this predate the cover of Herb Alpert's album *Whipped Cream*, with its famous cover photo? As we see Virna shooting the scene in her bikini-type costume, the announcer says her creamy outfit makes getting in and out of the cake "precarious—in more ways than one!" Really? What's the second way?

We segue to a "Welcome to Hollywood" party for starlet Romy Schneider, complete with cha-cha music. This stuff is irresistible to me. Charlton Heston is there, as is a pre-*Mannix* Mike Connors, Schneider's co-star in a movie called *Good Neighbor Sam*. Frankly, this party looks like the kind of official studio event that the people who were really having fun would be sure to avoid. The announcer concludes, "Romy Schneider—a name you'll want to remember!" Well, I do remember her name, but I can't remember a single movie she made. Credits reveal that all this stuff came from an outfit called Hollywood Newsreel Syndicate. I wonder for a moment about starting The Interstitial Channel, which would consist entirely of these leftover odds and ends. Would I be the only viewer?

Today is October 1, and October is officially Breast Cancer Month. Anyone who gets a mammogram in 1999 will get a free T-shirt from Rosie O'Donnell that says, "Don't be a boob." The theme continues on *The View*, as the women on the show talk about breast cancer and the importance of mammograms. And, appropriately enough, Ricki Lake's theme today is "You Can't STOP Me from FLAUNTING My CHEST!" (That's THEIR capitals, not MINE.)

Once again, the *National Enquirer* show fails to provide any gossip that a diligent reader of *People* or *Us* wouldn't already know. The lead story is about actor-comedian Andy Dick, who's having trouble with substance abuse. "His career, his future, and his life are at stake." So what's new? This piece could have run at any time in the last few years. Next up: "If you're an autograph hound, you should know if your favorite star is a signer or a whiner!" Not for the first time, television seems like an infinite series of mirrors, reflecting celebrity as far as the eye can see. This seems true of *The View* as well—now that they've stopped talking about breast cancer, Meredith Vieira holds up the covers of *Maxim* and *Bikini,* and goes over the whole Melissa Joan Hart thing again. As usual, Star Jones boils it all down to a catchy aphorism: "If the check comes every week, and the contract says you have to be squeaky clean, I'd advise you to get the Lysol, girl!"

I flip to Ricki. All I can hear in the free-for-all are the repeated words "low self-esteem," and occasional booing. Over to Jerry Springer, whose guests are a dominatrix and her slaves. The crowd chants "Jerry! Jerry! Jerry!" There's a tinge of Nuremberg in the air. In the friendlier realm of *The Price Is Right,* a spiky-haired kid can quit with $2,500, or keep playing to win a car. He goes on, and within minutes Bob Barker is yelling, "He wins the car! He wins the car!" Today Bob is wearing a black turtleneck under a sport coat, instead of his usual natty suit and tie—is it casual Friday on *The Price Is Right?* He looks like Steve McQueen in *Bullitt: The Retirement Years.*

Meanwhile, PBS has a kids' show called *Noddy,* which comes originally from the UK. Noddy himself is an elf or gnome with a peaked blue cap, a red nose, and eyelashes like Liza Minnelli. The cheapo puppet animation reminds me of the surreal Sixties religious show *Davey and Goliath.* It seems someone has dubbed over the original British *Noddy* stories, and repackaged them with new American wraparound material, an approach that proved very successful with the UK hit *Thomas the Tank Engine.* I don't think lightning will strike twice, however. Compared with the smart and entertaining children's shows I've seen so far this week— *Zoboomafoo, Zoom,* even *Beast Wars*—the Americanized *Noddy* makes me noddy indeed.

There are two new women onstage with Ricki Lake, both in spaghetti-strap numbers, arguing that you don't have to be big-breasted to flaunt your chest. Once again, everyone is yelling and I can't make out a thing. According to the running onscreen titles, "Niquisha says she's 'flat and all that,' and she gets anything she wants." On *Springer*, a guy rages at his woman, who's been visiting a female prostitute. "I'm busting my butt for you," says the guy, "and you're spending my hard-earned money to sleep with her!" "Well, she's beautiful!" replies his gal. "It's not like I'm sleeping with other guys." I don't want to cast aspersions on the veracity of Mr. Springer and his team, but today's proceedings look distinctly staged, with dialogue right out of *All My Children*. This guy is almost too perfect in his role, and I have a feeling he'll turn up as an actor on some commercial or other before the end of the day.

I'm beginning to sink into the familiar slough of despair, and there's only one refuge. "I have always wanted to have a neighbor just like you," sings Mr. Rogers, and the world seems brighter already. Does Fred Rogers wear the same cardigan every day, or does he have a closet full of identical sweaters? Like Rosie O'Donnell and Sarah Michelle Gellar earlier in the week, he's holding a doll—of himself. "A friend by the name of Beth made this," says Mr. Rogers. "He has a sweater like mine. And look at the shoes. Very much like mine." He walks the doll across the floor, then starts it dancing to jazzy piano music. "But you know, when I don't make it do things, it doesn't do anything. It just sits there. Because it's a doll, not a live person." That'll be a relief for any children watching the adventures of Timmy on *Passions*—not to mention Noddy.

On Cartoon Network, there's an animated version of *The Addams Family*, which is leagues better than the new live-action version I saw on Fox Family Channel last Sunday. For one thing, it sounds as if John Astin did Gomez's voice. For another, animation works very naturally for this show, allowing a kind of tall-tale exaggeration into every scene. The kids string Gomez up by his feet, as a boa constrictor curls around a pillar. Then Gomez does a somersault onto Lurch's shoulders before leaping off to kiss Morticia's arm. "You know what it does to me when you speak French, or one of its knock-off languages. Say some more—Eiffel Tower! Soup du jour!"

Channel 5 News does its part to maintain the television hall of mirrors with a piece on celebrity stalkers. So that's what Jerry Lewis was doing on TV the other day—not stalking, but testifying against his young male stalker in Las Vegas. Who would stalk Jerry Lewis? Could it be Jim Carrey? Adam Sandler? Pauly Shore? Equally improbably, the reporter interviews a young woman who's been accused of stalking George Stephanopoulos. "I think there's been some prosecutorial, uh, misconduct," she says. "Do you love Stephanopoulos?" asks the reporter. Pause. "I have good feelings for him," she finally whispers. The reporter holds up Stephanopoulos's recent book, in which he mentions his problems with a stalker. "Tangela, are you the stalker in this book?" Of course she can't admit it, because her entire worldview would collapse if she did.

Next up is the *n*th report on Melissa Joan Hart. Oh, come on already! This seems like a lovely time to take a shower, so I do. When I emerge, I get a succession of phone calls. I could hustle them all off the phone, but instead I throw duty to the winds and chat away, while Melissa Joan Hart and Britney Spears interview each other on MTV.

I finally hang up on the last call at 12:50, in time to catch ten minutes of a show called *Reading Club* on Channel 13, in which a group of articulate African-American women talk about books. What book are they talking about today? It's a Terry McMillan–style novel about infidelity, but they never seem to mention the title or the author. Then a woman reads aloud from the book, and I see the author's name is Benilde Little, but I still don't know the title. Their conclusion: "A good read. A subway read." *Reading Club* has its own website: www.thereadingclub.com. I'm delighted to see this show, and especially to see it on Channel 13, which often feels even whiter than the original three networks. At the end of the credits, we get a full shot of the book's cover—the title is *The Itch.*

Thank you. Meanwhile, on Comedy Central's game show *Vs.*, the winning team is Hollywood Gossips. This should come as no surprise to anyone.

It's time for *All My Children*. For the first time, I recognize every scene and character on the "previously." I'm like someone who's smoked crack four times, and is beginning to admit that it might be habit-forming. Most of today's episode takes place at the glitzy society party the characters have been talking about all week. It's a convenient location for people to meet each other and exchange exposition, since Friday seems to be Recap Day. The first fifteen minutes of the show are almost completely devoted to telling the audience what they might have missed since the previous Friday. By the time we get to something that actually qualifies as action, it's time for the next commercial.

At the break, I take a look around. American Movie Classics is showing *A Tree Grows in Brooklyn*, which I've never seen—and, alas, I'm not going to start now. VH1 does a *Where Are They Now* on the stars of *Fast Times at Ridgemont High*, perhaps the best-cast movie of all time: Jennifer Jason Leigh, Sean Penn, Forest Whitaker, Eric Stoltz, Anthony Edwards, Nicolas Cage, Judge Reinhold, and Phoebe Cates, all of whom were unknown at the time. Unlike the casts of nearly every other teen movie of the Eighties, most of these folks don't need a *Where Are They Now*. Next, the cast of *Dirty Dancing*. This seems like another odd choice. For heaven's sake, I just saw Jennifer Grey on Tuesday! Twice!

Back to *All My Children*. By now I'm starting to understand the mechanism that makes soap operas tick. They're all about imperative—the motor in a story that makes you wonder what's going to happen next. The show is divided into five long scenes, which are intercut throughout the hour. Literally every mini-scene ends with a character delivering a line that promises fireworks to come. Then the show cuts to another group of characters, while we wait to see how Character B will react to Character A's bombshell, or to see whether Character A will actually drop the bombshell. It's a cunning adaptation of the "coming-up-next" principle. The trick is to break down each of the long scenes into mini-scenes with their own moments of portent, without dragging things out unduly.

For instance, one mini-scene on today's *All My Children* ends with the hapless Edmund coming home from the party, only to discover his nemesis (and sister-in-law) Alex sitting on the beach. He turns away, but then she says, "No, come back!" This doesn't promise too many fireworks-to-come, and in a movie or a play, we'd see what happens next without a break—but because this is a soap, we cut away. When we return, Edmund is about to open his mouth, but it turns out Alex isn't talking to him—or even to Maximilian the horse—but to the missing-and-presumed-dead Dmitri. To my delight, Alex delivers a whole soliloquy: "Oh, damn you, Dmitri, you liar! You bloody liar! You vowed we were bound together, for sickness and health, and you gave up on me! You had no right! I could have saved you, but I'll never know, because you broke your promise! I'll never know if you leaving me was fate, or God's way of putting me in my place. Who the hell did I think I was? Your savior? Or were you mine? If I wasn't put here to save you, I don't know why God put me here at all!" Alex concludes with a dramatic collapse and mucho tears. Susan Lucci will have competition at this year's Emmys.

Before I can even recover from Alex's big speech, Princess Gillian delivers another one at the society party. Jake offers Gillian a ride home, but she declines because "going home would mean giving up, and Dmitri would never give up." It seems Dmitri liked chocolates, driving on the wrong side of the Autobahn, hot-air ballooning, swimming in the moonlight, and staying up all night to watch the dawn break. "You know, Jake, somewhere the sun is coming up and maybe Dmitri is watching it. Or maybe he's dancing in the light of the moon." Or maybe he's waiting out his contract negotiations by the pool at the Beverly Wilshire.

After a climax that involves several couples entering into remarkably steamy clinches—in different rooms, of course—I bid farewell to *All My Children*. I lean back in my chair and shake my arms like a swimmer. Gotta keep going. Not too long now. Gotta keep going.

To my delight, today's installment of *Passions* begins with a visit to Tabitha the witch and Timmy the talking doll, who have been AWOL for the last few days. Timmy is shaking cocktails for Tabitha, who's still exultant about learning that Charity is in a coma; apparently, Charity has magical powers as well, although she doesn't know it. "It means we can stay in Harmony, stirring up trouble!" crows Tabitha, who has a gift for stating the obvious. "And if Tabitha's safe, Timmy's safe!" says Timmy, who speaks in the third person like Bob Dole or Elmo. "That's right, doll face," says Tabitha. "What happens," asks Timmy, "if Charity wakes up and remembers everything?" Tabitha nearly chokes on her cocktail at the thought of it.

Tabitha resolves to finish Charity off. She tells Timmy to stay at home, but we see him sneaking out the door behind her. Naturally, in true soap-opera fashion, we cross-cut to two other scenes before we cut back to Tabitha as she bikes to the hospital. To my astonishment, Timmy is running after her in slow motion, accompanied by—the music from *Chariots of Fire*. My jaw drops to the floor. I know Penny watches *One Life to Live*, but I must tell her what she's missing on NBC. Thirty years from now, people will look back on *Passions* as a camp classic to rival the supernatural soap of the Sixties, *Dark Shadows*.

"Escape to Red Lobster," says an ad for the restaurant of the same name. Who would think those four words could sound so seductive? Meanwhile, Montel Williams is talking to eighteen-year-old Matthew, whose father married his ex-girlfriend. That'll trigger your Oedipus complex, all right.

Back on *Passions*, Tabitha is now creeping around the hospital, hoping to inject Charity "with one of my potent potions." Then the old *Mission: Impossible* theme starts up, a door opens—and there's Timmy, looking both ways. I am not making this up. At this point, Cosmo wanders into the room and sits right in front of the sets. I try to get him to move, but he's the worst-trained dog in the world, which is entirely our fault. He begins to snore loudly, and I turn the sound up higher on *Passions* to compensate.

After more of the bitchy WASP couple—whose constant drinking and bickering resembles a bus-and-truck production of *Who's Afraid of Virginia Woolf?*—we return to the hospital. In the corridor, there emerges a tiny figure in a tiny green outfit. "Now nobody will recognize Timmy in these surgeon's scrubs!" says the undercover doll. Like someone was going to recognize him *without* them? This raises so many questions that my head spins. Why does Timmy need a disguise, anyway? Wouldn't the sight of a doll in scrubs be even stranger than the sight of a doll in overalls? And where did he find this outfit? Does the hospital have a midget surgeon? What were the writers thinking? Then, carried away with his disguise, Timmy starts talking into his stethoscope: "Paging Dr. Timmy! Paging Dr. Timmy! Stat!" At this moment, *Passions* crosses the line from absurdity to sheer insanity, and I miss the next few minutes because I am laughing so hard that my eyes are cloudy with tears. I only come to when the credits finally roll.

I have to admit that I've enjoyed watching four days of *Passions* much more than I ever thought I would. And let me be fair to the show—beyond the supernatural hoo-ha and the Drama 101 plotting, it shares with the other soaps something that no other genre on television does. All the daytime soap operas I've seen have a keen awareness of class in America. For all its silliness, *Passions* is especially thorough in delineating the class structure of the mythical town of Harmony, from the topmost reaches (the wealthy Crane family) to the comfortable middle (chief of police Sam Bennett and his hilariously perfect wife, Grace) to the struggling workers (the intriguingly biethnic Lopez-Fitzgerald family, whose matriarch, Pilar, is the Cranes' housekeeper), with numerous gradations in between. You won't find that on *Friends*, or even *ER*. The soaps don't preach about class warfare; they just treat the diversity of their towns as a given. It's a remarkable shortcut toward instant believability, considering how few series on TV recognize these basic facts. And you *need* instant believability when your show features a talking doll named Timmy.

It's 3:00 P.M., and if I'm ever gonna make lunch, now's my chance. Only Mr. Swanson knows what today's TV dinner is supposed to be, but it's vaguely edible, and so I vaguely eat it as I watch *The People's Court*. Today, Judge Jerry confronts the second case in two days involving birds. This one involves a finch-smuggling ring, which seems more serious than a simple small-claims suit—but for some reason, nobody has been prosecuted. Will that change once this show airs? Judge Jerry punches holes in the defendant's story, and looks as if he'd like to punch the defendant too. I can't help wondering whether some of these poor schmucks regret taking their cases to the People's Court. Whatever the U.S. justice system had in store for them, it couldn't have been this humiliating.

Worried that I'm too drawn in to the Sheindlin family, I switch to *Judge Joe Brown* on Channel 9. The show's introduction says that Judge Brown's journey has taken him "from the streets of South Central Los Angeles to the halls of justice." The case: Ronald and Robin were lovers. They shared a condo, he moved out, and now he wants his property back—but she has a restraining order against him. She says he's controlling and abusive, but Judge Joe Brown decides immediately that she's not to be trusted, with a high-handedness that belies his laconic manner. In fact, her story sounds plausible to me; is Judge Joe operating on some judicial sixth sense, or is he simply not listening? The verdict: Ronald gets his stuff back. The more courtroom shows I watch, the more I feel like a court reporter myself, taking down endless testimony that has little or nothing to do with my own life.

Meanwhile, Judge Joy—excuse me, *Dr.* Joy Browne—seeks guests for "Is Your Daughter's Boyfriend Forcing Her to Do Something?" How do the staffs on these shows come up with these topics? Do they already have a guest who fits the bill, or are they just picking ideas out of a hat and hoping somebody shows up who fits their dysfunction-of-the-day?

At the end of the hour, I check out the Comedy Central game show *Win Ben Stein's Money*. Ben Stein is yet another former Nixon staffer; as far as I can tell, everyone in the Nixon White House went either to jail or to television, or both. The premise of the show is that Ben puts up $5,000 of his own money, and competes directly against the contestants, who are eliminated one by one. In the end game, Ben and the remaining contestant sit in isolation booths, ready to answer ten questions in one minute flat. The contestants are usually nerdy guys, but Ben's opponent today is a woman who looks like a cross between Michelle Pfeiffer and Reagan speech-writer Peggy Noonan. Oddly enough, her name is Peggy. Peggy goes first. In what section of an orchestra would you find the clar-inet? What famous English poet wrote "On His Blindness" in 1652? By what nickname was aviator Douglas Corrigan known? Peggy gets six questions right but Ben gets nine, so he keeps his money, adding graciously that "I'm somewhat humbled because you're so much better looking than I am." As for me, I know all of them (woodwinds, Milton, "Wrong Way"), and I experience the same pang I get whenever I watch *Jeopardy!* My store of useless knowl-edge is often as annoying to me as it is helpful—I remember who wrote and directed every Marx Brothers movie, but I can't remem-ber which drawer in our kitchen contains the egg beater. But on a quiz show, my trivia head suddenly works for me the way Gheorghe Muresan's height works for him in a basketball game.

It's my last weekday, so I can't possibly pass up Martin Short. He starts out by evoking the ritual opening of *Saturday Night Live*: "Pre-taped from Hollywood for syndication to a wide array of mar-kets and time slots, it's *The Martin Short Show!*" Catherine O'Hara will be a guest today. "Catherine and I worked together on *SCTV*," says Marty. "I was just looking at one of the old cast pictures of Catherine and me, and what a gorgeous, voluptuous creature. And she looked pretty good too." He follows up with a Leon Spinks joke, which falls flatter than Spinks himself. "I tell you, if it were 1979, that joke would have killed," says Marty ruefully. Next comes a taped bit in which Marty's sidekicks walk the streets of L.A. with petitions, trying to get him off the air. As they say in soccer, this is an own goal, because many of the people on the street don't seem to know who Martin Short is. It was one thing when nobody knew Conan O'Brien—but Short's been around for a long time, and his syndicators at King World will probably be chagrined to learn that much of his potential audience has never heard of him.

At the commercial I glance around to see Japanese animation abounding: *Digimon* on 5, and *Sailor Moon* on 22. Meanwhile, there's auto racing on ESPN, as there has been for much of the day. My friend Louis always insists that Formula One racing is one of the two most popular sports in the world (the other is soccer, of course), and ESPN certainly acts as if this were true. On Channel 4, Judge Judy is giving some guy hell: "Common sense, sir, suggests your argument is crazy." The other person in the case speaks up, and Judge Judy silences him with a "HEY!" that probably even shuts up her husband.

Fortunately—because I'm starting to droop—Martin Short's guest is the edgy comedian Dennis Miller, whose intensity burns a hole right through the niceties of daytime TV. "These reality-based daytime talk shows suck like an airplane toilet," he cracks. "I watch the panels on these shows, and I think, oh, I get it, this is what the people I see being arrested on *Cops* do during the day." Even Short's typically moribund audience begins to show signs of life. Miller, who joined *Saturday Night Live* the year Marty left, has obviously become used to the comparative freedom of HBO, where he has his own show. He talks about trying to pry loose the lid on a jar, which was "harder to get off than Martha Stewart on a set of dirty sheets." Too late, Dennis realizes this line may not be appropriate for a syndicated talk show, but Marty reassures him with a straight face, "We're on at 10:00 A.M. in some markets. It'll be just fine."

Here's Catherine O'Hara, looking fab. Am I the only person

who saw her *tour de force* performance as a scrappy Irish mom in the obscure movie *Last of the High Kings*? O'Hara isn't plugging anything today, which is such a relief I can't tell you. "I came out of guest retirement just for you," she tells Marty, "and I'd like to go back there." In fact, she seems to be on the show for one reason only, which is to tease the host. She says that when they were guests on *Letterman* together, Marty told an anecdote about being backstage at a Richard Burton play, complete with an impression of the Welsh actor. Backstage, she said, "I never knew you met Richard Burton," and he said, "I didn't. I met Shirley MacLaine—but I don't *do* Shirley MacLaine." Catherine and Marty reminisce about *SCTV*, which he calls "the best work I ever did—the rest has just been coasting and faking and imitating it, riding the coattails of that short period." This is one of those jokes that isn't really a joke.

Now Marty interviews someone whose celebrity quotient is so low he may never show up on another talk show—filmmaker Lawrence Kasdan, whose movie *Mumford* opened last week. Short has a small role in it, which explains what Kasdan is doing here. I identify with him, as another physically awkward movie guy with a beard. Kasdan says it's hard to make interesting movies, because you sell them to the public through thirty-second TV spots, and "if you have drama about human beings, it's much harder to convey in thirty seconds." Marty quips that if they made *Citizen Kane* now, Rosebud would be his skateboard. The discussion takes off from there about the dumbing-down of America, and it's more involving than any installment of ABC's *Politically Incorrect*. Short and Kasdan take the view that producers in showbiz pander to the lowest common denominator, while Miller plays devil's advocate, tongue in cheek: "Dumb people deserve premium entertainment for themselves. What's wrong with that?" Watching Miller, O'Hara, Kasdan, and Short, I get the feeling they're actually having fun; it's like a dinner party that really jells. My old London employer, Channel Four, used to have a late-night talk show called *After Dark*, which went on at midnight and just kept going until there was nothing left to say, at which point the station shut down for the night. This is the first bunch of talk-show guests I've seen this week who would have made a good episode of *After Dark*.

Too soon for me, the show wraps up. O'Hara asks Miller and Kasdan, "In all the years you've known Marty, has he *ever* given you this much attention?" "No," they agree instantly. "It's so scary to have you actually listening to me!" she tells Marty. "Don't worry about it," he says, "I wasn't really listening." Like I said, too hip for the room; insincerity'll get you every time. But this is why I love him; he's a pure creature of show business, and he knows it.

There's another side of show business on MTV's *Fanatic*, which brings obsessed fans face-to-face with their idols. This seems like a recipe for lawsuits or worse. In the first segment, a young woman named Veronica gets to meet George Clooney. "You're like the CIA here!" says Clooney, who's astonished by how much she already knows about him. In come Clooney's co-stars in *Three Kings*, Mark Wahlberg and Ice Cube, to meet Veronica and plug the movie. Something tells me a junket is in progress. I had no idea *Fanatic* was part of the plug machine too, but why should this surprise me? "Do you really like George?" asks Wahlberg. Veronica looks at him as if he's a moron: "I *love* George, hello?" Veronica seems less like a stalker than like a nice young girl who's into Clooney the way so many nice young girls are. (Remember, his character on *ER* was both a ladykiller *and* a sensitive pediatrician.)

Cut to a commercial for the upcoming movie *Drive Me Crazy*, starring Melissa Joan Hart, which is why she posed for those magazine photos in the first place. The announcer concludes that the movie is "now playing, only in theaters!"—as opposed to playing in Laundromats or shoe stores. But then I realize that for children of the Information Age, a movie could be premiering on video, or on TV, or even on the Internet. The problem isn't with the language of the ad, it's with my old-fashioned thought patterns.

All the while during the last hour and change, Comedy Central has been playing a mediocre Charlie Sheen movie called *Three for the Road*. At this point, Charlie is carrying Kerri Green through a swamp. Sheen and Green first came to my attention in the charming film *Lucas*, which also starred Winona Ryder and Corey Haim. This strikes me as a perfect little microcosm of showbiz: Ryder went on to stardom, Sheen self-destructed (despite frequent comebacks), Green disappeared, and Corey Haim made a lot of schlocky movies with Corey Feldman before they both joined Green in obscurity. One out of four is actually pretty good as these things go, but whatever happened to the charming Kerri Green? And where are the Coreys? You'd think they'd have a sitcom on the WB by now.

The second half of *Fanatic* features Enrique Iglesias, son of Julio; and his young Latina fan, whose name I don't catch. Enrique says he feels safe with his fans, which is hard to believe when we see a film clip of hordes of screaming girls baying for his firstborn. "So what's the first thing you notice in a woman?" asks Enrique's fan. "I like her smile, I like a good smile," he says, smiling. "Can I see you smile?" This guy flirts on autopilot, with not only his words but his body language—the whole time, he's holding on to her chair and leaning forward. A bit flustered, she presses on: "Are you paranoid about anything?" "Being in the studio, and being unable to write," he answers. Does he mean being unable to write in the studio, or was that two separate paranoias? Naturally, *she* was paranoid about meeting him. Enrique gives her a big hug at the end of the interview, then sits her on his knee. I have a feeling he kept her there once the camera turned off.

Under the closing credits, the women are babbling and happy, and Enrique's girl is crying. After watching five and a half days of TV's obsession with celebrity, I completely understand their reactions. They've been granted a Golden Ticket to the other side of the wall, where everything is perfect and glamorous, and they haven't been there long enough to learn that it's a lot like their side of the wall. That's something you can't learn until you live there instead of just visiting. I learned it when I was twenty-four. I had just moved to Los Angeles to work for Columbia Pictures, and was seated at an awards luncheon next to a movie star whose work I admired. He turned out to be friendly and talkative, and after an hour I felt the way the women on *Fanatic* are feeling right now, juiced from personal contact with a real, live celebrity. But two days later the actor dropped in at my office uninvited, and proceeded to make himself comfortable—using the phone and the copier, smoking a cigar, showing me a doctoral dissertation someone had written on one of his movies, and so on until I very politely threw him out. He wasn't a demigod after all, just a handsome surfer dude looking for an entourage.

Next up on MTV is *The Blame Game*, "the only show where real-life exes go head to head to win a vacation," which seems to exist in a genre netherworld between courtroom show, game show, and sexually explicit talk show. The set is a wacky version of a courtroom, but Judge Reed's robe is trimmed with leopard skin. The crowd is whipped into a frenzy from the very start. Today's real-life exes are both circus people; Crystal is a fire-eater with a pierced nose, and Zippo is a clown in full makeup. Only scant hours after the sight of Dr. Timmy, I reel from the surreality of it all.

Crystal and Zippo are each assigned a "lawyer" of the same sex, who start the game by asking their "clients" how they got together. We learn that they went to Vegas platonically, then stopped off at a monkey ranch. "It warmed my heart to see him play with the monkeys," says Crystal. "When did you finally make hot monkey love?" Zippo's lawyer asks him. "We did this show called 'Bird of Prey,'" says Zippo in a cranked-up obnoxious clown voice, "and then we went into the bedroom, and I was the bird and she was the prey." Crystal tells her lawyer that Zippo's constant clowning was cute at first, but that's all he knows how to do. Frankly, he's driving me crazy already; I don't know how she could take it for a night, let alone a relationship.

We cut to an ad for the *SNL* spinoff movie *Superstar*. It opens next Friday, but they're pushing it more heavily than many movies opening today. After the number of disastrous movies based on *SNL* characters, this could be make-or-break for Lorne Michaels's deal at Paramount.

When we get back, Judge Reed puts on a red nose and giant polka-dotted bow tie as he sets the stage: "It's the case of the fire-eating maneater and the buzzkill clown. This is the 'You Did It, Now Admit It' round. Whoever gets the most points gets to present a surprise witness." In this round, Crystal and Zippo dare each other to admit their embarrassing secrets, but these two will obviously admit anything. He admits he sleeps with a clown blanket. "He's twenty-eight!" snorts Crystal. She admits that she runs around the house naked listening to P. J. Harvey songs. "That's the first normal thing we've heard," says Judge Reed. He admits he's lazy about cleaning up after his puppy. She admits that she sometimes goes to the market dressed "as a cute little girl with pigtails." It's a tie, because they both admit everything, so they each get witnesses. Crystal's friend Daisy is a clown too—but unlike Zippo, she screams, "I know when to turn it off!" Zippo's clown buddy Zonkers can't understand why Crystal is so upset: "You gotta relax! He's a clown!" Then he throws a rubber chicken at her. Zonkers is as annoying as Zippo; Crystal seems relatively sane by comparison. Judge Reed announces that the audience was shown pictures of Crystal and Zippo before the "trial" even began, and based on looks, they found for her, fifty-nine percent to forty-one percent. What a novel concept! Think of how much time this would save for the few remaining lawsuits that haven't agreed to settle on *The People's Court*!

We go to another commercial, but I can't concentrate. I'm in one of those valleys. I stare at the screens, and the information washes over me like waves on a rock. And like the rock, I feel myself being worn away.

Back on *The Blame Game*, Judge Reed dons a multicolored Afro wig. He's now in full clown ensemble as he instructs the "jury"—the audience—to press button 1 if they think Crystal is to blame for the breakup, 2 if it's Zippo. The one who is found innocent gets a trip for two to Puerto Vallarta. Unsurprisingly, sixty-five percent say Zippo is to blame. Zippo now has fifteen seconds to apologize. He drops the annoying clown voice for the first time, and gets on bended knee to plead his case—but he's unaccustomed to sincerity, and mostly he just sputters. To wrap up, Judge Reed tells us to tune in next week, then hits himself in the face with a cream pie. As final proof of my complete mental and emotional deterioration, I begin to laugh uncontrollably.

American Movie Classics rolls the opening credits for *You're Never Too Young*, which is a Martin and Lewis remake of Billy Wilder's *The Major and the Minor*. If I'm feeling susceptible enough that a pie-in-the-face gag has me gasping for breath, I don't want to see what'll happen if I'm exposed to two hours of Jerry Lewis. Instead, I take Cosmo for a long walk.

I'm back at 6:30. To reward him for his in-depth Korean War piece last night, I watch Dan Rather and CBS. Rather's lead story is the former nuclear accident in Japan, which is all clear: "The radiation health risk is likely to be mild, outside the immediate area of the plant." This bureaucratic smooth talk makes me nervous; I can't help thinking of Don DeLillo's novel *White Noise*, in which the characters are preparing for a mysterious disaster known as "the Airborne Toxic Event." Next up is the Mexican earthquake. The death toll is at twenty, which would sound like a lot if we hadn't just had much bigger quakes in Taiwan and Turkey.

Looking around, I see Jennifer Lopez singing in a swimming pool on MTV. That goddam "I'm better than you are" car commercial. Fran Drescher plays slot machines in Atlantic City on *The Nanny*. Jerry Lewis dances in *You're Never Too Young*, while Jim Carrey makes Jerry-like faces on an *SNL* rerun on Comedy Central. Despite their similarities, you can see the sheer aggression that's a big part of Carrey's persona. He mugs like Jerry, but leads with his chin like Bob Hope. This makes me think of Dave Thomas's peerless Bob Hope impression on *SCTV,* and I long for a reunion all over again.

When Rather comes back on, I stare at the rest of the news like a zombie. My note-taking fingers have slowed to a crawl, like my mind. They say at the bottom of every human brain is the lizard brain that controls automatic reactions, and it feels as if that's what I'm reduced to now. I'm Jacosaurus—bite my big toe, and I'll say ouch in a few minutes.

The end of the CBS news segues to *Entertainment Tonight,* and the urgent headline "How Delta Burke Lost 60 Pounds!" I can't watch another celebrity fluff job. Out of sheer self-preservation, I switch to the TV-news satire *The Daily Show* on Comedy Central. I need a hit of intelligence. The camera zooms in toward host Jon Stewart, and an announcer declares that the show is "the most important television program—ever." I feel better already. The lead story is that Al Gore has moved his headquarters to Nashville, "to capture the up-for-grabs pedal-steel-guitarist vote." The problem is that "Gore is seen as possessing less of the common touch than such figures as Bill Clinton, Ronald Reagan, or the decaying body of the late Nelson Rockefeller." A bit on media responsibility features correspondent Vance DeGeneres—I think he's Ellen's brother—talking straight-facedly about how the media keeps sinking to new lows. "I have a clip," says DeGeneres, "but I must warn you, it involves shocking sensationalism that should not be shown—except as an example of what not to show." Of course, they show it twice. Then a story on Amazon.com's expansion. Says Jon Stewart, "Analysts say the move is a milestone in the history of E-business and, along with eBay, will cause a boom in E-commerce for such E-purchases as the collected works of E-e.e. cummings." Okay, I know Jon Stewart—he had a deal at Miramax when I worked there—but this stuff is funny by any standards, *and they do it four days a week.* Sam had a beloved English professor in college named Dale Harris, who died a few years ago, and she often quotes something he used to say: "If my standards are high, it is because they are available to everyone." By the same token, if other TV comedy shows aren't as funny as *The Daily Show*, it's not just because Jon Stewart is talented—it's because most of the competition is downright lazy.

Next, Jon interviews Bruce McCullough of The Kids in the Hall, who directed the ubiquitous *Superstar*. He's actually doing a double plug, having also directed a movie called *Dog Park*, which opened last week—and closed this week. Just as they begin to talk, I hear a screech of brakes and a crash. I run to the window, and see that a car has just hit a bicyclist at the corner of 110th and Amsterdam. The cyclist is on the ground—not dead, but not getting up, either. Traffic slams to a halt. I call 911. It turns out someone with faster reflexes has already called, and moments after I hang up, a cop is on the scene. Fortunately, we live four blocks from a hospital, and the paramedics show up only a minute later. If any of my neighbors have video cameras, they could probably send the whole thing to Fox for *World's Most Dangerous Bicycle Crashes*.

I sit back down and watch the end of *The Daily Show*, a bit shaken. Meanwhile, on American Movie Classics, Jerry Lewis sings in a tuxedo. It's a quick flash of the Jerry to come—telethon Jerry, pinky-ring Jerry, "Buddy Love" Jerry. The Final Jeopardy answer is James Herriot. The champion keeps going, with $45,200 to date. Clearly he bets intelligently, unlike certain past winners.

At 7:30, I unmute Cartoon Network and watch the original series *Dexter's Laboratory*. It's about a boy genius named Dexter, whose brilliant inventions are always foiled by his airhead sister Deedee. In some kind of loopy tribute to *Rocky and Bullwinkle*, Dexter has Sherman's glasses and hair, Mr. Peabody's height, and—most incongruously—Boris Badenov's accent. The show is fast and frenetic and not nearly as enjoyable as the ancient Bugs Bunny cartoons that make up much of Cartoon Network's programming.

Before I know it, it's 8:00 P.M. I am now officially a shell of myself. On MTV the *SNL* marathon has begun, hosted by *Superstar* stars Molly Shannon and Will Ferrell. It feels as if this entire week has been an *SNL* marathon, so deeply has the show permeated TV culture.

This may be the only time all week when two out of the three original networks feature minority performers: Bill Cosby in *Kids Say the Darnedest Things* on CBS, and D. L. Hughley in his sitcom *The Hughleys* on ABC. If you throw in Fox, UPN, and the WB, the number is three out of six. While I'm mildly curious about the paler drama *Providence* on NBC, I decide to go with the flow and watch *The Jamie Foxx Show* on the WB. I realize that I have no idea whether Jamie Foxx is related to the late Redd Foxx, because Jamie doesn't get covered in the media I read. How can this country remain so segregated, forty-five years after *Brown* vs. *Board of Education*?

The show is set in a hotel, where Foxx's character works. When he enters the lobby, the audience goes wild, the way they used to when Jack Benny would open his show. In this episode, Jamie's girlfriend Fancy wants to spend the evening with him, while he wants to play poker with his pals. The problem is that Fancy is played by a stunning actress named Garcelle Beauvais, and any heterosexual man who wouldn't rather be with her than play poker is a compulsive gambler, or else just plain nuts. I don't think either choice is what the writers of *The Jamie Foxx Show* had in mind.

Elsewhere on the sets, there's *Kids Say the Darnedest Things*, which my grandmother and her attendant Devorah Scott are watching right now—they're devoted to the show. Cosby and a cute little girl are making funny noises at each other, and if I had started the half hour with this, I'd be a happier man. On Fox, we see actual video of an exploding building, on yet another reality show, *Terror on the Job.* (Is this Mean Building Syndrome?) *The Hughleys* is about black folks in the suburbs, and it's not especially funny, even compared to the uneven Foxx show.

At 8:30 comes the unkillable *Candid Camera.* This show has been around forever—in fact, it started out on radio as *Candid*

Microphone. I remember enjoying it as a kid, but tonight's pranks fall flat, and the format seems not to have changed in decades. We don't even get close-ups of hosts Peter Funt and Suzanne Somers; are the cameras nailed in place? Peter Funt is the son of the show's creator, the late Allen Funt. He reminds me of another famous man's son, Christopher Tolkien, who writes interminable spinoffs of *Lord of the Rings* that never approximate the original trilogy's power. Like Christopher Tolkien, Peter Funt seems like the grim inheritor of a dated legacy with which he's determined not to tamper—but a little tampering might be healthier all around. Midway through the ordeal, Sam arrives with Chinese dinner, and I catch her up on the day's events. When I get to the adventures of Dr. Timmy on *Passions*, she's convinced I'm putting her on.

Nine P.M. brings *Sabrina the Teenage Witch* on ABC, which I consider watching as a logical conclusion to days of Melissa Joan Hart media mania. But I can't resist the new CBS series *Now and Again*, not to be confused with *Once and Again.* This is the second episode; in the pilot, a middle-aged man died in an accident, but his brain was placed in a young bionic body by a secret government agency. As they say in Hollywood—and they probably did—it's the old Rock Hudson movie *Seconds* meets *La Femme Nikita* meets *The Six Million Dollar Man.*

Am I crazy, or does this show have a CBS look? I don't think it's just the little eye logo superimposed in the corner of the screen; it's something about the grain of the image. *Chicago Hope* has it too. I know radio stations adjust their compression to give themselves a unique sound—is there such a thing as visual compression?

As the show begins, our hero, Michael Wiseman, escapes from his government handlers and runs through the streets of New York to his old office building, but they won't let him in. Instead, he does the logical thing—he takes off his shoes and climbs up the side of the building. Many stories up, he breaks a window and drops in on his pal Roger. Roger is terrified of him, and Michael doesn't do a very good job of keeping him from being terrified. "Who are you?" asks Roger. "I can't tell you that," replies Michael. "Why?" "Because." "Because why?" "Because when they know what you know, you die." Well, it seems like a question of degrees to me, since Roger probably already knows enough to lose a few vital organs. Michael keeps grabbing Roger and hurting him inadvertently, which should be funny but isn't. Under duress, Roger takes Michael to his old house, so he can watch his wife and kid doing the dishes through the kitchen window. Michael's wife, Lisa, is in debt, and I can see where the show is headed; as in the old musical *Damn Yankees*, I bet Michael will move in as a boarder to be near his family, and his rent will allay their money problems. Or something like that.

At the thirty-minute commercial break, I turn to Markie Post's sitcom *Odd Man Out*, listen to two minutes, then mute it again. Fox has yet another reality show, *World's Most Shocking Moments Caught on Tape.* "We love to watch others push the envelope," says the host breathlessly, "because we know there's always a chance the envelope might push back." We see a competitive motorcyclist losing control of his bike, which tumbles into the crowd. It hits five people and injures one. Then four vintage planes fly in formation in an air show, and two collide, which sends all four "to the ground in a fiery mess." Sorry, but this is one envelope I really don't want to see pushing back. Fox's cynical pandering reminds me of an old David Letterman sketch about new narrowcast cable channels, which proposed the Ninth Grade Boys' Channel: twenty-four hours of cars, trucks, trains, and planes crashing and sailing off cliffs.

Back on *Now and Again*, Michael and Lisa do indeed meet up. She's scared of him, since he's covered in scratches and bruises and his clothes are now rags—but then she buys him a pair of shoes at some Kmart-type place that is theoretically near Grand Central Station. Her rationale is that her husband is dead, her first date as a widow went badly, and she accepts that nothing happens the way you planned. Fair enough, but it's still unlikely she'd buy shoes for a scary young homeless guy who's bleeding. Then Michael is grabbed by government agents, so they can sic him on the trail of a mass-murdering psycho. I'm surprised this show isn't wittier or more original, considering that it's created by Glenn Gordon Caron, the guy behind my Eighties fave *Moonlighting*. But TV critics are eating it up; maybe it's one of those shows with a killer pilot, and a lame second episode?

Ten P.M. brings a show that Sam and I have been wanting to watch for weeks: *Iron Chef*. It's a Japanese show that first developed a U.S. cult following when it ran without subtitles on foreign-language cable channels. Somebody smart at Food Network picked up on this, and repackaged the show for America. It begins with an elaborate legend about an obsessive chef who built the world's first kitchen stadium, from which this event is broadcast. It seems there are four Iron Chefs: Japanese, French, Chinese, and Italian. "If ever a challenger defeats the Iron Chef," declares the unseen announcer, "he wins the people's ovation and fame forever." This must be a word-for-word translation from the original Japanese. "It's the way this is shot that's a riot," says Sam. She's right. *Iron Chef* is all heroic low angles, big music, and dramatic lighting, more Leni Riefenstahl than Emeril Lagasse. The participants don't seem to think this is funny, but it sure is for Sam and me—it's the kind of hilarious and hypnotic disconnect you only get in the cultural overlap between Japan and the U.S.

Tonight's challenge is in the Japanese arena. The Iron Chef won't cook tonight; he's designated his assistant, who is kitted out in full absurd regalia, complete with a multicolored, sparkly ruff. "He's like the Liberace of Japanese food," cracks Sam. Today's theme ingredient is sweetfish, similar to trout. The rules are less restrictive than on *Ready Set Cook*; as long as the chefs use sweetfish, they can do whatever they want. Their muttered comments are subtitled, occasionally. The host is joined by two Japanese celebrities, who comment on the action as it occurs in the stadium. At first I think they're speaking English, but then I realize they're dubbed. We've got dubbing, subtitling, and narration, all in the same show.

At the commercial break, Sam massages my note-taking

hands, which feel like limp sweetfish fillets by now. On Channel 9 news, we see a protest and counter-protest outside the Brooklyn Museum. One poster features a picture of Giuliani with dung on his head. Then there's the familiar Chris Ofili picture, shown as an example of what not to show.

I check out MTV's venerable franchise *The Real World* at 10:30, while keeping track of the increasingly frantic food preparation on *Iron Chef*. *The Real World* rounds up a bunch of strangers and plunks them into a house together, while videotaping their every waking moment. The show has been so successful for MTV that imitators and variations have sprung up in other countries, and now some of those more extreme formats are on their way back to the U.S. (The variation from Holland is called, appropriately, *Big Brother*. The show has an Internet site that allows you to watch whatever the stars/lab rats are doing at any moment.) It all goes back to Marshall McLuhan's notion of mass media turning the world into a global village. McLuhan was right about that, but the catch is that our own actual villages are fragmenting at the same rate that the global village is coalescing. One feeds the other; you may not know your next-door neighbors, but the folks on *The Real World* are everybody's neighbors. As Penny said about the soap characters, you can gossip about them without hurting anybody—because their secrets have already been revealed to millions of viewers.

This season's house is in Hawaii, although tonight's episode follows the mediagenic roommates on their vacation in India. The Hawaii shows have attracted more media attention than usual, not only because several of the roommates take off their clothes a lot (with tasteful digital fuzzing), but also because one of them is a mixed-race bisexual alcoholic named Ruthie whose drinking problem got her kicked out of the house. Tonight Ruthie isn't even mentioned, which is a shame. In an episode I saw a few weeks ago, she was the focus of everything, and it was far more dramatic. Without her, we're watching a bunch of whiners standing in the way of beautiful Indian scenery. "It's all just turning into one big puff mush in my brain," says the neurotic Amaya, and I completely agree with her.

Back on *Iron Chef*, the host is excited: "On the challenger's side, they're in disarray!" But the substitute Iron Chef can't savor his imminent victory: "I'm exhausted," he says. "Once is enough. I prefer being an assistant." The food looks sensational, though. The judges discuss each dish in turn, and their verdict is that the substitute upholds the honor of the Iron Chef, denying the challenger the people's ovation and fame forever.

Before I walk the dog, I check out tonight's *Blind Date*. It couldn't be more different from last night; this couple hits it off instantly, and seems to develop a promising romantic connection. It's still pleasant, but the dates are clearly a lot more fun when they don't go well, like last night's; or when one of the daters is what novelist Martin Amis would call "an obvious goer," like last night's gal.

I take Cosmo for a trot on the street. "One more day," I keep telling him, "one more day." As usual, he's more interested in other dogs' markings than in my existential crisis.

Back in the apartment, I place Cosmo on the bed at Sam's sleeping feet, and return to the sets for the 11:30 talk shows. Edmund Morris is on *Charlie Rose*. I figure this out before I turn up the sound, not because I recognize Morris but because once again I think it's Steven Spielberg, and I know Spielberg doesn't have anything to plug right now.

HBO has *The Chris Rock Show*. The moment Chris Rock takes the stage, you know he's something different. It's not because he's young, or even because he's black; it's because he's *focused*. Journalists always compare Rock to Richard Pryor, but he reminds me more of Lenny Bruce in his combativeness, and in his willingness to go where others fear to tread. He starts right in on Chris Ofili's dung-encrusted Madonna: "What's the big deal? I mean, every statue in New York is covered with pigeon shit!" Apparently, *Hustler* magazine is opening a casino in Atlantic City. "Not to be outdone, *Black Tail* magazine is opening a three-card monte stand on 125th Street."

After the traditional five-minute delay, Letterman and Leno join Rock in the late-night talk-show brigade. Dave's monologue, like Jay's, rests upon the unspoken assumption that every celebrity can be defined by one or two traits. For instance, Bill Clinton = gluttonous hornball; Hillary Clinton = self-righteous shrew; Al Gore = wooden dullard. Dave's riff tonight is typical. In New York this week, Gore "went into the new wax museum in Times Square, and they wouldn't let him out." He continues, "This year, the goal for Gore is to be less stiff. And, gee, that should have been Clinton's goal." There's applause, but even Letterman seems embarrassed by this joke, adding, "And let me remind you, this is award-winning comedy."

Meanwhile, Jay Leno says that NBC has canceled *Mike O'Malley* after two episodes: "They're going to replace it with *The Best of the Mike O'Malley Show.*" My only question is, what took them so long?

Chris Rock hosts the Reverend Al Sharpton, who is trying hard to change the traits people use to define him—from "rabble-rousing street hustler" to "dedicated community activist." I can't say I'm a fan of the blustery reverend, but he's certainly a better talk-show guest than, for instance, Brooke Shields. "Now, Giuliani's crazy," says Rock, to enthusiastic whoops from the audience. Chris settles them down; this isn't *Ricki Lake.* He asks Sharpton if Giuliani's craziness helps Giuliani's opponents in the end. It does, Sharpton says. Shutting down a museum over a painting "makes as much sense as me calling to shut down HBO because one guy cusses too much on Friday night." "It don't even look like Mary!" says Rock. "It looks like Moesha!" Adds Sharpton about Giuliani, *"We* wouldn't have known it was elephant dung, but he knows a lot more about dung than we do."

And on it goes, while Letterman reads a weak Top Ten List of "university classes taught by Oprah Winfrey," and Leno plays a game with the audience called "Idiots for a Day." Frankly, Chris makes both Dave and Jay look toothless. I know this is exactly the kind of comparison that drives the networks crazy. After all, how can you compare HBO shows, with their freedom of language and subject matter, to network shows? However, I notice the networks stopped complaining after *The Practice* beat *The Sopranos* at this year's Emmys. An unfair contest is a contest you lose. If you win— well, then it must have been fair, at least until next year's contest.

As *The Chris Rock Show* nears its end, the music show *Sessions at West 54th* begins on Channel 13. The show was hosted last season by David Byrne; this season it's rocker John Hiatt, a cult figure whose cult includes me. Hiatt is wearing a sharp suit, but looks stiffer than Al Gore's reputation. He introduces tonight's guest, Ruben Blades, by reading haltingly off the TelePrompTer with a deer-caught-in-the-headlights expression. Despite my love for Hiatt's music, I can't help wondering how he got this gig. Then Blades plays his first number, an instrumental, with a huge multi-cultural ensemble. It's pretty on top, with polyrhythms beneath, and I just listen for a while, happy to respond to something that defies analysis.

Jay Leno, of all people, yanks me out of my musical reverie by bringing out the adorable Keri Russell. She wears a red halter over black pants, and she's cut her hair stylishly short. Jay has dug up an old clip of Keri from her days in *The Mickey Mouse Club*. "Oh, you are such a jerk!" she admonishes him. They roll the clip, and it's true— he really is a jerk to show this. Keri is awful, mugging all over the place. "I think I was like fifteen years old," says Keri, covering her face with her hands. As she sits in the chair, she keeps kicking up her legs like the quads last night, which reminds me just how young she still is. For a moment I feel like Humbert Humbert.

Politically Incorrect has another insanely eclectic panel: actress Jeri Ryan, who plays the alien Seven of Nine on *Star Trek: Voyager*; Niger Innis of CORE; comedian Adam Carolla, host of MTV's

Loveline and Comedy Central's *The Man Show*; and violin prodigy Joshua Bell, who was on *Martin Short* yesterday. Coincidentally, Jeri's show is on Channel 9 at the same time. Adam's show is *supposed* to be on MTV, according to *TV Guide*, but they're showing a marathon of the *Beavis & Butt-head* spinoff *Daria* instead. Bill Maher kicks things off by bringing up the Edmund Morris book, saying that people who think Reagan is a saint had better think again. Just to pick a fight—I don't think they actually like Reagan—Niger and Adam line up against Jeri, a staunch liberal, and Bill, who's truly iconoclastic but hates Ronald Reagan. Everybody talks at once except Joshua, the kid at the grownups' table. Meanwhile, on *Queen Latifah*—yup, it's Melissa Joan Hart.

I have officially hit the wall. If I were a more dedicated individual, I would stay up late, then watch cartoons tomorrow morning with little or no sleep. But because I am a dedicated individual in a different way, I decide to get some sleep and keep a tiny portion of my brain intact for tomorrow's grand finale. I turn off the sets, and the resulting quiet seems like a promise. ♉

Pokémon—The Untold Story

I wake up just before 8:00 A.M., with a mixture of excitement and dread. The good news is, I only have to do this for one more day. The bad news is, I have to do this for one more day.

I turn on the sets for the last time, and I hear the now-familiar cacophony of electronic Babel-babble before I mute them all. When I was a kid, Saturday-morning TV was a wonderland of cartoons, and I knew the ins and outs of every show. Cartoons are still plentiful in 1999, but now there are channels that don't seem to know it's Saturday morning. In a twenty-four-hour universe, things aren't as time-specific as they used to be. *Oprah* is a daytime show, but I saw it again late Thursday night. Comedy Central plays reruns of *Saturday Night Live* constantly, whether late at night or early in the morning. Then there are channels that do only one thing, and they do it around the clock. Cartoon Network does cartoons, The Weather Channel does weather, the news channels do news, and the sports channels do sports, regardless of time of day or day of week.

On this particular Saturday morning, PBS is showing *Wall Street Week,* whose strict talking-heads format would send any kid running to the bright cartoon world. Meanwhile, NBC has a Saturday edition of *Today,* with another good long look at the Chris Ofili picture. Chris Rock was right—it *does* look like Moesha.

The commercials, however, are the same old mix of cereal and toy ads I remember from my youth, like an ad for Nesquik cereal featuring the inevitable animated bunny. "Sugar and chocolate!" says Sam, who has woken to the sound. "What a great way to start the day!" I think she's joking.

I've invited our friend Suzanne and her four-year-old son Nicky to join me this morning. On Suzanne's suggestion, I promised to pay Nicky one dollar for his consulting services, a sum that Suzanne says is only slightly less than one million dollars to him. I'm hoping Nicky will explain the mysteries of *Pokémon* to me, and I'm curious to see Saturday morning in 1999 through his eyes. Will it look to him the way Saturday morning in 1967 looked to me? This makes me realize that I was Nicky's age when Sopkin did his TV-watching stint. I look up the Saturday-morning section of *Seven Glorious Days, Seven Fun-Filled Nights,* and notice that for the most part Sopkin skipped past the cartoons to grab on to any adult programming he could find, including televised shorthand lessons. Of course, Sopkin didn't have any childhood associations with Saturday-morning cartoons, because when *he* was four years old, it was 1936. These sudden mental shifts make my head ache.

To prepare myself for Nicky's arrival, I start watching cartoons. On CBS are the *Rescue Heroes,* who all have names like Rocky

Canyon and Wendy Waters. The WB has Batman and Superman, in niftily animated new adventures that beat anything I remember from my superhero-besotted youth. ABC counter-programs for girls with *Pepper Ann*, a gentle and fairly realistic show about a contemporary kid. On Fox Kids, I'm expecting more adventures of Shirley Holmes, whom I last saw on Sunday—*The New York Times*'s TV grid just said "S. Holmes"—but it turns out to be an animated Sherlock and Watson in "The Hound of the Baskervilles." This show is faithful to the original story, but with one tiny, insignificant change: it takes place on another planet. Holmes uses his spaceship's computer to track any satellites in the area, before donning a space suit and venturing onto the planet's surface. This hound doesn't leave huge footprints, because it's not a dog but some sort of alien hologram. This all reminds me of one of my least happy experiences in the film industry, when I was ordered to develop a version of *Cyrano de Bergerac* in which the hero didn't have a big nose.

At 8:30 comes a brilliant programming maneuver by ABC. Instead of just running shows on the half hour with animated interstitials in between, like every other network in the Saturday-morning kid business, ABC has turned its kid-vid schedule into one big show, *Disney's One Saturday Morning*. The idea is that once you're in the Disney/ABC universe, you'll be out of synch with the rigid time schedules of the competition and just stay in the Disney flow. Viewers are invited to log on to Disney1.com as well, and swirling onscreen are the user names of some of the kids who did. The show takes place amid a bizarre conflation of three-dimensional studio sets, computer-generated imagery, a live elephant, and God knows how many extras. The overall effect is overstimulation, which makes me feel right at home. Our host is a lively African-American girl who goes unnamed. "Today is Saturday," she says cheerily, "and that means you don't have to do anything. Well, that's not true. You do have to breathe." Then we go to the first segment, *Centreville*, which features a jagged cut-out animation style that was reserved for avant-garde filmmakers only a few years ago. The segment takes place on a school bus, and the kids are still photographs whose mouths move. After every joke, the driver repeats ritualistically, "In your seats! In your seats!" It's positively surreal. I wonder if Philip Glass and Robert Wilson have seen this show?

Nicky and Suzanne arrive at 8:35. Suzanne joins Sam, who is reading the newspaper in the dining room, while Nicky's eyes grow wide at the sight of all the TVs. I ask him if he's ever seen this many in one place. "Only on a commercial," he replies. I tell him I'm trying to watch a little bit of everything, but I can't watch everything at the same time. Nicky nods sagely. "You'd have to move your head that way and that way, back and forth and back and forth," he says. He takes a look around, then quickly gravitates to "the one I really like," which is *Pokémon* on Channel 11. I was hoping he would say that.

The heroes of *Pokémon* are a young boy named Ash and his two friends. "They're Pokémon trainers," says Nicky. "I'm already a Pokémon master." The three kids are on a Pokémon-hunting safari with an an expert on Pokémon named Dr. Westwood, and the show's mascot, a yellow, angular, happy-faced thing named Pikachu. Nicky tells me the names of all the *Pokémon* characters, not that I can possibly follow them. He knows a lot—he really is a Pokémon master. Apparently, each Pokémon has many aspects, like stats on a baseball card, the most important of which is its fighting ability. The dual objectives for Ash and his real-life devotees are to further their anthropological understanding of Pokémon (which is its own plural), and to train them to fight each other, nonlethally. It's as if Jane Goodall turned her chimpanzees loose on Dian Fossey's gorillas.

The bad guys, siblings Jesse and James, are called Team Rocket. They have a pet Pokémon, Meowse, who states their aim: "We want to steal all the Pokémon we can get our hands on!" Team Rocket attacks Ash and friends to steal their latest discovery, and in the middle of the fight two Pokémon merge into a new species. Dr. Westwood takes continuous notes "to present to the symposium,"

CAN'T TAKE MY EYES OFF OF YOU

and after the fight he gives a mini-lecture on the new Pokémon. Can Nicky really be following this? I'd be hard-pressed to make any sense of it even if I were operating at full mental capacity, which I certainly am not. But he seems to be completely up to date on the evolutionary diversity of all 150 species, and sings along with every word of the closing theme song. As childhood crazes go, this seems benign. Will there be a boom in college anthropology classes in ten years?

Next up is *Batman Beyond,* a series I've actually watched a few times on my own. Here's the ingenious premise: In the future, Gotham City is terrorized by a clown-faced motorcycle gang called the Jokerz, while a teenage boy named Terry is trained as the new Batman by the elderly Bruce Wayne. The animation is stylized and kinetic—it's rave TV. Nicky is a fan of this show too. In this episode, the Jokerz steal an experimental flying police cruiser and take it on a destructive joyride through the *Blade Runner*–ish city. Batman/Terry teams up with the woman who designed the vehicle, and fights the Jokerz, kung-fu style. "Ooh—that's gotta hurt for that guy," says Nicky as Batman flips a bad guy across the room. Nicky reacts to each punch, making all the sound effects that would have run onscreen in the old *Batman* show: "Ooh! Aah!" What's both refreshing and worrisome is that *Batman Beyond* is pitched entirely at the level of a smart postmodern action movie like *The Matrix* or *Speed* (and Terry looks a lot like Keanu Reeves, to boot). There's no moral, no message, just a lot of really cool action.

The commercials arrive. Cosmo sits in the big chair with Nicky, and promptly falls asleep on his lap. Nicky points to an ad for the Hot Wheels Tune-Up Shop. "I know how much that is," he says. "How much?" I ask. "Five hundred dollars," he replies with a straight face—then he laughs. "Actually, I think it's eight bucks," he admits. Meanwhile, the once-as-popular-as-*Pokémon* Power Rangers continue their slow fall to oblivion on Fox, fighting a squad of sorry-looking ninjas. "I hate those guys," says Nicky. "Who, the Power Rangers?" I ask. "No," he says, "the guys fighting the Power

Rangers. Yeah, they're bad." If Nicky can be bothered to hate the Power Rangers' enemies, maybe there's life in the old franchise yet.

It's 9:30, and I point to *Rugrats* on Nickelodeon. "That's a really good show," I say. "I know," says Nicky, "but I saw it 160, 150 times." Well, I've only seen it once, so I'm in no position to argue. He also passes up a show called *Xyber 9: New Dawn* on Fox Kids (even the name is tiring), a cartoon version of the movie *Beetlejuice* on Cartoon Network, and a show called *Recess* on *One Saturday Morning*. Nicky knows what he likes, and what he likes is action involving outlandish creatures, so we stick with the WB to watch the animated *Men in Black*. The aliens are more exotic and variegated than in the movie, even if there don't seem to be 150 species. But *Men in Black* turns out to be more about snappy dialogue than action, and before long Nicky is restless. "What do you think of this show?" I ask him. "Okay," he grunts. This is the four-year-old version of damning with faint praise. Then he brightens. "After this, I'm going to get a Poké–ball," he says. "It's a dollar. I have fourteen dollars." I think this is a coy hint about the dollar I'm supposed to pay him. On Channel 9, Linda Evans is hosting an infomercial for some sort of electronic face mask. Does it measure vital signs? Stimulate something? Smooth your wrinkles? Nicky points to the mask, which is called Rejuvenique. "I know how much that costs," he says. "How much?" I ask, resigned to being his straight man. "As much as I have, fourteen dollars," he says—not that he either wants or needs a Rejuvenique mask, he just likes feeling he can afford it. Actually, it's four easy payments of $49.75 each.

The ads are upon us now, and Nicky is more interested in them than he was in *Men in Black*. Here's one for Cookie Crisp, the cereal that looks like little chocolate–chip cookies. I take this opportunity to do some market research; I'm obsessed with micro-brewed root beers, and have spent an embarrassing amount of time thinking about starting a Root Beer of the Month Club, and even about milling a root-beer-flavored breakfast cereal called Root Loops. Sam thinks this sounds disgusting, but I'm convinced that a real kid will feel differently. So, with Sam in earshot, I ask Nicky if he'd eat a cereal that tasted like root beer. To my chagrin—and Sam's delight—he makes a disgusted face. "No," he says, "but I love Cookie Crisp!"

Men in Black returns. Nicky is positively bored now, and fidgeting in his chair. I enjoy the show more than he does, but I can understand how after the nonstop rush of *Batman Beyond*—or the minutely detailed alternate reality of *Pokémon—Men in Black* seems slow despite its witty details. Nicky only stirs when an alien jumps out of someone's face.

Not a moment too soon for Nicky, the WB begins its second *Pokémon* of the day. Apparently there's a third to come. This episode is much easier to follow, since there are fewer varieties of Pokémon in it, and thus no evolutionary lectures from Professor Westwood. Instead, we get a simple plot about a surfer and his pet pikachu ("Pikachu" seems to be not only the name of Ash's pet, but also of its species), who are preparing for the Humungadunga wave that comes only once every twenty years. Team Rocket steals the pikachu, but Ash and his friends come to the rescue in time for the big wave. The announcer tells us this proves it's never too late for dreams to come true, adding, "Don't go away—Pikachu Jukebox is next!" "Boy, that was exhausting," I say. "Yeah, really exhausting," agrees Nicky.

More ads, of course. *Doug's First Movie*, a spinoff of the Nickelodeon series, is out on video. Nicky has already seen it, and he tells me there's a great line in it—"The guy says, 'Smelly underwear, sir!'" Nicky repeats this line over and over. For a four-year-old, this is the soul of wit. Then an ad for a toy set, WWF Bashin' Brawlers, with action figures of star wrestler Goldberg. I love that a famous tough guy can be named Goldberg. Who's next—Rosenbaum? Finkelstein?

"Pikachu Jukebox" turns out to be a Pokémon music video, and Nicky knows this song too. When the closing credits roll, we switch to Nickelodeon; Nicky wants to watch a cartoon called *SpongeBob SquarePants*, about the adventures of an underwater sea sponge. It seems perfectly pleasant, but unlike Nicky—who could clearly keep this up for hours without blinking—I'm cartooned out. While he watches, I play with the dog and talk to Suzanne about what I've seen. Then Nicky points excitedly to a promo on Nickelodeon. "They put slime on the teacher, then Britney Spears comes, then they serve Chuck E. Cheese pizza." It's the Nick Takes Over Your School sweepstakes; Nickelodeon understands its audience very well. Next is a commercial for what looks like Olympic Gymnastics Barbie. I ask Nicky if he's ever played with a Barbie. "No way," he says instantly.

At eleven, I show Nicky and Suzanne to the door and pay Nicky a dollar for his *Pokémon* fund. I express my gratitude, but he's already debating which color Poké–ball to buy.

Back before the sets, I take a deep breath, and for the first time this morning I contemplate adult programming—relatively speaking. American Movie Classics is risking the wrath of the Asian-American community by showing a very non-PC Charlie Chan marathon. I'm just in time for the end of *Charlie Chan at Treasure Island*, in which Chan deduces the identity of the evil Dr. Zodiac—it's the magician Rhodini, played by Cesar Romero. Number One Son is full of awe for his brilliant father: "From now on I'll be just like you. I'll keep both feet right on the ground." Number One Son then tumbles through a trapdoor onstage. This was one of the later Chan pictures, starring Sidney Toler; next up is the earlier *Charlie Chan in Egypt*, with Warner Oland.

As Sam leaves to go shopping, I realize that after three hours of cartoons—and especially after *Pokémon*—I'm running on fumes. I decide to take an unorthodox step, and nap early so I can concentrate later. I pick up the pug and carry him to the bedroom, where he happily plops down on Sam's pillows. Within minutes we are both dead to the world.

At 1:38, Jaime Wolf calls—the writer, not the lawyer—to check up on me. Otherwise, there's no telling how long Cosmo and I might have slept. I still feel bleary, but then I think about the scene near the end of *The Hustler*, when it looks as if Fast Eddie will finally beat Minnesota Fats. Just when things seem rockiest, Fats calls a halt, washes up, changes his shirt, and reemerges refreshed and ready to play pool. In honor of the late Minnesota Fats (and the late Jackie Gleason), I decide to get up all over again, showering and dressing for the second time in six hours. Sure enough, the trick works, and by 2:00 P.M. I feel vaguely like a person.

On Channel 2, *Entertainment Tonight* has a special on *"Bewitched*—The Untold Story." When VH1's *Behind the Music* series took off, somebody must have realized that the format would work equally well with old TV shows instead of old rock stars. I've always liked *Bewitched*, not least because it's about a woman named Sam. But I'm a bit reluctant to watch this exposé, since at this point I need no further convincing that television is the ultimate subject of television. However, the competition is mostly sports-related—the Basketball Hall of Fame on NBC, college football on ABC, baseball on Fox—and my ignorance of sports is so vast that I don't expect to make heads or tails of any of it.

Before giving in to the meta-TV hall of mirrors, I scan through the rest of the channels. There's a documentary history of circus sideshows on The Learning Channel, and yet more *SNL* reruns on Comedy Central. But the mother lode is on Channel 31, which has an infomercial for Nad's hair-removal gel. (Does it remove hair from your nads?) I've been neglecting infomercials, despite the astonishing amount of air time they command these days. I really should pay more attention, since their very existence is something Charles Sopkin could never have imagined. Constructing a thirty-minute commercial disguised as a TV program must have seemed like a crackpot idea once upon a time. But now the practice is so respectable that even my old employer Miramax routinely buys blocks of air time on local stations, to publicize likely Best Picture contenders around Oscar time.

Unfortunately, the Nad's infomercial isn't a prime example of the form. We see the history of the product, and how the Australian inventor, then a housewife, experimented with different formulas for twelve years. But in no time the perky blonde host is signing off with "See you next time, from another exotic location!" as if somebody might be clueless enough to think this is a real show. Then she plays a didgeridoo under the closing credits. I'm not kidding. Next up is an infomercial for the Fuzuoku 9000, a polite electric "massager" for people who don't want to set foot in a store that sells sex toys.

At this point I give in and dive headfirst into *Bewitched* trivia. Here's an interview with Erin Murphy, who played the young Tabitha. She's as old now as Elizabeth Montgomery was then. "She was close to Montgomery, whom she called Manthamommy," says the narrator. "Unlike many child stars, Erin led a normal life, and her parents carefully managed her money." Boy, they're really tearing the lid off. Then *ET* turns to the two Darrins, who are both dead now. The first, Dick York, was addicted to painkillers. After leaving the show, he couldn't get an acting job, and at one point worked as a janitor. We see a pathetic late interview with York— broke, toothless, and hooked up to oxygen for his emphysema. The image of York as the perfect suburban husband is so indelible that this counter-image feels truly horrific. It reminds me of the supermarket tabloids, always going out of their way to find the least attractive pictures of glamorous stars. Sir Isaac Newton was right: "To every action there is always opposed an equal reaction," and this debunking of celebrity is the equal reaction to the kind of celebrity worship I've been watching all week.

More upbeat—in a noble TV-movie way—is the story of the second Darrin, Dick Sargent, who was one of the first TV actors to come out of the closet. Unlike *The Brady Bunch*'s Robert Reed, Sargent was in a long-term relationship with a man, who died not long before he did. Then we get the story of Elizabeth Montgomery's romance with Robert Foxworth, and her own untimely death from cancer. At all points, the narrator promises further revelations to come. Well, who's left, Gladys Kravitz the nosy neighbor? Got it in one—coming up next, the two actresses who played Gladys Kravitz. I feel like the sitcom equivalent of a Pokémon trainer. But I know nothing compared with onscreen expert Herbie Pilato, author of the authoritative *Bewitched Forever*, who knows *everything*. Still, I can't be too disparaging of the uses to which he's put his intellect, since I'm using mine to watch twelve television sets for a week.

The *pièce de résistance* comes after a brief interview with Bernard Fox, who played Dr. Bombay. The host mentions that Fox has been busy lately—appearing on *Passions*, summoned by none other than Timmy! Did Dr. Bombay put Charity in her coma? This isn't just TV about TV, it's TV about TV about TV! Next weekend on *Entertainment Tonight*: the secrets behind *The Brady Bunch*, rehashing all the stuff I already saw on the Fox special on Tuesday. How many years until we get the secrets behind *Entertainment Tonight?* How much are Mary Hart's legs insured for? "John Tesh—torn between two careers!" And we're certainly not far away from an E! *True Hollywood Story* on Arnold Ziffel, the pig from *Green Acres*.

In fact, even infomercials can be about TV. There's one for Tivo, the new digital video recorder/player that allows you to pause live TV while you're taping it. That's right, this is a long commercial for a product that will encourage people to avoid watching commercials. We are truly down the rabbit hole now.

The next infomercial is called *Y2K: A World in Crisis*, and it seems to star long-ago TV star Hugh O'Brian. But then we pan over to another host, someone named Deborah Winters. And another, Richard Roundtree. The hosts bring us up to date on the Y2K bug and how it will cause chaos unseen since the days of bubonic plague. They keep throwing more hosts at us, and we pan again, to Richard Anderson. Whom will they pan to next—Jimmie Walker? Bob Denver? No, it's Dick Van Patten! I wouldn't be surprised to see Arnold Ziffel. Then back to Anderson, who tells us, "In early 1999, the CIA informed us that current..." I don't follow the rest of his spiel because I'm tickled by the idea that O'Brian (star of the high-tech secret-agent series *Search*) and Anderson (formerly the government contact for *The Six Million Dollar Man* and *The Bionic Woman*) are speaking authoritatively about something the CIA told us. What are they selling? Their spiel is interspersed with sound bites from "experts," not one of whom I recognize, but all of whom promise disaster to come. Interestingly, one expert actually decries the media hype on the subject, but goes on to say that beneath the hype are some disturbing facts. "The systems are broken. I know you don't like hearing that, I know you think it's hype and exaggeration, but it's a fact." It's a clever gambit; because he undercuts his own sell, he's the guy you trust.

The first outright commercial is for a computer security program, Secret Enkrypt, which also protects e-mail. "Insiders, competitors, and even government agencies can't get into your files!" says the unseen announcer. We hear testimonials from "an I.T. executive"—and, ominously, a "South African security adviser," who is white. I half expect him to say that if Botha and De Klerk had used Secret Enkrypt, that rascal Mandela never would have come to power. The next ad is for Global Village Market food, which seems to be vast canisters of textured soy protein. It's outrageously expensive. We see men with long beards, wandering around a post-apocalyptic studio landscape. "Guarantee your family's food supply!" says the announcer. Then we're back to the "program." So the show itself doesn't sell anything—it wraps around the exact products it sets you up to buy. I have a feeling we'll see more of this approach in the future. Don't just sell deodorant—embed the commercials in a program about America's smelly-armpit crisis!

I flip from set to set. Now, after six and a half days of watching, I'm acutely aware that meta-TV is everywhere. On E!, there's *Inside Pro Wrestling*, a documentary, featuring an interview with my new hero Goldberg. He says he played pro football, but he got hurt. "My accountant said to get up off my butt and go make some money." Cut to a promo for an upcoming profile of Soleil Moon Frye, once the child star of the sitcom *Punky Brewster*. The only thing I know about her adult life is that she had breast reduction surgery a few years ago. Sure enough, "People didn't see Soleil," says an unidentified woman, "they saw Soleil's breasts." That does it—I need to watch something that isn't completely self-referential.

It's time to face up to my own sports illiteracy. I watch a few minues of baseball, but while I enjoy the game at the ballpark, it always falls flat for me on TV. Maybe it's the static way baseball is shot. Maybe it's the lack of hot dogs. Then I turn to CBS, which is competing with ABC in the college football business. Who's playing? Alabama versus Somebody. They're playing in Gainesville, Florida, so I guess it's Florida. (I do know that Alabama is called the Crimson Tide, but only because Steely Dan mentions it in the song "Deacon Blues.") Kickoff. Returned. A little box gives the stats for a player named Doug Johnson. Back to the overhead shot. Pass, incomplete. A flashy info-screen lists the offensive starters for Florida. It's not that I don't understand the rules of the game, but I can't imagine what it would take to get me interested in its outcome. If I knew one of the players personally? If I knew someone who knew one? I stare at the set numbly and wish I could watch golf instead. The simple human drama of each shot—especially on the putting green—is easier for me to grasp, and it would give me a chance to think about my golf-loving dad, and my late golf-loving father-in-law. But because I have no emotional connection to football, the spectacle feels dehumanized to me. The padded, helmeted creatures might as well be Pokémon.

Seeking a more accessible sport, I turn to Fox Sports Net. It's men's beach volleyball, direct from the Hard Rock in Las Vegas. We see stats on the players, some of whom are my age, but in much, much better shape. That's another reason I prefer to watch golf—some of the pro athletes are actually older than I am. Serve, volley, bounce. Snore. If anything, I feel more alienated from this than I do from football.

I look at Sopkin's book to see how he dealt with the Saturday-afternoon doldrums.

Answer #1: Saturday was his first day rather than his last, so he was still full of beans.

Answer #2: He watched sports. Even Charles Sopkin, that urbane, cocktail-quaffing sophisticate, watched sports.

I might as well admit to myself that I'm a freak of nature—a straight guy who enjoys watching a behind-the-scenes documentary on *Hello, Dolly!*, but can't get excited about a bunch of manly men throwing a ball around.

So what to do, with my options dwindling and my mental reserves on low? I could always watch *Raiders of the Lost Ark* on Channel 11. Ronald Lacey as the evil Nazi is preparing to torture Karen Allen, a lovely actress whose film career has mysteriously dried up. (She's badly in need of a TV series.) But watching a movie that I've seen dozens of times—that everyone has seen dozens of times—feels too much like cheating. Why do they even bother to show *Raiders of the Lost Ark* anymore? Why don't they just run the title onscreen, and let us fill in the rest with our memory?

Here's how desperate I am—I'm tuning to American Movie Classics, where a host introduces Sidney Toler in *Charlie Chan in City in Darkness*. I look it up in Leonard Maltin's invaluable reference book *TV Movies*, which gives the date as 1939. "In Paris, Chan takes on an arms dealer who's supplying weapons to the Germans. Mediocre entry with a topical angle." I sit poised to transcribe some hilarious lines of pidgin English, but this movie is so goddamn dull that I can't find any. Are there really people out there enjoying this? As I detach from the routine plot, I speculate on Sidney Toler's ethnicity. I'm pretty sure Warner Oland was Swedish—however, all I can tell about Toler is that he sure isn't Asian. AMC is either gutsy or stupid to run a full day of Caucasian actors in yellowface. Meanwhile, the cast includes one Douglass Dumbrille, who more memorably played the villain in the Marx Brothers' *A Day at the Races*. This makes me wish for a Marx Brothers movie—any Marx Brothers movie. Under the circumstances, I'd even watch one of the crappy ones, like *The Big Store* or *Love Happy*.

Four P.M., and all's hell. (Or *H-E-Double-Hockeysticks*, which is the title of an upcoming Disney Sunday Movie trailed incessantly on ABC.) *The Brady Brides* are on Fox Family again, but while once was astonishing, twice promises to be excruciating. I'm reduced to a rerun of *The Big Valley* on Channel 31 until Sam comes home from shopping and notices grizzly bears on Channel 9.

The grizzlies are on *Wild Things*, a syndicated nature show. This segment is hosted by a soft-voiced British wilderness guide who seems more interested in photographing the bears than in capturing them. As we go to commercial, they throw us a trivia question: How fast can a zebra run—sixty, forty, or twenty miles per hour? "Forty," says Sam confidently. Then she thinks for a moment. "Could be sixty." The show comes back on and we learn it's sixty, but only when it sprints. Next up, a trip to look at lions in the Serengeti. Now our guide is Megan, who heads up the Serengeti Lion Project. A lioness hunts down a wildebeest, and it's dinnertime for the cubs. "Look how many of them there are!" says Sam, happy as always to be watching animals. It's a good thing our cable system doesn't carry Animal Planet, or we'd never get anything done.

Before we know it, it's time for more commercials. The first is a cute ad for Budweiser. Two dalmatian puppies are in love, but they're tragically separated. Two years later—fourteen dog years—they pass each other on the road. One is on a fire engine, and the other rides with the Clydesdales. Their eyes meet. It's like the end of *The Way We Were*, except with spots. Then we get a McDonald's commercial that's been bugging me all week, in which a boy asks his father, "Am I too old for a Happy Meal?" Dad agrees he might be, and buys him his first Big Mac. The ending is cute—the kid stares at the big sandwich and asks, "Dad, how do you start this thing?"—but it's a problem of syntax. If the kid said, "*Don't you think* I'm too old for a Happy Meal?", hinting to his father, then we'd know he's ready to move on. But that's not how he phrases it, and the logical response to his question is that you're never too old for a happy meal. It gives the whole ad a bizarre sadness, like the one I felt when

I saw the quadruplets on Leno. It's as if this kid is growing up faster than he wanted to.

Back to *Wild Things*, visiting a chimpanzee sanctuary. Yeah, they're funny, but we also see them bite a human's ear. The chimps are living in cages, which isn't quite my idea of a sanctuary. "Breakfast is a two-course affair, consisting of a breakfast-type cereal and—of course—bananas." It immediately occurs to both Sam and me that our banana-loving pug might be part chimpanzee. Then a baby chimp climbs on its keeper's head, much the way Cosmo likes to sleep on *my* head, and now we're convinced this is true. Aha—the chimps are only in cages as a stage in the process of letting them back into the wild. They're orphaned chimps that need to be introduced gradually to the wild chimps in the area. "This is a good show," says Sam.

It does have a lot of commercials, though, like this ad for a psychic hot line: The psychic asks a young woman, "Did you have police officers over to your house? Did one of them ask you out?" The woman assents. "You should go out with him!" says the psychic, beaming. "This is totally amazing! I'm going to tell all of my friends to call!" says the caller. The psychic speaks directly to the camera: "Believe in us, we're for real!" Now I'm picturing a whole scenario, in which a hunky policeman broke down this woman's door to arrest her no-good boyfriend for armed robbery. Based on this one phone call, she'll go on a date with the policeman, and the boyfriend will escape from custody and shoot both of them. Could it be that I've been watching way too much TV?

Wild Things ends, just as golf finally begins on ESPN. My green oasis returns. I move to the couch and let Cosmo sit on my shoulder and lick my neck. I feel better. Sam and I mute everything for a moment to watch the apocalyptic climax of *Raiders of the Lost Ark*, which doesn't seem to have been edited for television. It's pretty grotesque for 4:54 P.M.

Time to walk the pug. Sam joins me, and we take the longest

walk of the whole week, around the cathedral and over to the bodega on the corner. Our local Dominican numbers runner gives Cosmo a banana, a daily ritual for both of them. "It's official," Sam tells the numbers runner as Cosmo gulps down the banana, "he's half chimpanzee."

When we return, Sam and Cosmo and I watch some of a syndicated series called *Relic Hunter,* starring Tia Carrere as a combination of Indiana Jones—she's an anthropologist who teaches at a bucolic college—and the buxom video-game heroine Lara Croft. In this episode, Tia and her two sidekicks seek the jeweled .45 of Al Capone. It's familiar stuff, right down to the old sliding-bookcase bit.

On Channel 11 is a rerun of *Star Trek: The Next Generation.* The characters seem to be just standing around talking, as usual. No, I take that back—Riker and Worf are actually sitting. This may have been the most cerebral series in TV history. It makes even a cerebral guy like me long for flashing phasers and hand-to-pseudopod combat with aliens. Now Data the android has a tête-à-tête with a woman in a fringed suede jacket. "Is she supposed to be an alien from the Seventies?" cracks Sam.

On PBS, it's *This Old House,* in which the guy who isn't Bob Vila tours a house that's been ravaged by fire. "We sort of would like to help in any way we can," he tells the house's owner. Do I detect a lack of real enthusiasm here? "I thought you only worked on old houses," says the owner, who may be picking up on this as well. No, assures the host, they'll help—on next week's show. That's it for this week, brought to you by Ace Hardware and State Farm insurance and Minwax wood finish and Saturn automobiles. At this point there's not even a pretense that these aren't commercials. Then an ad for *This Old House* magazine, and the tie-in CD-ROM. I try to remember why PBS fired Bob Vila years ago—wasn't it for making a commercial endorsement?

The array of football games on all three original networks looks like one giant game on three screens. It's a home IMAX movie. I imagine a quarterback passing the ball on Channel 2, seeing it sail past the team on Channel 4, and a receiver catching it on Channel 7.

On MSNBC, the characters from *Sesame Street* do a kick line in Rockefeller Center. Jane Pauley comes on—it's *Time and Again*'s salute to *Sesame Street*. I haven't watched the end of *Time and Again* before, and it's genuinely cool. In quick succession, we see all the NBC logos over the last fifty years, accompanied by the many sound variations on the famous chimes.

Six P.M. Late Saturday afternoon seems to be the time for syndicated adventure shows, perhaps as a nod to the old movie tradition of Saturday-afternoon serials. Channel 9 has *Peter Benchley's Amazon*; like *Relic Hunter*, it seems to be shot entirely through some sort of orange filter. They probably did some market research that showed orange appeals to middle-income males in their thirties. On Channel 11, *Earth: Final Conflict* turns out to be another variation on *V* or *The Invaders*; aliens are on earth, and our heroes are in the Earth Resistance. *Star Trek* producer Gene Roddenberry is credited as the creator, but since he's been dead for years, this might be like all those posthumous best-sellers by L. Ron Hubbard. "What are you watching?" says Sam. "This is dreadful!"

My dad calls to root me on. He urges me to rest when I'm done. I need no urging. When I hang up, Sam is staring at the sets and shaking her head. "This is a wasteland," she says. I don't know if she's deliberately quoting former FCC chairman Newton Minow, or just being descriptive. "Is anything on tonight?" she asks. I tell her. "And then you're done," she admonishes me, "and you're never watching television again. At least not twelve of them. At least not in my house." Once again, I need no urging.

But huzzah, there's something fun on Channel 13: New York culinary hero Ed Levine, author of the essential book *New York Eats*, on a show called *Going Places*. He does a remote from Barney Greengrass, the Upper West Side deli whose heavenly smoked-salmon-and-sturgeon sandwich deserves the Nobel Prize for appetizers. Then Ed takes us to the Fulton Fish Market, and before I know it we're on a tour of every obvious New York landmark: the Brooklyn Bridge, the Flatiron Building, the United Nations, Radio City Music Hall. This program isn't exactly full of surprises, but it does remind me that there's a city out there, and that I'll get to enjoy it again starting tomorrow. The funniest moment is when the show goes to the eighty-sixth-floor observation deck of the Empire State Building, from which we see—the Chrysler Building. It's like the sign Harpo Marx wears in *Duck Soup*: "Join the Army and See the Navy."

Sated with virtual tourism, I yawn. It's the boredom that kills me. I've spent much of my life avoiding boredom—mainly by reading—and now it's finally caught up with me. Not for the first time this week, I think of the old Stan Freberg commercial I heard on WFMU radio before I started this kamikaze brain dive. Freberg was telling a little girl about how radio stretches the imagination. "Doesn't television stretch the imagination?" asked the girl. "Up to twenty-one inches, yeah," snickered Freberg. But once again, just as I'm on the verge of a negative generalization about the medium, I glimpse something that gives me hope. In this case, it's a biography of Rudolf Nureyev on Bravo. Here he is in his prime, dancing "Le Corsaire." Wow.

Dazzled by Nureyev, I forget about everything for several minutes. Then *Going Places* abandons the tourist trail and goes back to food, and both Sam and I lean forward. Ed Levine takes us to Sylvia's in Harlem, then to Katz's Deli on the Lower East Side, then to Chinatown—this is food porn. We end with our genial host, James Avery, urging us to take a day or a week and visit NYC. As diverting as this show is, it would be better if it weren't *selling* all the time, like an infomercial or a Simpson-Bruckheimer movie. Who produced this, the New York Tourist Bureau?

Sam leaves me to my own devices at 7:00 P.M. On NBC is the thirteenth annual Hispanic Heritage Awards, from the Kennedy Center in D.C., hosted by former MTV VJ Daisy Fuentes and somebody named Bobby Cannavale. Daisy and Bobby promise guest appearances by every Hispanic celebrity you've ever heard of, except Ricky Martin and Jennifer Lopez. Then an ad for Denny's restaurants, in which the company's CEO talks about how happy Denny's is to sponsor the awards. "Thanks, Denny's!" says Geraldo Rivera. I suspect it's no coincidence that Denny's settled a big racial-discrimination suit.

Meanwhile, on Channel 41, there's a different kind of Hispanic heritage: *Sabado Gigante*, a four-hour-long Spanish-language variety show that has run continuously for decades. Host Don Francisco, who has a head like a granite block, stands in the audience and introduces six women who sing and dance in bikinis. I don't speak Spanish, so all I can do is marvel at the full-strength showbiz glitz of it, at a level unseen on English-language television since Cher had her own show in the Seventies. What's remarkable in 1999 is that I can't detect any irony here. There's nothing parodic about the bikini-clad women; it's as if thirty years of feminist media criticism had never existed.

I feel as if I'm going through Mr. Peabody's Way-Back Machine. Channel 21, the Long Island PBS station, is rerunning another variety warhorse: Lawrence Welk, whose schtick was already creaky when I was a tot. The camera pans across the orchestra, bubbles blowing, to land on Welk, who does a champagne-cork *pop!* with his thumb. I try it myself, but I don't have his level of experience. Out come the cleanest, happiest singer-dancers you've ever seen, including former Mousketeer Bobby Burgess. Then Myron Floren and his accordion lead the Champagne Music Makers through a medley from *The Sound of Music*, which splits the difference between sprightly and stately. Does anyone under sixty-five watch this stuff? What is it doing on PBS? Can reruns of *Hee Haw* be far behind?

For the postmodern variety of variety show, check out *The Man Show* on Comedy Central. The hosts are Adam Carolla, who was on last night's *Politically Incorrect*, and Ben Stein's sidekick, Jimmy Kimmel. Their show is a TV response to the recent boom in non-porn men's magazines like *Maxim* and *Gear*, whose cheerfully laddish surface conceals more than a bit of rage at women for changing the old rules. Tonight's show is the *Man Show* Wedding Spectacular. A couple face the preacher, doing the traditional wedding thing, until Adam and Jimmy stop them and suggest a few changes. For instance, an alternative set of vows, including, "Do you promise to love him at least three times a week? And honor his credit-card limits? And respect his football-watching time?" Have Adam and Jimmy been hanging out with Jamie Foxx? Next step is to lose the ring; as Adam says, "If I'm going to spend two months' salary on a ring, it had better be a Super Bowl ring." Then they bring out the Hymen Repair Kit—"It'll be like prom night all over again!"—and the exploding wedding cake, which is "one last diversion to allow the groom to run like the wind." This isn't funny—it's sad and misogynistic. I prefer the simple, unreflective sexism of *Sabado Gigante* to the sneering, angry, wink-wink retro-sexism of *The Man Show*.

I have a massive case of déjà vu; it feels as if I've seen *everything* before. *Pensacola Wings of Gold* is on Channel 2 again. Yet another version of *Star Trek*—this one is *Deep Space Nine*. Another rerun of *Third Rock from the Sun*. *Baywatch Hawaii*. TV is a big hamster wheel, and I have five more hours to run. On *The Man Show*, Jimmy Kimmel reports on Vegas wedding chapels, and I'm tempted to watch because Sam and I renewed our vows before an Elvis impersonator at the Graceland Wedding Chapel—but I'm still annoyed with the show's attitude, and so I bail.

Instead, I take the high road and concentrate on the Hispanic Heritage Awards. They're honoring dance teacher Tina Ramirez, the founder of Ballet Hispanico, and her gracious acceptance speech is followed by a dazzling dance number. For a moment, with Ballet Hispanico on NBC and Nureyev still leaping on Bravo, the sets are alive with dance. And that's not counting the latest bikini antics on *Sabado Gigante*, or the scantily clad babes bouncing on trampolines of irony under the closing credits of *The Man Show*.

Next up on the awards are Energy Secretary Bill Richardson—last seen on *Meet the Press*, ages ago last Sunday—and the first Hispanic astronaut, Dr. Ellen Ochoa. Then an award to Placido Domingo. This is a noble enterprise, but dull television. I can't help wondering whether this would have made the network schedule at all if the NAACP hadn't been making noise about minority representation on TV.

Sabado Gigante seems to consist almost entirely of women in bikinis. Now I know why the show has lasted so long. The only exception is a segment called "La Gran Oportunidad," in which a woman with a big "4" on her dress sings while a masked man in a sombrero dances behind her. It must be some kind of talent show for the bikini-impaired.

Nureyev is sitting naked on a rock as we roll credits on Bravo. Sam approves: "More naked people on television, that's what I have to say." Steve Allen she's not. On Channel 21, *Lawrence Welk* gives way to another ancient rerun, *The Tennessee Ernie Ford Show*. After that, according to *TV Guide*, it'll be Guy Lombardo. I can't imagine this is what Congress intended when it established public broadcasting in America.

Eight P.M. Finally, back to network episodic programming. I'm passing up the drama *Early Edition* on CBS, the movie *Twelve Monkeys* on ABC, and the season premiere of *Hercules* on Channel 11, because NBC's *Freaks and Geeks* is the obvious choice. TV critics are raving about this show; I know this from a promo that's been running all week. Besides, *SCTV*'s Joe Flaherty plays the dad, and it's set in 1980, when I was a high-school geek myself.

The show starts at the family breakfast table. The house seems a little underdecorated to me, but the use of wood paneling is accurate for the period. It's nice to see a dial phone too. Oddly, Flaherty's character is complaining about the Sex Pistols. Sam smells an anachronism at once: "The *Sex Pistols*? When is this set?" I know she's right—the Pistols had already been broken up for two years by 1980. Then we follow the kids to school. At least they all look like real teenagers rather than the young-looking adults I've seen on the other "teen" shows. At a school assembly, they watch a skit about drunk driving, and Sam and I argue about whether this is anachronistic too. She thinks it is; I remember that Mothers Against Drunk Driving was already around, but this kind of skit does seem more like junior high school than high school. However, we agree that the next skit is definitely anachronistic; *nobody* was talking about cocaine in high schools in 1980, except maybe in Beverly Hills. Why are they spending so long on this stuff? Well, it turns out the freak girl is throwing a keg party, and her geek brother and his friends substitute a nonalcoholic keg. "This is the most contrived plot I've ever seen in my life!" says Sam, and I have to concur, not least because I can't imagine who would sell nonalcoholic beer by the keg in 1980. They probably don't even sell it by the keg in 1999. This doesn't feel anything like my high-school experience—and if anyone knows about freaks and geeks in 1980, it's me. Maybe the critics who like this show were born later. Besides, this kind of revisionist look at substance abuse is a dull subject to center a show around, compared with all the other things I remember.

I know I should do due diligence and watch the entire hour, but I'm pissed off and worn down and trying to summon the strength to get through these last hours. Instead, I order a pizza from V&T's, which is conveniently located downstairs, and stagger from show to show, unwilling to watch *Hercules*—which I might actually enjoy—because I've already spent an hour on it earlier in the week. *Sabado Gigante* rolls on like the Columbia. A lizard hatches on Channel 15. A&E's *Biography* covers Danny Thomas, leaving no TV stone unturned. I'm almost ready to surrender to *The Secret World of Stock Cars* on The Learning Channel when I realize what I must do.

It's *Cops*, on Fox, in which cinema-verité crews follow real-life policemen on their rounds. I can't read the backs of their uniforms clearly, so I don't know where this is taking place. Aha—it's some-place called Riviera Beach. As I said, I don't know where this is taking place. There's a "31 in progress—two females, possibly drug-related." We're never told what a 31 is, but when the cops get to the house, one woman says someone cut her daughter with a knife. "What is this all about? Let's be honest," asks the young cop, who looks not unlike *NYPD Blue's* Rick Schroder. "He cut her, he cut her, oh my God," cries the woman. A voice from offscreen con-fuses matters: "She was being held hostage in this house by some-body." Who was that, a cop? A bystander? A crew member? Just then the pizza arrives, so I miss the rest of the case—but Sam assures me the cops caught the slasher.

"I wonder what Frederick Wiseman has to say about shows like this?" asks Sam, referring to the cinema-verité pioneer who directed such classics as *Titicut Follies* and *Welfare*. *Cops* may use Wiseman's tools—no narrator, handheld camera, jagged editing—but the result doesn't feel at all like Wiseman's work. That's because Wiseman is always looking at the system as a whole, at how things work and why. By contrast, *Cops*—like virtually all "reality pro-gramming" on television—is looking at the thing itself, with no context, no analysis, and no follow-through. The material is undoubtedly rich enough for a true Wiseman approach, and I don't think the audience would be any smaller. The problem is that Wise-man takes a year or more to make each of his films, and *Cops* does five shows a week. I remember this trap from when I worked at HBO. HBO has higher standards than most TV companies, but TV is all about filling time slots. It's the nature of the beast that you only have so much time to make it as good as it's going to get, and then it goes out to millions of people.

Comes 9:00 P.M. I miss *Pretender* on NBC and the season pre-miere of *Xena* on Channel 11 (now I'll never find out how Xena and Gabrielle return to their earthly bodies), to catch up with *Martial Law* on CBS. It stars the Hong Kong actor-director Sammo Hung, of whom I am a longtime fan. Sammo is a portly guy who looks nothing like anyone's idea of a martial-arts master—which is why it's so effective when he kicks ass. On top of that, he's a powerful and nuanced actor, at least in Cantonese.

I haven't seen *Martial Law* since its premiere last season, and have been looking forward to reconnecting with it. In the interim, the show has been completely revamped—which it certainly needed—and Sammo now co-stars with Arsenio Hall, in a blatant attempt to recreate the dynamic between Jackie Chan and Chris Tucker in the hit movie *Rush Hour*. Unfortunately, it soon becomes clear that whatever they've changed, it wasn't enough. *Martial Law* is a throwback to the kind of by-the-numbers cop show that I thought died out with *Simon & Simon*. Sammo has very little to do as an actor (admittedly, he's hampered by his lack of fluency in English), and, surprisingly, not much more to do as a martial artist. The plot is something about going undercover to infiltrate a ring of jewel thieves. At the end, everyone chuckles about the events of the last hour, like Ben and Hoss and Little Joe at the end of *Bonanza*.

Determined not to repeat my abortive experience with *Freaks and Geeks*, I manage to last through the entirety of *Martial Law*. I don't think I'm reading too much in to detect America's distrust of the Other in the way that the explosive Sammo Hung is contained within a safe, dull formula. With the exception of the kinetic director John Woo, the same thing has happened to the rest of Sammo's contemporaries in the Hong Kong film world, performers and directors alike; they've been domesticated by Hollywood, and they've sacrificed their wildness and originality in the process.

At 10:00 P.M. I could watch American ass-kicker Chuck Norris on *Walker, Texas Ranger* on CBS, or *Profiler* on NBC, but I just can't take another lame drama series. Don Francisco is still going strong on *Sabado Gigante*—the man is indomitable. My hero Bob Barker tapes for five hours to do a week of *The Price Is Right*, but the fact that Don Francisco does one four-hour show at a stretch may be even more impressive. Meanwhile, there are imported British mysteries on Channel 21 and on A&E. Does it never occur to anyone on this side of the Atlantic to construct an intelligent, multipart mystery series?

To be fair to the brave new world of cable sitcoms—which I have hitherto neglected—I go for *Oh Baby* on Lifetime, a channel I have neglected as well. Actress Cynthia Stevenson plays a hip single mother named Tracy. In an inventive touch, the show has a framing device, in which Tracy plays the episode's events on a VCR, pausing to make direct-to-camera comments, and fast-forwarding to the good bits. Tonight's episode is about getting someone to watch the baby while Tracy goes on a date. Rather than rely on her overbearing mother, Tracy takes the baby along—without telling her boyfriend. The police show up because Tracy's mother thinks the baby has been kidnapped. This feels even more contrived than the nonalcoholic keg earlier this evening. When Carl Reiner was producing *The Dick Van Dyke Show*, he had a guiding principle for writers: "Tell me about yourself, not about other television shows you've seen. That's how we'll get a story." Of the shows I've watched this week, only *Once and Again* really passes that test—and *Oh Baby* certainly doesn't. Besides, the start-and-stop of the VCR framing device is annoying me. My whole last week has been start-and-stop. What I long for is a narrative sustained enough and involving enough to keep me from feeling like a gnat in mid-flit.

At the end of the show, Sam retires to check her e-mail, and I mute everything while I decide what to watch next. The resulting moment of silence is deafening. I sit on the couch with my head in my hands, thanking my lucky stars that no huge crisis preempted regular programming this week. If I had to do this again, I might honestly die.

It's 10:30. The three channels that have ten-o'clock news shows—5, 9, and 11—now do the weather simultaneously. Fluffy clouds seem to drift from one set to the next. Meanwhile, a topless woman on another set has me checking my grid to see if I've accidentally turned on The Playboy Channel. But no, it's *Jonathan Creek*, the British mystery series on Channel 21, the same channel that was airing Guy Lombardo only hours earlier. On yet another set, Channel 55 has an infomercial for an inflatable mattress. It reaches an unexpected point of hilarity when two sumo wrestlers grapple on top of the mattress, to show it won't deflate that easily.

Rather than join one of the network shows halfway through, I unmute MTV's *Downtown*, a gritty animated series that seems to owe a debt to the nuevo-boho East Village musical *Rent*. It starts out as a funny and well-observed story about our nerdy hero Alex's date with a black-clad babe, whom his friends refer to as "the vampire chick." Alex lives a not-unrealistic New York life, hanging out at both coffee shops and copy shops, and listening to genuinely hip bands like Elastica. It's fun to see tattooed cartoon characters who aren't Popeye. But halfway through, we get lost in Alex's fantasies, and the entire show is sidetracked into a battle with giant slugs. This is a case of writers who don't trust their own material.

Meanwhile, on Channel 13, a pattern begins to form out of garment buttons. Is this one of those European animated shorts they use to fill out the time slot when a British import comes up short? Well, no—the buttons eventually spell out S-Y-M-S, for the clothing store. It's more enhanced underwriting, complete with the slogan "An educated consumer is our best customer." And the educated consumers who watch PBS are our best demographic. The ensuing show turns out to be the TV version of Andrew Lloyd Webber's *Cats*—my wife's least favorite Broadway show of all time, which I've managed to avoid somehow. Why is *Great Performances* starting this at 10:51 when it isn't even pledge week? As the dancing felines begin to chant a number about Jellicle cats, I wonder idly if "Jellicle" is short for evangelical, and if it has something to do with T. S. Eliot's religious convictions. Then it occurs to me that "gelical" might be an obscure word that isn't in my vocabulary. I look up both "Jellicle" and "gelical" in the dictionary—but no, Eliot must have made it up. This should give you an idea of how eager I am to be doing something other than watching TV. Once again I despair at my alienation from the mainstream of popular culture. I never saw *Cats*, I don't watch TV much, and I don't care about sports. Do I exist at all? If a cultural elitist falls in the forest, does he make a sound?

I'm also sobered to realize that *Cats*—a nearly twenty-year-old musical—is yet another example of the British domination of dramatic programming on PBS. One of my first jobs in show business, in 1985, was working for a New York producer named John H. Williams. At the time, John had a booming business producing drama for *Great Performances* and *American Playhouse*, including shows like Sam Shepard's *True West* and Clifford Odets's *Rocket to the Moon*. Fourteen years later, John and I both make movies, and *American Playhouse* is no more. Oddly, it was the controversy over *Tales of the City*—one of the highest-rated shows in PBS history—which helped to kill *American Playhouse*. These days PBS airs almost no original American drama. It makes me think of a campaign trip with my father in southwestern Virginia, when I met an implacable cracker sheriff in the little coal-mining town of Grundy. I was fourteen years old, but I had noticed something strange about the town. "Sheriff, how many black people are there in Grundy?" I asked. "None," he replied. Clearly he hadn't understood the question, so I rephrased it. "No," I said, "I mean, how many black people live in the whole town?" His eyes flashed at me. "Ah said none, boy. Zee-ro. Are yuh *deef*, boy?" At that moment I understood *why* there were no black people in Grundy. Whenever I think of former PBS chief Ervin Duggan, the undoubtedly suave and cultured man who pulled the plug on *American Playhouse*, I can't help picturing him as that sheriff.

At 11:00 P.M., blessed relief appears in the form of HBO's *Sex and the City*. Sam joins me on the couch; this is one of our favorite shows, and it's the penultimate episode of the season. It starts with a parody of the multiple-boxes opening of *The Brady Bunch*, to introduce the members of a group-share house in the Hamptons. In short order everyone sleeps with each other and the group falls apart, so

CAN'T TAKE MY EYES OFF OF YOU

they invite our four New York single gals—Carrie, Samantha, Charlotte, and Miranda—to take the remaining weekends of the summer. Someone asks whether the house is a good deal. "Of course it's a good deal," says Carrie, who is played by Sarah Jessica Parker. "It's haunted by cheating boyfriends and sexual rejections." Sam already loves this episode; she loathes the Hamptons, having spent one hellish summer programming the Hamptons International Film Festival while surrounded by men driving Humvees and women wearing denim cutoffs with nine-carat diamond rings. I love the show too; sure, things are exaggerated for comic effect, but this definitely passes the Carl Reiner Test. The empowered and defiantly witty women of *Sex and the City* are unusual only in the bland world of television, not in real life.

But the-women-go-to-the-Hamptons is only one of the two intertwined themes of this episode, the other one being that the show's thirty-something protagonists are thrown in with a bunch of twenty-somethings, and feel their age as a result. It's smart construction; you could get an entire show out of either theme, but doing both at once gives you real texture. Plus, as always with *Sex and the City*, each of the four women has her own story thread, and all of them dovetail and resolve. Like *Seinfeld*—and unlike Monday night's mistake, *Ally*—it shows how much you can pack into thirty minutes if you know what you're doing. And on top of everything else, there are genuinely funny lines. Says Carrie, "The Hamptons Jitney is just like the bus to summer camp, except instead of singing songs, everyone ignores each other and talks on their cell phones." My *only* problem with this show is that Sarah Jessica Parker, while an inspired comedienne, is painfully thin. I want to invite her and Calista Flockhart and Lara Flynn Boyle and Sarah Michelle Gellar to a dinner party, and serve them lipids.

The show ends, and we turn to NBC for the season premiere of *Saturday Night Live*. It's the only possible ending for a week that started under the shadow of the 25th Anniversary Special. Cosmo snuggles on Sam's lap as we all see out the week together.

Before *SNL* begins, there's the Sprint PCS commercial with Judd Nelson, which might be the single most repeated ad of the week. À la Kevin Costner's encounter with Donald Sutherland in *JFK*—and with a dash of *The X-Files* thrown in—Nelson meets an older man in the middle of a park. The man gives him a cellular phone and shows him the various features, which include Web browsing. "Do you think they're ready?" asks Judd. "Some are," says the man. "Others will follow." In its blatant use of snob appeal, this is of a piece with the "I'm better than you are" car commercial, and it's only marginally less annoying.

Saturday Night Live is here at last. The end is in sight! As the opening credits unfurl, Sam says, "Do you know how long it's been since I watched this show?" "As long as it's been since *I* watched this show," I reply—maybe ten years, maybe even more. As Sam points out, the number of regular cast members has mushroomed to roughly the size of the Mormon Tabernacle Choir. Then announcer Don Pardo gets to "musical guest, David Bowie!" "Who?" asks Sam. "I trust you're being facetious," I say. "David Loewy?" asks my genuinely confused wife. "Who is David Loewy?" "David *Bowie*," I tell her, a lifelong George Burns to her Gracie Allen. She can't believe it: "That didn't look anything like David Bowie!"

The guest host tonight is Jerry Seinfeld, whose introductory monologue is about how he spends his time now that he's not doing his show—watching TV all day, just like me. After what I've seen this week, I certainly hope he's kidding.

The fake ad is for an old, respected brokerage firm that waited just a little too long to get a Web page, so now their Internet address is www.clownpenis.fart. Then Jerry stars in an actual ad for American Express. The lines between real and fake commercials have blurred considerably in the last twenty-five years.

Next is a parody of a *Regis & Kathie Lee*–type morning show. Their guest is Jerry, playing the author of a diet book called *The Realm.* "It's got a little more room than *The Zone*," says Jerry. As an in-joke, his character is named "Dr. Jedediah Purdy," after the young writer whose recent book *For Common Things* decries the kind of postmodern irony that is Seinfeld's stock-in-trade. I'm not surprised that someone at *SNL* has picked up on this. Nothing infuriates a liberal media worker like a conservative culture critic, as evidenced earlier this year when the raunchy teen movie *Cruel Intentions* had a character patterned after Wendy Shalit, the antifeminist defender of modesty and virginity. I only wish that Seinfeld were playing a character based on the real Purdy, so *SNL* could address his thesis head-on instead of just taking a swipe at him. But does this show dare to even mention the idea that irony might be unhealthy for America? Like Seinfeld's own show, *Saturday Night Live* was built on irony. If it ever appeared to take something seriously, the whole house of cards might collapse.

Quicker than you can say "cross-promotion," a commercial for *Superstar* gives way to a sketch featuring Molly Shannon as Mary Kathleen Gallagher. St. Monica's is playing Yeshiva Academy, and Mary Kathleen takes a shine to Seinfeld, a student from the other school. "I just want to say you make a really great Jew basketball player," she tells him, and she invites him out for a knish. "Kno," replies Jerry. This episode of *SNL* is a lot funnier than the last one I saw, back in the Cretaceous Era. My appreciation continues through a spot-on parody of a local eleven-o'clock news show and its endless "coming-up" gimmicks: "The President has been assassinated. The President of what? We'll tell you later." "This is genuinely funny," I tell Sam. "I think you've watched too much TV this week," she says sternly.

And on it goes. The venerable news segment, still called "Weekend Update," suffers from comparison to the sharper writing on *The Daily Show*. There's only one truly biting joke, about the nuclear accident in Japan: "Officials said it was nothing compared to having two atom bombs dropped on them." But I can't help noticing some of the same misogyny I saw earlier tonight on *The Man Show*, which fits right in on a show that's famously inhospitable to female performers and writers. There are the inevitable gags about Monica

Lewinsky, and less likely ones about Wynonna Judd, in each case revolving around weight. Now that so many subjects are off limits in the age of political correctness, fat jokes are the last acceptable frontier—but I don't find them particularly acceptable myself. I like to think I'd feel the same way even if I were thirty pounds thinner.

Here at last is musical guest David Bowie, pushing his new CD, of course. Am I crazy, or is Bowie getting younger as he gets older, like F. Scott Fitzgerald's character Benjamin Button? No wonder Sam didn't recognize him. Then to a commercial; the breaks are getting longer and more frequent. "This is what I remember most about *SNL*," says Sam, "which is that in the last half hour, the commercials multiplied exponentially." A promo for *The Real World*, back in Hawaii again. Long-distance services abound. An ad for Bowie's CD, naturally. There are capering capybaras on the Discovery Channel, and digitally fuzzed breasts on Howard Stern. "Do you think they're ready?" "Some are. Others will follow."

Back on *SNL*, the funniest bit all night. It takes off from the final episode of *Seinfeld*, which ended with Jerry and the gang in jail. In this filmed sequence, Jerry is transferred to Oz, the brutal maximum-security prison on the eponymous HBO series. The coup is that Jerry is on the real set with the real actors, behaving like his neurotic *Seinfeld* character in the midst of violence and grit—lining the toilet seat with toilet paper, flossing instead of dropping the soap. The sketch includes parodies of classic *Seinfeld* lines: "But the makeup sodomy is the best part of being nailed to the gym floor!" Like the *Regis & Kathie Lee* skit earlier, it's yet more TV about TV—but it's hilarious. It's a win-win situation for HBO too, because by network standards, nobody watches *Oz*. The publicity can't hurt.

More commercials, including the first ad I've seen for the new Scorsese movie *Bringing Out the Dead*. Then the Traditional Sketch That Goes On Way Too Long, about toll-free numbers. More commercials. "Are you still buying chicken from those burger boys?"

drawls the Colonel. "Drop the chalupa," says the Chihuahua. "Do you think they're ready?" "Some are. Others will follow."

Just when I'm ready to zone out, *SNL* comes back with another funny sketch—about TV, of course. The premise is that *Two Guys, a Girl, and a Pizza Place* will lose the humans instead of the location, becoming *And a Pizza Place*. We see the network strategy session: "Can you name the girl? Can you name even one of the two guys? But can you name the place where they meet?" "But who's in it?" "Whoever likes pizza." Unfortunately, this turns out to be the Traditional Sketch That Doesn't Know How to End, which is a shame—it could have been a contender.

Once again, David Bowie, doing "Rebel Rebel"—a song that isn't on his new CD, wonder of wonders. The choice of song is ironic, considering that both Bowie and *SNL* are rebels who have become institutions themselves. Time'll get you every time.

More commercials. Then the last sketch, I think. Sam identifies it as a parody of the Mel Gibson movie *Payback*—I haven't seen it, so I wouldn't have known. Jerry is beaten up by some thugs. He has no pulse, so they hook him up to a defibrillator and revive him, as they would on *ER*. Once he recovers, they start beating him up again. Then it all happens again, and again. It leads into a *Patch Adams* bit. It's the Traditional Sketch That Just Isn't Funny *And* Goes On Way Too Long. Like so much else about television since I last watched it steadily—or even since Charles Sopkin watched thirty-two years ago—*Saturday Night Live* is different, yet the same.

More TV shows on the other channels. More ads. Sam and Cosmo are asleep on the couch. I have three minutes left before my week of video masochism ends. I promise never, ever, ever to do this again.

At last, everybody is on the *SNL* stage for the traditional good-night wave to the audience. Those bluesy piano chords, which tap directly into the cortex. I flash back to the first time I heard this music, twenty-five years ago, when I was a teenager and my sister

Eve was up past her bedtime. And like a rapid montage, I remember in quick succession the dozens (hundreds?) of other times I've heard it—in other cities, in other states of mind, with other people who are no longer in my life. It's the feeling Brazilians call *saudade*, the melancholy ache that recognizes that the past is past. For a moment I wonder if someday I'll watch the 50th Anniversary Special of *SNL*. Will I think back with *saudade* to when I spent a week watching twelve television sets?

Frankly, I don't think I will. With the greatest of pleasure, I turn off the sets, and go to sleep for a long time. 📺

So I survived. In fact, once I caught up on my sleep, I felt better than I had in some time. I woke up every day with a smile on my face, knowing that I didn't have to watch twelve TV sets that day— or any other day for the rest of my life. I was like the proverbial guy who banged himself over the head repeatedly with a hammer, because it felt so good when he stopped. Watching a week of TV isn't a mental-health regimen I'd recommend to everyone, but it worked for me.

Two men from Time Warner Cable arrived the next Monday to pick up the cable boxes. They shot me odd glances while they gathered up the cords, as if they suspected me of harboring some

EPILOGUE

The Long Arm of Sturgeon's Law

unspeakable—or perhaps unfathomable—perversion. The TV sets took longer to get out of the apartment, to Sam's distraction. John Taylor from Zenith asked me kindly if I wanted to keep one, but at that point watching more TV was the farthest thing from my mind. Eventually the sets were picked up as well, leaving the apartment as it was before I began my experiment—except that we now have six grounded outlets in our hallway. They're very useful whenever I run the vacuum cleaner, although I hate to think of how many times I'll have to vacuum in order to fully amortize their cost.

Over the next few months, television events took their course. I wasn't at all surprised when *Work with Me* was canceled soon after *The Mike O'Malley Show*, and only slightly less so when *It's Like, You Know . . .* and *Action* met the same fate. At this writing, *The Martin Short Show* is still hanging on, although on December 15, 1999, *The New York Times* reported that WCBS would move it from 4:00 P.M. to 1:30 A.M.—not a good sign, to say the least.

In retrospect, there are shows I wish I had watched, like *Everybody Loves Raymond, Buffy the Vampire Slayer*, and the one that turned out to be the biggest new hit of the 1999 fall season, *Judging Amy*. There are whole channels to which I should have paid more attention, like Bravo, TBS, and The Weather Channel. I'm also embarrassed by the possibility that my residual loyalties to HBO might have led me to give short shrift to its erstwhile rival, Showtime. At the other extreme, I could have written more about VH1, but most of its programming is catnip for a rock-and-roll obsessive like me, and I didn't want to gush. Still, I think I covered about as much of the TV landscape as anyone with only one pair of eyes could manage.

Once I began to reconnect with my friends, I was continually asked whether my week of immersion had changed my attitudes toward TV. Did I hate it now? Did I love it now? The fact is, I emerged feeling neither hate nor love for the medium itself, any more than I do for books or theater or radio. I don't think TV is the evil monolith its most vociferous critics fear it to be; nor is it the panacea that the visionaries of the Fifties and Sixties hoped for. It's just a medium. As in Charles Sopkin's day, ninety percent of what's on television is crap—because, as science-fiction writer Theodore Sturgeon famously said, "ninety percent of *everything* is crap." (Critic David Bianculli quotes Sturgeon's Law in his 1992 book in defense of TV, *Teleliteracy.* Bianculli's book is a refreshing corrective to all those jeremiads about the murder of culture at the hands of television.)

What infuriates me isn't the existence of the crap, or even the popularity of some of it, but what lies behind it. What I saw in the unfunny comedies, the undramatic dramas, the unenlightening news shows, and the unstimulating talk shows was a pervasive cynicism that saddened me. Again and again I got the feeling that people working in TV had accepted inwardly the most scathing criticisms of the medium—and that their work was hasty and uninspired because they felt that was all anybody expected. Sure, some of the writers and producers and executives are merely untalented. But they work for and with others who know better, and it's the cynicism of those people that saddens me most.

By contrast, the best work I saw on TV was always a product of one thing: *sweat.* Behind *The Daily Show* or *The Rosie O'Donnell Show,* behind *Zoboomafoo* or *Zoom*—and even behind some shows I didn't love, like *The Practice* or *The West Wing*—I could sense that people were working their asses off to make their shows entertaining, to make them more substantive than anyone would expect, to make them *better.* That's simple, honest craftsmanship, the pride in your own work that keeps you from issuing a shoddy product even if the time saved is money in your pocket. TV's insistent demand for immediate results discourages craftsmanship, and encourages laziness and sloppiness, as I remember all too well from my own stints in the TV world. This makes me cherish the carefully crafted shows all the more, because I know how difficult it must have been to produce them at that standard. When something like HBO's series *The Sopranos* comes along, it's nothing short of miraculous.

If TV is both better at its high end and worse at its low end than it was thirty-two years ago, that's probably due to the process of evolution. Just as animal species develop the attributes that will best ensure their long-term survival, so TV shows build on the proven successes of the past, incorporating useful mutations along the way. *Once and Again,* for instance, wouldn't exist without its direct ancestor *thirtysomething,* and maybe *Family* before that. By the same token, Jerry Springer's show wouldn't exist without its own long TV tradition, which includes the innovative format of Phil Donahue, the outrageousness of the nearly forgotten Morton Downey Jr., and the showmanship of Geraldo Rivera. There was a time when *Geraldo* seemed like a new all-time low for TV. It took a devolutionary leap for *Jerry Springer* to sink below that; in doing so it made Geraldo's show look tame, and outlasted it.

The audience keeps moving forward, and to keep up with us, TV keeps evolving too—but while the specifics are always different, the parameters are always the same. So it shouldn't be surprising that I came to some of the same conclusions that Charles Sopkin did. It's the nature of the medium. Thirty-two years from now, if there's someone masochistic enough to spend a week watching twenty-four televisions, that chronicler will probably conclude yet again that the good stuff is scarce but exciting, and that the crap is plentiful and depressing.

Of course, it's possible that, by then, television as a medium might be replaced by some interactive technology of the future. Right now the buzzword is "broadband," which promises to turn the personal computer, the video store, and the television set into one big repository of instantly accessible entertainment. I shouldn't play the prognostication game—after all, I'm still waiting for the rocket car and the teleportation devices I was promised as a child—but I strongly doubt that television will die. TV didn't kill off radio, and movies didn't kill off live theater. When a new medium comes along, the old media tend to shift a bit, but they don't usually die. What seems more likely to me is that our definition of television will simply expand to include channels of entertainment and information that are now considered part of the Internet. Just as TV exploded from Sopkin's six channels to my seventy-five, that chronicler thirty-two years from now may be navigating through literally hundreds of channels. But my bet is that we'll still call it television.

That explosion of channels is one of the real ways TV has changed since Charles Sopkin despaired for the medium's future. In a multichannel world, there's nearly always *something* worth watching, on one channel or another—and if you don't agree, then you probably shouldn't be watching television in the first place. With the advent of VCRs and pay-per-view and now digital video recorders, TV is becoming more and more like a bookstore. It stocks best-sellers that everyone buys, as well as specialized titles that appeal to a smaller but no less devoted readership. If you're not interested in a book, you can pick out another one. And if you're disappointed in a book, the fault isn't with the bookstore, but with the writer—and with the publisher. Like a real bookstore, TV can respond to its customers if they're persuasive and persistent enough. During my TV week, I was struck by something I didn't expect: The average quality of children's television was not only higher than anything I remembered from my own childhood, but also significantly higher than the average quality of TV for adults. On reflection, I think this is due to years of dogged activism by people like Peggy Charren of Action for Children's Television, who pressured broadcasters and legislators for decades.

One peculiarity of the TV bookstore is that there weren't many best-sellers in the Nineties, just a lot of specialized titles. This is the downside to narrowcasting. In their zeal to deliver target audiences to advertisers, TV executives pursued individual demographics so ferociously that a show like *Felicity*—with its low ratings but perfectly delineated viewership—was considered a hit. (Those ratings became even lower after my TV week; I was one of the only people who liked Keri Russell's new haircut.) In late 1999, however, a big-money prime-time game show called *Who Wants to*

Be a Millionaire shocked those same executives by appealing to absolutely everybody. Once again the conventional wisdom turned out to be just that—conventional.*

In his wonderful book *Adventures in the Screen Trade*, screenwriter William Goldman coined the truest maxim about the art of making movies: "Nobody knows anything." It applies equally well to television. When I worked at HBO, the conventional wisdom was that the networks directed their programming largely at women, so HBO should aim for men. That's why HBO has always featured boxing and shows with naked ladies. Then my colleagues Colin Callender and Keri Putnam pushed through an original movie called *If These Walls Could Talk*, about abortion in America. Despite much internal skepticism, it went on to become HBO's highest-rated original movie ever, bringing in millions of female viewers and revealing that HBO wasn't a channel for men after all. Rather, it was a channel that tended to ignore half its potential audience. HBO learned its lesson, as evidenced by the success of *Sex and the City*.

This stuff isn't just TV-industry gossip; it relates directly to the issue of quality and craftsmanship. Why was *The Cosby Show* so astoundingly popular around the globe? Yes, Bill Cosby is a uniquely gifted performer—although that hasn't lifted his current sitcom, *Cosby*, to the same level. Yes, the show told us something we all wanted to hear, in portraying an African-American family who were happy and loving and successful in the modern world. But I think the fundamental reason is that it was a damn good show, as good as any in the history of television. It was written with honesty and wit and real insight into the way families work; it was skillfully performed and directed; and once again, you could sense the blood, toil, tears, and sweat of a team of people doing the very best they could do. There's no substitute for quality—and if you can't deliver

---

*Ironically, after spending so much concentrated time as a TV viewer, in February 2000 I ended up on the other side of the screen as a contestant on *Millionaire*. I won $125,000, not least because three of the questions were about TV shows. Maybe I should be *grateful* that the eternal subject of TV is TV.

quality, what the hell are you doing working in a medium that's viewed by millions of people every day?

So did I learn to enjoy television again, as I had hoped? When it's good, yes. When it's bad, no. What would it take for me to become a regular viewer? Nothing less than a new flowering of the American work ethic, and how likely is that? Still, I don't think the future of TV is hopeless—unlike Charles Sopkin, who decided at the end of *his* week that "the only way to solve television's problems was, literally, murder—i.e., send in squads of machine-gunners and summarily execute every executive at every network and start from scratch." Fortunately, Sopkin added, "I have cooled down a bit since then."

So have I. I don't resent TV for being what it is, and I don't resent the millions who enjoy it. I can't condemn the medium as does Bill McKibben, who wishes TV would go away so we could all enjoy the great outdoors—an outcome that seems about as likely as my wish for a renewed work ethic. Nor can I, like David Bianculli, wholeheartedly celebrate the medium, although I'm certainly more sympathetic to his position than to McKibben's.

One of my differences with Bianculli is that his concept of "teleliteracy" causes him to celebrate the insistent intertextuality of television—which was one of the things that drove me crazy during my TV week. When Bianculli wrote *Teleliteracy*, it was still somewhat novel for a television show to refer to other television shows. As an outstanding example of self-reflexive TV, Bianculli cited the 1985 episode of *St. Elsewhere* in which a delusional patient at the hospital thought he was Mary Richards from *The Mary Tyler Moore Show*. I saw that episode too, and it was indeed terrific. But fourteen years later, what was once groundbreaking has become rote. I was staggered by the degree to which TV is now about TV—and the proportional degree to which areas of real life are out of the loop. Television is the number-one subject of TV talk shows; it takes up a surprising amount of time on both local and national TV news; it makes fun of itself on comedy shows; and the half-hour sitcom has become a formula exercise that is primarily concerned with attaining the rhythm and shape of other, funnier sitcoms of the past.

In this way, TV is a unique medium after all. Sure, there's self-reflexivity in literature (the meta-fiction of Philip Roth and Robert Coover, for instance), in popular music (one name says it all: Beck), and in the movies (often in very good films, like *Pulp Fiction* or *Boogie Nights*), but it's never been as pervasive as it is in contemporary television. Maybe this is a result of the cable boom itself, and the way channels like Nickelodeon—first with its nightly rerun block, Nick at Nite, and then with its spinoff channel, TV Land—have brought the pleasures of the past into the present. But after watching exposés of behind-the-scenes doings at *Bewitched*, *The Partridge Family*, *The Brady Bunch*, and even *Three's Company* in one week of television, I have to conclude that the serpent is in danger of devouring its own tail. Believe it or not, there are still people in America who don't watch television at all—and how much of what they're missing might actually have some bearing on their lives? Along with wishing for a renewed work ethic, I wish everyone working in TV would heed the words of Carl Reiner: "Tell me about yourself, not about other television shows you've seen."

And I say this as someone who's just spent 272 pages telling you about television shows I've seen. I'd better shut up now. 📺

The Credits

Like any movie or TV show, this book owes its existence to the efforts of many people. First on the list is Suzanne Gluck, who became my agent before there was even a proposal for her to represent. Without her guidance, my desire to write a book would probably still be as unfulfilled as my desire to found the Root Beer of the Month club. (If Suzanne ever turns her attentions to the beverage industry, I'll be the happiest man alive.) I'm also indebted to her ICM colleagues—Karen Gerwin, Caroline Sparrow, and John Delaney—and to Nicky Dyja, who more than earned his consultancy fee.

Doug Pepper of Crown Publishers is the editor most writers wish they had. The book is immeasurably better for his constant care and attention, and any remaining gaucheries are attributable to me alone. A tip of the crown, too, to Steve Ross, Barbara Sturman, and Jennifer Hunt.

John Taylor at Zenith lent me twelve beautiful new TV sets for a week—an act of generosity that still amazes me. As a result of his kindness, I am happily indebted to three Chicagoans I've never met: John; his assistant, Kim Parker; and Geoff Pomerantz at Hill & Knowlton. Those Zeniths, their respective cable boxes, and the electricity to supply the whole setup were hooked up by Donovan Dawkins, Tony Picon, and Yvette Baskerville at Time Warner

Cable, and Leo Nazco and Harold Howard at The Electric Connection. A special thanks to Ricardo Palacios at Time Warner Cable, a true gentleman.

Throughout this project, I have walked in the footsteps of the late Charles Sopkin. I'm sorry I never got to meet Mr. Sopkin, but I'm grateful for the patient assistance of his family, specifically Nicholas Sopkin and Alexandra Mayes Birnbaum.

For background information on one of the great sitcoms of all time, I'm indebted to a delightful book by Ginny Weissman and Coyne Steven Sanders, *The Dick Van Dyke Show: Anatomy of a Classic.*

Many thanks also to John Sloss and the gang at Sloss Law Office; Ken Greenhut; everybody at Miramax and at Radical Media; Dr. David Cordisco; Sam Bayer; Steve Gallagher; Cary and Tim Irving; Robert Leighton; Kathryn O'Kane; Penny Paul; Caroline Payson; Bari Pearlman; Mark Saltzman; Devorah Scott; Steve Shainberg; Jonathan Weisgal; Jaime Wolf; and the other Jaime Wolf.

Finally, I'm delighted to acknowledge the unfailing support of my family. My mother, Susan Lechner, is my foremost television connection, and her help in this project has been invaluable. For their love and assistance, thanks also to my father, Ira Lechner; my sister, Eve Lechner; my grandmother, Hannah Schwartz; my stepmother, Eileen Haag; my in-laws, Sallie Maser and Sally Anne Maser; and my late father-in-law, Dr. Marvin Maser.

This book is already dedicated to my wife, Sam Maser—but I could easily double its length by enumerating all the ways it's been enriched and enabled by her wit, her editorial panache, and her remarkable forbearance during a process that would have fazed most spouses. She's the heroine of the book, and of my life.

CREDITS